The Art of
Clinical Supervision

Integration Books

STUDIES IN PASTORAL PSYCHOLOGY,
THEOLOGY, AND SPIRITUALITY

Robert J. Wicks,
General Editor

also in this series

Clinical Handbook of Pastoral Counseling
R. Wicks, R. Parsons, and D. Capps (Eds.)

Adolescents in Turmoil,
Parents Under Stress
Richard D. Parsons

Pastoral Marital Therapy
Stephen Treat and Larry Hof

The Art of Clinical Supervision

A Pastoral Counseling Perspective

Barry K. Estadt
John R. Compton
Melvin C. Blanchette
editors

Integration Books

paulist press/new york and mahwah

Library of Congress Cataloging-in-Publication Data

The Art of clinical supervision.

    (Integration books)
    Includes bibliographies and index.
    1. Pastoral counseling—Study and teaching—
Supervision.   I. Estadt, Barry K., 1934-
II. Compton, John R.   III. Blanchette, Melvin.   IV. Series.
[DNLM: 1. Clinical Competence.   2. Counseling.   3. Pastoral
Care.   WM 61 A784]
BV4012.2.A/7   1987   253.5′07′15   87-13634
ISBN   0-8091-2904-3   (pbk.)

Published by Paulist Press
997 Macarthur Boulevard
Mahwah, NJ 07430

Printed and bound in the
United States of America

Contents

Introduction

Clinical intuition—even when it is accurate—is of little long term value to persons in the helping professions unless it can be broken down, elucidated and examined. To develop one's skills and level of understanding of the whole therapeutic process, there must be a definable, logical approach to reviewing one's professional work with a more experienced colleague. The heart of this process is what is commonly known as "supervision." In *The Art of Clinical Supervision: A Pastoral Counseling Perspective* a very clear understanding of this undertaking to increase clinical acumen is presented.

Using a number of paradigms and employing numerous illustrations, the contributors provide a thorough understanding of such essential supervision issues and concerns as: the alliance that needs to be formed between intern and supervisor; the primary factors affecting the actual supervisory process itself (i.e. the use of a learning contract, countertransference, etc.); specifics to take into account when certain types of treatment modalities are employed (i.e. crisis intervention, short/long term counseling, family/group counseling, addiction counseling, etc.); and religious, ethical, and social justice aspects of pastoral counseling supervision. The final chapters present a methodology for theological and pastoral integration in working with others. The epilogue encourages a deep spiritual as well as psychological appreciation of the value of supervision and the sensitivity that must be involved if it is to be truly effective.

The Art of Clinical Supervision is not merely a technical manual, although it provides clear, clinically-proven approaches. It is a volume designed both to increase one's motivation to employ the supervisory process in an intelligent, well thought out fashion, and to encourage a deep desire to respond to the call to be both professionally and spiritually attuned to the "mission" of supervision. This book takes a comprehensive approach and presents itself as an introductory view of the whole panorama of supervision as an *opportunity*.

Intense supervision is an opportunity for supervisors to be role models. It is an opportunity to focus on practice techniques, treatment philosophies, and theological/psychological hermeneutics so as to encourage supervisees to become mature as pastoral counselors. It is an opportunity for all involved to see their limits as well as their talents, to see how they can aid a client's welfare as well as hurt it. And, finally, it is an opportunity for the supervisor as well as the supervisee to grow. Although the object is to teach the novice, the supervisor must be open to learn as well; and although supervision is not treatment, in a different form it does help the novice to appreciate his/her own unconscious/conscious issues and needs so they can be dealt with in ongoing self-analysis and personal therapy.

In light of the opportunities that *The Art of Clinical Supervision: A Pastoral Counseling Perspective* offers, it is a useful book for both supervisors and supervisees in clinical/counseling psychology, social work, human services, and pastoral counseling graduate programs, as well as in practical theology courses and in field work. There is as much to be learned here about counseling supervision in general as there is about the specific areas of pastoral care/counseling. Given the background of the contributors (who have education and experience in both the behavioral sciences and ministry), as well as the presence of professionals representing psychology, counseling and social work, I suppose this should not be surprising.

Robert J. Wicks
Series Editor

Part 1

Overview of the
Supervisory Alliance

1

Toward Professional Integration

Every profession is concerned that its candidates be prepared for the effective practice of that profession. This requires that the candidate, during the course of preparation, acquire the theoretical body of knowledge proper to the profession as well as the professional skills which will enable the candidate to function effectively. Becoming a professional requires that the candidate master both theory and skills through discipline, concentration, patience and diligent practice. It means mastering the art of the profession.

An art is not something which can be taught; it can only be learned. The necessary steps in learning any art are outlined by Erich Fromm in *The Art of Loving.* He writes:

> The process of learning an art can be divided conveniently into two parts: one, the mastery of the theory; the other, the mastery of the practice. If I want to learn the art of medicine, I must first know the facts about the human body, and about various diseases. When I have all this theoretical knowledge, I am by no means competent in the art of medicine. I shall become a master in this art only after a great deal of practice, until, eventually, the results of my theoretical knowledge and the results of my practice are blended into one—my intuition, the essence of the mastery of any art (p. 4).

Most professional groups have incorporated internship experiences which provide candidates with an opportunity to work toward a "mastery of theory" and a "mastery of practice." Professional schools dealing with the preparation of counselors have faced an additional challenge since mastering the art of counseling goes beyond mastery of theory and practice. It includes, in addition, the personal qualities of the counselor which facilitate personality growth.

In the 1960's, Rogers pointed clearly to the importance of the person of the counselor as he outlined the necessary and sufficient conditions for personality growth to occur. Within the Rogerian framework, the capacity of the counselor for entering into a warm, accepting, empathic relationship characterized by unconditional positive regard, along with the ability to communicate to the client one's acceptance and understanding, is critical to the counseling and therapeutic process. This point has been strongly underscored by Carkuff, well known for his systematic work in training counselors in specific skills. Although much of Carkuff's focus is on skills training, he stresses the importance of the counselor's personal actualization in his preface to *Helping and Human Relations*, Vol. II:

> If the helper cannot actualize his own potentials, he cannot enable another to do so. The focus of training, as the focus of treatment, then, is upon the change or gain of the trainee himself. This is most critical, for without an effective person in the helping role, all else is futile (p. xii).

Authors in counseling and therapy typically present a list of the personal qualities of the therapist in keeping with their theoretical presuppositions. Corey, for example, in his introductory text for counselors, offers a list of nineteen qualities of effective therapists. Although each list varies in content and length, the points of convergence are significant in establishing an overwhelming consensus within the professional counseling community of the importance of the personhood and behavior of the counselor in the counseling process. Weiner, in *Principles of Psychotherapy*, summarizes the thinking in the field as follows:

> Some approaches to psychotherapy have focused largely on technical skills with little attention to the personal qualities of the therapist. Others have stressed the personal interest and warmth of the therapist as the major agent of change in psychotherapy and have minimized the importance of technique. Yet most psychotherapy practitioners and researchers concur that effective psychotherapy requires a balanced combination of personality and technical skills, which Strupp (1970, 1972) aptly refers to as the general and specific factors promoting change in psychotherapy (pp. 34–35).

Mastering the art of counseling requires an integration of a vast body of theoretical knowledge with clinical skills. It also involves developing in oneself the personal qualities which facilitate personality growth in clients within the context of the counseling relationship. Learning how to integrate theory, skills and personal qualities in working with many different types of clients is part of the long process of mastering the art of counseling.

Supervision——A Primary Catalyst

Within the counseling professions supervision of the candidate's ongoing counseling work has come to be regarded as the primary catalyst in facilitating an integration which includes: (a) an incorporation of the body of knowledge common to the field of counseling theory and practice; (b) the acquisition of specific counseling skills; (c) the development of a general way of being that facilitates personal growth in the client; (d) the formulation of one's personal understanding of counseling as a helping professional. The goal of supervision in counselor training is to assist candidates in working toward this fourfold integration.

Concepts of supervision vary among the various counseling specialties and within any given specialty. The term supervision is used to refer to administrative supervision, to beginning skill training as well as to a more intensive clinical process. While all forms of supervision play a role in the training process, the authors of this book presume that administrative supervision appropriate to the specialty and to the setting is being provided. In addition, they assume that basic courses in Helping Relationships, Crisis Intervention, Personality Development, and Psychopathology have been completed. The attention of the authors, therefore, is primarily directed toward the unique interpersonal process of supervision which seeks to address the growth of the candidate in mastering the art of counseling.

With this focus in mind, supervision is defined as a special kind of tutorial relationship in which a person with less experience presents his/her work for the scrutiny and critique of a person with more experience. In the counseling professions, the preferred work-sample is a recording (audio or video) of a complete counseling session along with a clinical case report or summary which situates the counseling session. The recording grounds the supervisory session on the actual performance of the counselor and the interaction of the counselor with the client(s) along with the variety of issues which the work sample generates.

A. Supervisory Formats

Programs utilize *a variety of formats*. Individual supervision, based on a dyadic tutorial model, is deeply personal. It allows the supervisor to give consistent, ongoing, uninterrupted attention to the work of the counselor. The counselor is enabled to proceed at one's own pace and to deal, in a non-competitive setting, with one's personal learning needs.

Small group supervision is based on the premise that participants can learn a great deal from one another as well as from the group supervisor. Making presentations to the group strengthens one's ability to conceptualize the client's problems in clear and concise terms. It also allows for response from a variety of persons, thereby giving the counselor a broader based feedback. Frequently small groups, because of the personal nature of the interaction, develop into strong support groups in which counselors become increasingly comfortable with responding to one another with both positive and negative feedback.

The interdisciplinary case conference has been designed to allow the counselor the opportunity to present a counseling case in depth, demonstrating to one's supervisors and peers a level of competence in the total management of a case at the same time that one utilizes the group for consultation. A detailed grasp and organization of the case is required as well as the demonstration of clinical skills, a theoretical grasp of the psychodynamics of the client and the counselor-client interaction, and an understanding of one's own identity as a counselor. Participants have the opportunity of learning about a variety of clients through the in-depth presentations of their peers.

B. Supervisory Focus

The *focus* of supervision involves three primary interrelated functions: monitoring client welfare, promoting the supervisee's professional growth as a counselor, and evaluating the supervisee. For the agency supervisor who has direct responsibility for case management, the initial and sometimes primary concern will be for client welfare. The agency is directly and immediately accountable for services provided to the client. Quality control is required at every step in the delivery of services including intake, diagnosis, the development of treatment plans, ongoing counseling, and referral or termination.

Agencies which develop training programs and utilize students in the delivery of services frequently find that the quality of services is significantly enhanced. Teaching and supervising trainees stimulates staff to set standards of excellence in the delivery of services and provides a forum for ongoing reflection and evaluation of services rendered. The supervision of students provides unique opportunities for collegial peer interaction around diagnosis, the development of treatment plans and a wide range of potential treatment modalities. Frequently agency morale is enhanced as staff divide their energies between direct service and the supervision of students. Paradoxically, the utilization of student interns typically enhances the quality of service provided by an agency to clients.

Developed counseling programs supplement agency supervision with program supervision directed primarily at the *professional growth of the candidate*. This frees the supervisor from the pragmatic need to focus on crisis management and other needs of immediate concern, thereby allowing the supervisor greater freedom to deal with the growing edges of the counselor in depth without neglecting client welfare as issues emerge. The focus of supervision varies with the level of training of the counselor: the beginning counselor versus the near-graduate. Needs of counselors-in-training also vary widely because of diverse backgrounds and varying degrees of prior counseling experience. The supervisory hour with beginners may deal with basic diagnostic and counseling skills while supervision with intermediate students assumes basic skills and concentrates more on an integration of theory and technique. The advanced level student would be expected to have achieved a technical proficiency in terms of theory and technique focusing now on the process issues of therapy and one's identity as a professional counselor.

C. Evaluation

Evaluation is an inescapable part of the supervisory relationship, whatever the supervisory setting. The primary issue is whether evaluation is done well or poorly. In this regard, the criteria on which a student is evaluated need to be made explicit, communicable and appropriate to the training level of the candidate. Problems in student evaluation emerge when the expectations of each level of training are not shared by student and supervisor. It has been my experience as administrator of a counseling training program for ten years that some supervisors have a special gift for dealing with beginning students, accepting their theoretical and clinical limitations, enabling them to move from neophyte status to an intermediate level, while other supervisors function more effectively with intermediate to advanced level students. It is important to match students and supervisors.

Counseling programs utilizing external field placements face the challenge of working at a common understanding of expectations regarding levels of expectation. The experience at Loyola is that program expectations are generally higher than agency expectations requiring an ongoing dialogue between the program and the agency. Special problems emerge when the prevailing therapeutic modalities at an agency differ notably from those of the counseling program itself. Although such differences in approach are enriching for the intermediate and advanced student, challenging the student in one's personal integration of theory and technique, it is confusing to the beginning student and must be taken into account in the evaluation process.

Supervision Distinct from Therapy

The impact of the personal qualities of the counselor in the therapeutic relationship makes it inevitable that the counselor's personal therapeutic issues will emerge within the context of supervision. While individual therapeutic issues can be addressed in relationship to a given work-sample, extensive focus on the counselor's therapeutic issues in supervision will side-track and contaminate the supervisory process. Supervision focuses primarily on the dynamics of the candidate-as-counselor: how the counselor interrelates with clients in a growth-producing manner. Therapy with a supervisee would divert supervision from its threefold focus on: (a) client welfare, (b) professional growth of the candidate, and (c) evaluation. The therapeutic focus would involve changing the contract that a supervisor has with the supervisee and with the agency or program involved.

Such a shift thoroughly contaminates the process of supervision and demonstrates the supervisor's inability to establish and maintain parameters. Supervision frequently brings therapeutic issues to light since, in working with clients, counselors come face to face with unresolved issues in their own lives. When issues for personal therapy are brought to light, counselors can be invited to address the issues in appropriate ways: through personal self-reflection, dialogue with significant persons in their lives, growth groups or personal therapy. Whenever personal issues seriously interfere with counseling and the ongoing supervisory process, the supervisor must address the need for personal psychotherapeutic investigation as part of the evaluative process. While there may be different nuances of thought on the role of personal therapy and its requirement of all counselors-in-training, individual counselor training programs should have a clearly defined policy understood by faculty, supervisors, and students alike.

Supervision: The Core Process

For decades supervision of the candidate's practicum experience has been accepted as integral to the training of counselors and related mental health professionals. Hundreds of supervisory hours are invested in every counseling candidate to assist the counselor in the task of integrating theory, clinical skills, therapeutic personal qualities and professional identity. Yet surprisingly little attention has been given to the training of supervisors. In most professional groups it has been assumed that if one has gone through the supervisory process as a trainee, one is qualified upon completion to take on the role of supervisor. The American Association of Pastoral Counselors (AAPC) is notable in distinguishing between the role of practitioner and supervisor. In AAPC the highest level of practitioner is the "Fellow." This status is awarded to the seasoned practitioner who has demonstrated an advanced level of integration of counseling theory and technique with one's clinical skills, pastoral identity and the ability to reflect theologically on one's counseling work. Fellows who wish to aspire to supervisory status must normally possess a doctoral degree and undertake to be a supervisor-in-training, accumulating a prescribed number of hours of doing supervision under supervision. The assumption underlying these requirements is that supervision is an activity different from counseling requiring careful self-reflection and professional critique. Supervision of supervision, however has been carried on without the benefit of a systematic understanding of the process of supervision.

In recent years efforts to understand the supervisory process conceptually have been appearing. Typically, attempts to understand the process have involved drawing parallels with theories of counseling and psychotherapy. There are articles on supervision from a variety of approaches: Psychoanalytic, Client-Centered, Cognitive Developmental, Rational-Emotive, Social Learning and others. All are interesting and insightful to some degree; some are highly complex; others appear to focus more on the theoretical model rather than on the supervisory process itself. What is attempted in Chapter 2 is an examination of the *core process* of supervision as a basic process which underlies one's theoretical orientation. What precisely is the process of supervision? What are its stages? How is the process facilitated? What are the supervisory issues commonly addressed? An attempt is made to look at the *process of supervision* much as Carkuff, Egan, and others have looked at the process of counseling and psychotherapy addressing the core process of supervision which is fundamental irrespective of one's theory of counseling and psychotherapy.

References

R.R. Carkhuff, *Helping and Human Relations.* New York: Holt, Rinehart and Winston, 1969.

Erich Fromm, *The Art of Loving.* New York: Bantam Books, 1956.

I. Weiner, *Principles of Psychotherapy.* New York: Wiley, 1973.

2

The Core Process of Supervision

Supervision is *a process of attending leading to awareness, of exploring resulting in insight, and of personalizing culminating in integration.* In the typical supervisory process there are three stages: The Early Phase: *Building the Alliance;* The Middle Phase: *The Work of the Alliance;* The Final Phase: *Concluding the Alliance.* In each of these three stages there are unique supervisory issues to be addressed. In the Early Phase, the primary issues involve building a relationship of trust and developing the supervisory contract. In the Middle Phase, a multitude of supervisory issues emerge which can be categorized under the headings: Counselor Issues, Counselor-Client Issues, and Counselor-Supervisor Issues. The Final Phase deals with the process of summation and termination. During each of the stages identifiable supervisory attitudes and skills facilitate the work of the respective stages.

The development of the "core-process" model of supervision summarized above has been both deductive and inductive: deductive in that I have attempted to examine the parallels of the supervisory process with that of the counseling process; inductive, in that I have been studying the weekly written responses of graduate students to their ongoing experience of the supervisory process. Quotations from counselors-in-supervision are utilized throughout the chapter to illustrate aspects of the supervisory process under consideration.

I. The Core Process of Supervision

Supervision is a process of attending—leading to awareness, of exploring—resulting in insight, and of personalizing—culminating in integration. This core process is an ongoing cooperative effort of supervisor and counselor throughout the supervisory process from the first to the last session. At each stage of supervision, irrespective of the issues addressed, the core process involves attending, exploring, and personalizing with a view to awareness, insight, and integration. The following diagram illustrates this ongoing core process:

EXPLORING

ATTENDING   Inquiring   PERSONALIZING
                             Clarifying
                             Interpreting
                             Confronting

AWARENESS   INSIGHT   INTEGRATION

A. Attending Leading to Awareness

Quality "attending" is the first component of the supervisory process. As supervisor, I invite the counselor into the supervisory relationship by a physical and emotional presence which communicates to the counselor that I am ready to become involved in the task at hand. Physical presence assures full attention to the counselor without calls and interruptions. Emotional presence requires that I bracket personal concerns and issues, attending fully to the counselor, to the work-sample, and to the issues brought to the supervisory session by the counselor. Attending implies *listening* to both verbal and non-verbal messages. It means listening to words but also the messages that are contained in the counselor's tone of voice, pauses, gestures, facial expression and posture. Through active attending the supervisor seeks to understand the frame of reference of the counselor just as the counselor seeks to understand as fully as possible the communication of a client. Attending implies understanding along with a communication of that understanding to the counselor through responding accurately to the content and to the emotional components of the counselor's communication. Counselors undertaking supervision, like clients beginning counseling, need the assurance that they are being understood.

Quality "attending" by the supervisor is powerful. It conveys many deeper underlying attitudes but it says up front to the counselor that review of one's counseling work is a serious undertaking which requires full attention. Quality "attending" as supervisor conveys the important message that nothing is more important to me during this hour than the counselor's professional growth.

Frances, a new master's level candidate, comments after an early supervisory session:

When I asked him if he was willing to listen to my taped session, he said yes and then listened for a long time. His comments told me that he understood and was really into the process with me. I could tell that the tape captured his interest and that he wanted to help me explore what was there. The session left me feeling very good.

The counselor's experience of the supervisor's presence, interest, and being *into the process with me* is the characteristic result of quality attending. As supervisor and counselor together attend to the work at hand, they move inevitably to an awareness of a supervisory issue. The identification of a supervisory issue may be initiated by either supervisor or counselor; sometimes the awareness comes simultaneously to each. Once an issue is identified, supervisor and counselor move into the second component of the core process of supervision, i.e., Exploration.

B. *Exploration Lending to Insight*

Our quest for knowledge is insatiable. In *Four Quartets,* T.S. Eliot exclaims: "We shall not cease from exploration. And the end of all our exploring will be to arrive where we started and know the place for the first time." This is especially true in the supervisory process. Supervisors and counselors bring their individual and collective energies to penetrate into the inner dynamics of the therapeutic process, examining in detail each aspect of the counseling relationship. They study microscopic details reflecting upon the effectiveness of individual responses and the power of a single word. They explore extensively, contemplating the manifold directions of the counseling process, the power of the therapeutic relationship and the source of energy from within the human spirit. It is an exciting process in which supervisor and counselor set out to discover vistas and depths which neither could reach individually. The process of exploration in supervision, by its nature, calls upon collective energies. Divers do not explore the depths alone nor do climbers scale peaks by themselves. The process of supervision, whether it involves two individuals or several, is essentially a shared exploration in which the participants arrive at a place which, individually, they would not find. In supervision the place of arrival is often the point of beginning: through my own personhood and my potency for leading others into contact with the source of their unique energies, a fuller and more complete understanding and presence is realized.

Successful exploration is not random. The discovery of the unknown requires prior mastery of the known. The location and recovery of the treasures of a sunken galleon require that the explorer possess a wealth of knowledge and consummate skillfulness. The dangers to be avoided parallel the treasures to be found. The exploration into the inner dynamism of the therapeutic process involving counselor, client, supervisor, and their interrelatedness is equally challenging. Successful exploration requires mastery of the known, professional skillfulness, and commitment to the task at hand.

The process of exploration in supervision is as varied as the combined ingenuity of supervisor and counselor allow as they move from awareness of a supervisory issue into an examination of the issue. Styles of exploration vary given the personal characteristics of both supervisor and counselor, the level of training of the counselor, the stage in the exploratory process, the expertise of the supervisor and the theoretical orientations of both counselor and supervisor. The theoretical orientation of the supervisor will have special impact since it represents at least a "tentative cognitive map" which the supervisor will instinctively utilize in the exploratory process.

Most of the exploratory initiatives of the supervisor, notwithstanding significant differences in approach, will be classifiable under four headings: Inquiring, Clarifying, Interpreting, and Confronting.

1. *Inquiring* involves a request for information. Through an inquiry, the supervisor invites the counselor to focus attention on a supervisory issue. If the inquiry is done within the context of a trusting relationship, supervisor and counselor embark upon a mutual search. When threat from the supervisor is absent, both counselor and supervisor can join energies in addressing the real challenge presented by exploration into the dynamics of the therapeutic process. An inquiry is seldom a simple yes or no question. Rather an inquiry is frequently the beginning of an exploratory search which may readily lead far beyond and beneath the particular point of departure for the inquiry.

Frances, a forty-five year old celibate religious enrolled in a master's degree program in pastoral counseling, comments on facets of the exploratory process opened up in her third supervisory session:

> To open up a question and to talk about it bring not only clarification but energy and enthusiasm to go on. I think B's nonverbals told me more than his actual words. For me, that was an excellent process. I learned that everything is not all wrapped up and neat at the end, but it is precisely in process . . . it goes on!

The inquiry in this early supervising session focused on the need of the counselor to have everything wrapped up at the end of each session. Inquiry led to insight into how her own excessive need for closure was interfering with the therapeutic process. More important than this special insight, however, was the fact that Frances found the process of exploration energizing. She was beginning, early on, to grasp the learning potential of a search in which supervisor and counselor together seek the truth in a spirit of mutuality. Rather than being defensive or feeling criticized, Frances reports on this early session: "Supervision feels good. I felt comfortable, calm, at peace, supported and helped."

2. *Clarifying* initiatives on the part of the supervisor go a step beyond inquiring. Clarifying involves making something clearer or more understandable. Sometimes it involves freeing the counselor from confusion. The supervisor, because of a more substantive theoretical and experiential background, can be of enormous assistance to a less knowledgeable or less experienced counselor. Counselors may need assistance in understanding the psychodynamics of the client or in arriving at a clear diagnosis. Frequently enough they need insight into how their own personal issues are interfering with their counseling work with individual clients. During the fourth supervisory session with Frances, I assisted her in clarifying how her own issues were impacting the counseling process. She comments:

> B. affirmed me in my assessment that Susan was stuck. He then suggested to me a way to help her get unstuck. His third step in this process surprised me as he checked out in my personal life if I had the "credits to spend" or if from my own experience I had the "authority" to "demand" of Susan that she plan for and make time each week to do something life-giving for herself. B. wanted to know if I take time each week for my own refreshment and recreation. In other words, he checked out if I would be "practicing what I preach" when I ask this of Susan. B. did this gently and respectfully and I felt supported and cared for rather than feeling that my privacy was invaded.

3. *Interpreting* in supervision, as in counseling, is an exploratory strategy aiming at bringing about insight by calling attention to some aspect of the counselor's behavior or experience which has not yet risen to the level of full awareness. Interpretations may consist of observations, inferences, probabilities, or hypotheses offered by the supervisor which seek to facilitate the counselor's further understanding of oneself, the client, the counselor-client or supervisor-counselor interaction. Learning what to interpret and when to interpret is a significant part of mastering the art of supervision. In Chapter 5 Blanchette defines interpretation as a

process of communicating understanding. After listening and gaining an appreciation of the client's difficulties and the questions life might be asking, the therapist, through interpretation, attempts to put into words the meaning of what is happening. Blanchette also deals in depth with the various forms of resistance which block and impede the client's path toward freedom.

4. *Confronting* in supervision, as in counseling, has as its primary goal the facilitation of further insight and learning on the part of the counselor. The supervisor, through confrontation, attempts to bring to the counselor's awareness blind spots and inconsistencies which impede the counselor's effectiveness as a therapeutic person. At the same time the supervisor models for the counselor the delicate art of confrontation: calling attention to "growing edges" in an atmosphere of acceptance and trust. There is a growing body of literature in many fields supporting the fact that the majority of people learn best within the context of a positive working alliance. In the *One Minute Manager*, on the New York Time's Bestseller List for twelve months, the authors underscore the fact that "reprimand" to achieve its goal must have two critical components: during the first half of the reprimand they stress *immediate* and *specific* feedback about performance; in the second half of the reprimand, the focus is on reaffirming the individuals of the fact that you think well of them but not of their performance in this specific situation. Confrontation, in its many forms, focuses on behavior and performance, not on the individual's worth as a person.

Effective confrontation requires both a high level of skill and an established working alliance. In the ninth supervisory session with John, a forty-year-old high school instructor enrolled in a graduate program in Pastoral Counseling, I invited him to reflect on his abrasive style of confrontation. John writes:

> In this session B helped me to focus on my need to smooth out my style. He felt that I am too abrupt and confrontational. He was very firm in insisting that I respond more empathically. This was a side of B I had not previously encountered. Don't get me wrong! His response was gentle but firm. This confrontation led me to re-read my weekly reflections on the supervisory process. I found it fascinating. Under "Type and Quality of Response from the Supervisor," I almost invariably comment on the fact that B is gentle, affirming the positive and nudging me to focus on my growing edges. I feel that he has been demonstrating what I should be doing with my clients. I need to smooth out my style. I am too abrupt. My statements should be in the form of inquir-

ies. I do not adequately convey the fact that I am in my client's corner. I have been too confronting and not sufficiently empathic.

The counselor's comments reveal the fact that the firm insistence of the supervisor that he re-evaluate his attitude and manner of approaching the client led the counselor to a deeper understanding of his growing edges. At the same time, the supervisor modeled for the counselor how one can be simultaneously both firm and empathic.

In another supervisory session with John, I pointed out to him how inconsistent the therapeutic working alliance is with accepting a dinner invitation from a client and how he was giving a mixed message to the client by accepting. John realized his error. Nonetheless, he felt accepted and valued as a counselor at the same time that he was brought to realize that he had made a mistake.

I felt that I had blundered when B told me I had made a mistake by accepting a dinner invitation from my client. I felt that I had to correct my blunder and did so without generating hard feelings in the client. B, as always, was most gentle even with what one might call a "reprimand." I gained a greater understanding of the limit setting necessary to respect the therapeutic process.

C. Personalizing Leading to Integration

The process of *attending* leads to *awareness*. The process of *exploration* through inquiring, clarifying, interpreting, and confronting leads to *insight*. The third step in the core process of supervision is *personalizing* leading to integration. Personalizing is the process by which a counselor takes ownership of the insights arrived at through the exploratory process. It implies an intellectual grasp of a concept as well as the presuppositions and implications of the concept. Personalizing involves reflection, judgment, deliberation about possible courses of action, an evaluation of alternatives and a determination to carry out decisions related to the insights. Insights, over a period of time, must become part of a therapeutic way of being with clients.

The personalizing process takes place at many levels. The empirical experience of the counselor in relationship to clients is the primary data on which the supervisory process is grounded. Attending to the data gives rise to an awareness of supervisory issues. Exploration through inquiry, clarification, interpretation and confrontation leads to insight. Incorporating insight into one's way of being is a process of assimilation over time. The assimilation process might be compared to the digestive process in its complexity. Through the attending and exploratory processes of the supervisory hour the counselor takes in a variety of insights regarding clients and oneself in relationship to clients. In the period of time between supervisory sessions the counselor is engaged in the assimilation process, at times conscious but much of the time at a level beneath immediate awareness. Frances comments:

> In a way it is like the counseling process. It is a mysterious reverent adventure into the unknown. It is a time of exploration, leading to a deeper understanding and greater insight both about the client and myself. My client and I are growing together. It is not that she is growing and I have finished growing. It is always new for both of us.

Weekly supervisory sessions serve as a catalyst to the spiraling process of attending, exploring and personalizing. Successful supervision leads the counselor not only to the assimilation of insights but also to an incorporation of the core process of supervision itself as part of one's professional way of being. Over a period of time, the counselor attends, explores, and personalizes in the absence of regularly scheduled supervisory sessions as the process of integration becomes internalized.

II. The Stages of Supervision

In the pages above, the core process of supervision has been defined in terms of three integral components: (a) attending leading to awareness, (b) exploring resulting in insight, and (c) personalizing culminating in integration. This core process can be described as an ongoing spiraling process which is repeated over and over again throughout the supervisory working alliance: Attending, Exploring, Personalizing leading to Awareness, Insight, and Integration. The process, however, takes on different nuances as it moves through three major stages: Stage 1 (Early Phase) Building the Alliance; Stage 2 (Middle Phase) The Working Alliance; and Stage 3 (Final Phase) Concluding the Alliance.

During each phase the supervisor effectively contributes to the work of facilitating the process of attending, exploring, and personalizing. Each stage, however, has its unique and special issues. Supervision, like counseling, is not a random process. It has identifiable characteristics and tasks in each of the stages. It is a developmental process which moves from the foundation laid in the Early Phase to the substantive work of Middle Phase and subsequently to the consolidation work of the Final Phase.

Chart I outlines three stages of supervision: Stage 1 (Building the Alliance), Stage 2 (The Working Alliance), and Stage 3 (Concluding the Alliance). In each stage the supervisor facilitates the work of the supervisory alliance by attitudes and behavior which recognize the quality of the supervisory relationship as well as the special tasks of the given stage. While there is continuity in the supervisor's way of being with the supervisee throughout the process, the task of *Stage 1*, developing a relationship of trust and a learning contract, is facilitated by an attitude of basic acceptance and by demonstrating empathy and genuineness in the supervisory relationship. After the learning contract is clear and relationship of trust is established, supervisor and counselor are ready to move into the substantive work of *Stage 2* which addresses three major categories of concerns: (1) counselor issues, (2) counselor-client issues, and (3) counselor-supervisor issues. As the supervisory relationship nears conclusion, the task is one of summation, evaluating the progress made and the growing edges which remain for subsequent supervision. The process of summation is facilitated through an evaluation conducted with an attitude and stance of collegial affirmation. Chart I gives an overview of the supervisory stages, noting the supervisory tasks of each stage and the manner in which the supervisor facilitates the work of each stage.

CHART I
The Stages of Supervision

STAGES	*Stage 1* (Early Phase)	*Stage 2* (Middle Phase)	*Stage 3* (Final Phase)
	Building the Alliance	The Working Alliance	Concluding the Alliance
SUPERVISOR FACILITATES BY	Acceptance Empathy (Primary) Genuineness	Empathy (Advanced) Immediacy of Interaction Supervisor-Counselor Supervisor-Client Counselor-Client Parallel Process	Collegial Affirmation and Evaluation

SUPERVISORY TASKS	Learning Contract	*Counselor Issues*	Summation
	Trust Relationship		Termination
		Skill Acquisition	
		Self-Knowledge	
		Therapeutic Capacity	
		Ethical Sensitivity	
		Professional Identity	
		Counselor-Client Issues	
		Knowledge of the Client	
		Therapeutic Relationship	
		Counselor-Supervisor Issues	
		Supervisability	
		Supervisory Competence	

A. *Stage 1 (Early Phase): Building the Alliance*

The early phase of the supervisory relationship focuses on two tasks: (1) establishing a relationship of trust and (2) developing a supervisory learning contract. Both tasks are facilitated when the supervisor approaches each counselor with an attitude of full acceptance as a person and as a counselor-in-training. Every counselor-in-training is unique, bringing to the supervisory relationship the richness of one's personhood along with all of the experiences which contribute to the counselor's "strengths" and "growing edges" as a counselor. In respectfully communicating acceptance to the counselor as person and trainee, the supervisor models for the counselor the acceptance which the counselor is expected to offer to each client in the initial phase of the counseling relationship. Each step of the supervisory alliance parallels the counseling process providing counselors-in-training with a parallel experiential learning process. Effective supervisors model for counselors-in-training a qualitative professional helping relationship and the specific clinical skills and techniques which are required for effective counseling. The skills of primary empathy and genuineness modeled by the supervisor during the early phase of supervision are the precise skills needed by the counselor in the early phase of counseling.

The supervisor communicates primary empathy by understanding what the counselor is experiencing at this initial phase of supervision, entering into the counselor's world and looking at the process of supervision through the counselor's frame of reference. Prior supervisory experiences, ranging from highly positive to profoundly negative, affect the readiness of the counselor to enter into a relationship of trust with the supervisor.

The supervisor, by attending and listening carefully to the counselor's verbal and non-verbal communications during the process of negotiating the supervisory learning contract, can come to an understanding of the counselor's inner frame of reference.

Compton, in Chapter 3, "The Supervisory Learning Contract," discusses the rationale for the supervisory learning contract and explores in detail areas of concern to be defined in the contract including the collegial process of constructing the contract, a mutual understanding of the evaluation process and negotiating changes in the learning contract. The establishment of a clear learning contract and the building of a trusting relationship lay a firm foundation for the professional working alliance between supervisor and counselor.

B. Stage 2 (Middle Phase): The Working Alliance

During Stage 2, the middle phase of supervision, supervisor and counselor focus their energies on counselor issues, counselor-client issues and counselor-supervisor issues. The skilled supervisor can facilitate an examination of these issues by communicating to the counselor advanced-level empathy and by effectively dealing with issues as they arise in the immediacy of the supervisory relationship, skillfully attending, at the same time, to parallel process issues. In the pages to follow, we will briefly address the concepts of advanced empathy, immediacy and parallel process before moving to a discussion of (1) counselor issues, (2) counselor-client issues and (3) supervisor-counselor issues.

Advanced Empathy

During the middle phase, the supervisor gains considerable insight into the personal dynamics of the counselor, the counselor's style of dealing with clients and the counselor's strengths and growing edges. This knowledge of the counselor, together with a wealth of experience in both counseling and supervision, allows the supervisor to facilitate the process through advanced-level empathy skills. The supervisor, a half-step ahead of the counselor, can lead the counselor into insights about self, the counselor-client relationship and the relationship with the supervisor. In supervision, as in counseling, if the supervisor moves too many steps ahead of the counselor, interpretations and confrontations may not be able to be absorbed. The supervisor models, by sensitivity to the counselor's readiness for interpretation and confrontation, a therapeutic way of being which the counselor can translate into the counseling relationship. Joyce, a forty-five-year-old vowed religious enrolled in a graduate program in Pastoral Counseling, wrote after her eighth supervisory session:

B has a way of pulling things together and taking them a step further. I am amazed at his ability to clarify issues by a simple comment or question! B's comments were "to the point" and gentle, a hard balance to achieve. B has a way of saying what he thinks in a non-threatening style, so that I feel able to accept it.

Immediacy

One of the keys to effective supervision is the opportunity it provides for "in vivo" learning in the *immediacy* of the moment. Joyce comments, after her ninth supervisory session:

B knew before I did how uncomfortable I was. His encouragement for me to "get in touch" with how bad I was feeling was sensitive and understanding. Struggling through my tears, I let go of the superwoman concept. I felt incredibly vulnerable . . . like a client and not a counselor. I felt relieved and freed up to be myself. B gently acknowledged the growing edges which I shared but also affirmed my strengths. I felt respect and support for me as a person and as a counselor.

Sometimes counselors can be invited to get back in touch with the feelings that were going on during a segment of the taped interview. John, during the ninth session referred to above, was asked to bring into focus the feelings he experienced when the client invited him to dinner. He commented:

I experienced myself being sucked into the client's talent for organizing people around her. I didn't like it but I said yes because I didn't want to offend her.

In guiding the counselor back into an experience of the segment of the counseling session in question, the supervisor provided an opportunity for the counselor to tune into his inner experience during the counseling session. Had he followed his inner instincts, he would have refused the invitation. John continues after Session 8:

The supervisory process is making me more aware of what is going on inside of me during the therapeutic session.

Another aspect of immediacy involves the feelings generated in the supervisor by the counselor or the client as the supervisor attends to the work-sample, i.e., the supervisor-counselor or supervisor-client relationship. In Session 12 with Frances, I shared my feelings toward her client as I found myself identifying with the client's husband. Frances commented:

> I gained new insight into Susan from B's transparency in sharing his negative "counter-transference" feelings toward my client during our last session. This helped me to grasp a male's response to Susan which has been helpful in understanding some of the dynamics of Susan's relationship with her husband, Harry.

Parallel Process

A third area of learning during Stage two involves the many *parallel process* issues which occur within one triadic supervisor-counselor-client relationship. John gained insight into *parallel process* issues in Session 3 as he wrote:

> I really wanted B to stop the tape and say, O.K., John this is what you are doing wrong, or this is what you're doing right. He never did that! He asked me if I felt I was doing O.K. I wanted answers from him! I laughed when I realized that I was expecting from B the very same thing my client was expecting from me, namely, answers!

At times, supervisors will find their own supervising style with counselors unconsciously modeled by counselors in relationship to clients. Recently I was interested in assisting a counselor to risk greater intimacy with his client, nudging him to break through the client's resistance to make contact at a deeper affective level. In a role play I took the part of the counselor attempting to enter into a deeper level of contact with the client. As I demonstrated the risks involved in attempting to engage the client more fully, I was, in effect, taking significant risks in penetrating the resistance of the counselor in dealing with affect in the supervisory relationship. Only later did I recognize the ongoing parallel process between my own careful gradual approach to the counselor and the counselor's equally cautious approach to the client. I had been modeling, and in reality unwillingly reinforcing the counselor's approach by my own. When I wanted my supervisee to deal differently with his client, I found that I had to deal differently with my supervisee.

1. Counselor Issues

Supervisory issues vary from week to week as counselors enter into relationship with a variety of clients. The focus of supervision is affected by the counselor's level of training, prior supervisory experiences and the types of clients being served. Nonetheless, under the general heading of counselor issues, one would expect, over a period of time, to deal with issues of skill acquisition, self-knowledge, therapeutic capacity, ethical sensitivity and professional identity.

In terms of *skill acquisition*, beginning counselors require supervisors who have the "gift" for allowing them to be beginners. Entering into counselor training is incredibly demanding as candidates seek to apply in their counseling practicum what they have learned cognitively in their courses in theory and techniques of counseling. The supervisor needs to have a sensitivity to the fact that the development of counseling skills takes place over a several year period, assessing in the development of the learning contract the level of competency of the counselor and the status of the counselor within the overall training program. In the Loyola program, for example, courses in The Helping Relationship, Crisis Intervention, and Psychopathology precede the counseling practicum. This gives the supervisor some base-line of expectation regarding programmatic expectations for the beginning counselor. In the rating form for Loyola master's degree students, the following progression is expected in terms of basic skill development:

Beginning Counselor
   a. an *ability* to accept clients in a non-judgmental way.
   b. an *ability* to attend to the client's internal world of feeling.
   c. an *ability* to respond empathically to the client.
More Advanced Counselor
   a. Attending, responding, and initiating skills (à la Egan, Carkhuff) are a *relatively effortless part* of the counselor's repertoire.
   b. The above skills manifested in a *consistent* way within the context of the counselor's personal theoretical orientation.

The movement from beginning to more advanced skill development takes time, practice and an ongoing careful review of the trainee's taped counseling sessions. A work-sample on audio or video tape gives no room for "creative recall" or for a reconstruction of the session in keeping with the supervisor's expectations. The taped session, revealing the reality of the counselor-client interaction, gives the supervisor a powerful tool for teaching basic and advanced skills. In reviewing the work of a neophyte counselor, the supervisor might do well to follow the suggestion of Blanchard and Johnson in the *One Minute Manager:* "Help people reach their full potential. Catch them doing something right."

John, after Session 3, comments:

> I was glad that B was listening to my tape. He affirmed some responses and drew out of me alternatives in responding to the client or moving the client back to dealing with her own issues. The supervisor's approach felt good: He never said I was wrong in my responses, but he led me to improved responses. Perhaps under B's guidance, I will discover the professional therapist within me and leave the rookie behind.

The counselor's final comment indicated that the professional working alliance was well underway. The counselor experienced acceptance from the supervisor and was eager to have him as a "coach."

Self-Knowledge

Supervision, as counseling, is a deeply personal kind of learning. It requires that the counselor risk sharing, in relationship, with the supervisor, the intimate details of one's counseling sessions. As supervisor and counselor together attend to the intrapsychic processes of the client and the inter-personal dynamics of the counseling relationship, counselors inevitably reveal, in the process, a great deal about their own intrapsychic processes and inter-personal way of being. In many ways, the supervisory process creates a double jeopardy situation: the counselor risks entering into relationship with the client; then the counselor proceeds to risk an examination of that relationship in the process of supervision. The authenticity of the counselor is doubly tested!

As one enters into counseling training, even after personal therapy, new discoveries are made about self, especially as clients confront the very issues which the counselor has not yet adequately explored. Unresolved issues of loneliness, anger, sexuality, power, or depression can lead a counselor to respond in ways which are not therapeutic. Such personal "counter-transference" issues emerging in the course of supervision come under intense evaluation in the supervisory process. Blanchette, in Chapter 6, explores in depth, issues of transference and counter-transference. Frequently, counselors complement supervision with personal therapy as unexplored blocks come to light through the supervisory process. The process of supervision—*attending* with a view to awareness, *exploring* seeking insight and *personalizing* with the goal of integration—is a powerful ongoing process which requires that we look at ourselves and our work with clients with forthrightness and honesty as we strive to become increasingly therapeutic in our counseling relationships. Enhanced self-knowledge is one of the personal therapeutic by-products of the process of supervision.

Therapeutic Capacity

A critical variable in the training of counselors is the development of the counselor's capacity to be a therapeutic person. Corey, in a chapter entitled "The Counselor as a Person and a Professional," makes the point that therapy can be for better or for worse. "Clients can become more actualized, or they can become less healthy. In my judgment, the degree of aliveness and self-actualization of the therapist is the crucial variable that determines the outcome." Corey, in thinking about counselors who are therapeutic persons, comes up with a description of nineteen personal qualities and characteristics important for promoting personal growth. The primary qualification, he emphasizes, is a willingness by counselors to examine their own lives with a profound sense of hope, taking the risks and making the effort to make life-oriented choices. He writes:

> My view is that it is through our own realness and our aliveness that we are able to significantly touch our clients. If we make life-oriented choices, radiate a zest for life, are real in our relationships with our clients and let ourselves be known to them, we can inspire and teach them in the best sense of the word. This does not mean that we are self-actualized persons who have "arrived" or that we are without our problems. Rather, it implies that we have not given up our willingness to look at our life and do what is necessary to make the changes we want to make. Because we have a sense of hope that we can change, and that changing is worth the risks and the efforts, then we can hold out hope to our clients that they have the capacity to become their own person and to like the person they are becoming (p. 268).

Being a therapeutic person requires the emotional capacity of the counselor to enter into an empathic, non-possessive helping relationship. This involves an ability to adhere to the parameters of a "working alliance" which focuses on the needs of the client. A degree of self-knowledge, self-acceptance, and understanding of one's own inner dynamics is required to enter effectively into a counseling relationship dealing with the inner life of a client. The same qualities are required of the supervisor who deals with a more complex set of relationships involving both counselor and client. The supervisor is expected to be sensitive to the intra-personal dynamics of both counselor and client, the inter-personal interaction of client-counselor as well as the nuances of the supervisor's relationship to both client and counselor. Effective supervision requires that the supervisor be a therapeutic person.

Ethical Sensitivity

Counselors, by profession, are committed to uphold the dignity of the human person. The entire counseling enterprise is built upon respect for individual rights but within the parameters of the human society. Consequently, over the years, the helping professions have developed standards and codes of ethics. The American Psychological Association, for example, developed its *Ethical Standards of Psychologists* in 1953. It has been followed by a series of revisions and casebooks dealing both with ethical principles and their application to individual cases. Other professions have made similar attempts to enunciate principles which guide professional conduct. Davenport, in Chapter 17, deals with some of the foundational ethical issues in counseling and supervision while Callahan, in Chapter 16, looks at some of the specifically religious issues which emerge.

Supervisors, by their personal sensitivity to ethical issues, including those touching upon the supervisory relationship, model for counselors the kind of careful attention to the rights of the individual and of society which emerge within the counseling relationship. While the response to some ethical issues is mandated by law, as in the case of child abuse, most responses are discretionary requiring attention both to principles and to persons in working through difficult and sensitive ethical issues. Often enough the rights of one person are pitted against the rights of another, requiring that the counselors have a refined moral sense and the ability to lead clients to a consideration of their personal rights as well as their ethical responsibilities. Counseling is not, nor has it ever been, value free. The values of the client, the values of society and the values of the counselor are ever-present in the counseling relationship. In the supervisory relationship, the values of the supervisor are added to those of the counselor, client, and society. The supervisor, by modeling, in the ongoing process of supervision, sensitivity to the values of counselor, client, and society, will assist the counselor in developing a sensitivity to ethical issues along with an understanding of how to address them in the concrete realities of individual situations.

Professional Identity

The growth of the contemporary helping professions in the United States since the beginning of 1940 has been phenomenal. This half century has seen the emergence of a wide variety of professions dedicated to addressing the psychic well-being of the human person and of society. Psychiatry, nursing, psychology, social work and a wide variety of counseling professions have emerged, each addressing human needs from a somewhat different perspective with the accumulated richness of method, experience, philosophy and the theoretical orientation of the given discipline. Today we find members of many different professions practicing the art of their respective professions in addressing the needs of very similar clients. Psychiatrists, psychologists, social workers and counselors are all engaged in individual therapy, couples counseling, family counseling, and group counseling. They all treat clients with developmental defects, anxiety, depression, mid-life crises, bereavement issues and the like. There are notable differences between professions and within professions, yet there are also striking similarities in underlying philosophical assumptions, theoretical constraints and the range of treatment modalities. In this state of pluriformity in the helping professions, the candidates in-training need to come to an understanding of their profession, integrating an understanding of self as a helping professional within the context of a given profession.

As the helping professions have emerged, the public has been keenly interested in addressing the competence of those who lay claim to provide human services. *Certification laws* require demonstrated competence to utilize specific titles. *Licensure laws* generally restrict the performance of a range of services to those who have been duly authorized to provide the services in question. Both certification and licensure laws are intended to protect the public from the unqualified and to ensure minimum standards of practice. Many professions go beyond licensure setting standards for board certification and diplomate status.

As a candidate prepares for entry into any of the recognized helping professions, a congruity needs to emerge between the individual's capacity to help and the expectations of the profession. A respect for the integrity and historical development of one's profession and a proper sense of loyalty and identification is fitting and proper. However, today, given the unique contributions offered by a variety of professional groups, the trainee in the helping professions needs to come to an understanding of and respect for professions other than one's own. Quality service to the public by competent helpers is a far more important value than protecting one's own professional prerogatives. While there will always be questions of competence as new professions emerge and legitimate concerns about standards of service, the helping professional-in-training today needs both a strong sense of *professional identity* and a recognition of professional *inter-dependence*. A case could be built that the maturity of a profession is in direct proportion to the profession's ability to recognize the legitimate claim of other professional colleagues. There are striking core similarities among the groups as well as distinct differences. Mutual understanding and acceptance of similarities and distinctiveness leads to healthy self-understanding as well as inter-professional cooperation.

2. Counselor-Client Issues

In the preceding pages we have looked at some of the generic *counselor issues* which are typically dealt with over the course of supervision, issues including skill-acquisition, self-knowledge, therapeutic capacity, ethical sensitivity, and professional identity. Under the heading of counselor-client issues, we will address two broad topics: Knowledge of the Client and the Therapeutic Relationship.

Knowledge of the Client

As the counselor approaches a client, the stance is properly one of curiosity, open to exploring the inner world of the client with a view to understanding the richness of the human person. The counselor, as a student of human behavior, is interested in discovering two types of knowledge: What is *generic* and what is *unique?*

In dealing with the "generic" dimension of knowledge, the counselor is asking the questions: What kind of person is this? What is the individual underlying personality structure? What does a psychic X-ray reveal? What is the basic skeletal reality or diagnosis? Christiaan Barnard, in *The Body Machine*, describes the human skeleton as follows:

> The skeleton is the body machine's structural support system onto which the muscles are anchored. Although skeleton derives its name from the Greek word meaning "dried up," live bone is anything but dry. Bone is one-third water and one of the most biologically active tissues. The body's mineral banks are stored in the bone and millions of red blood cells are manufactured every minute in the marrow, the soft core of the bone. As a chassis, the skeleton is unique. It twists and bends to permit a wide range of movement unequalled by any manmade machine. Equipped with highly sophisticated shock-absorbers and a re-

markable lubrication system, the skeleton is more durable than
any manmade creation (p. 33).

The analogy of the skeleton with the underlying personality structure
of an individual is appropriate. As people of different body builds share
skeletal similarities, so individuals develop a variety of identifiable psychic
patterns in their efforts to satisfy their needs within the context of their
environment. Students of human behavior, over the centuries, have noted
various types and typologies describing identifiable patterns of behavior.
Contemporary psychology and psychiatry have added a wealth of knowledge in understanding patterns of behavior, offering the helping professional the technology to do at least a rudimentary psychic X-ray albeit not
a psychic CAT-scan. Arriving at an accurate diagnosis, a knowledge of the
underlying psychic skeleton is integral to the counseling relationship since
effective treatment will follow upon the nuances of the counselor's diagnosis.

In counseling, as in medicine, the diagnostic X-ray reveals the health
or pathology of the skeletal structure; the diagnostic X-ray is not, in itself,
treatment but provides knowledge essential for treatment. The art of counseling requires an additional type of knowledge of the individual—a knowledge which can come only through the process of a therapeutic
relationship in which counselor and client come to discover and appreciate
how the skeleton is enfleshed in a totally *unique* and idiosyncratic manner.
It has been said that "discovery is seeing what everyone else has seen but
thinking what nobody else has thought." Counselor and client discover the
nuances and richness of meaning in the unique personhood of the client
through the therapeutic alliance. The supervisor has the opportunity of
modeling this sense of discovery in the supervisory relationship itself, approaching the counselor-in-training with a sense of mystery, open to explore the inner world of the counselor as the counselor attempts to enter
into a therapeutic relationship with clients.

Therapeutic Relationship

The supervisor has two areas of concern as regards the counselor's
therapeutic capacity: (a) Is the counselor able to establish and maintain a
therapeutic relationship with this client? (b) What are the implications of
the counselor's work with this client for other therapeutic relationships?
As counselors-in-training work with a variety of clients, they are experimenting, seeking to discover their current level of effectiveness with given
clients and types of clients with a view to identifying strengths and growing
edges. Improvement can only be based on knowledge and knowledge on
experience.

Henri Poincaré made an interesting comment on experimenting to the effect that submitting to experiment is not enough unless we uncover, in the process, the dangerous hypotheses which are tacit and unconscious, for unless we come to know them, we are powerless to abandon them. One of the most important functions of the supervisor is to assist the counselor in becoming aware of the personal issues, frequently tacit and unconscious, which limit a counselor's therapeutic capacity with individual clients and types of clients. (Blanchette, in Chapter 6, "Transference and Countertransference," deals in depth with blocks to the therapeutic relationship.) The supervisor, by openness regarding personal countertransference issues, can model for the counselor an acceptance and non-defensiveness regarding issues of personal limitation. Such transparency helps to deliver the important message that counselors are professionals with limitations. Limitations are problematic only when they are unknown or ignored; learning how to work within one's strengths and limitations is part of the process of becoming a professional helper.

3. Counselor-Supervisor Issues

In the pages above, we have addressed supervisory issues under the headings: *counselor* issues and *counselor-client* issues. A third important dimension of the supervisory process remains, i.e., *counselor-supervisor* issues. Under this rubric we will consider two topics: counselor supervisability and supervisory competence.

Supervisability

Beginning students are not expected to be skilled; they are expected however, to be supervisable. This includes, for the beginning student, an openness to presenting one's work for critique in a variety of supervisory settings: individual and small group supervision and interdisciplinary case conferences. They need to have the ability to "hear" both positive and negative feedback from supervisors and peers as well as the capacity to incorporate feedback by appropriate follow-through on supervisory recommendations. Sometimes it happens that extremely bright students who have a history of high-level academic achievement find the collegial process of give and take disconcerting. A compulsive need to prove oneself through achievement and "A" work can be counterproductive, interfering with the counselor's ability to engage in self-reflection and self-critique.

The more advanced counselor is expected to take the lead in initiating pertinent discussion in supervisory sessions. As the candidate gathers experience, supervisors rightly look for a growing ability to make an objective analysis of one's performance, highlighting strengths and growing edges with respect to the client in question and clients in general. The more experienced counselor utilizes the supervisory process to gain insight into transference and countertransference issues. In brief, the advanced counselor is expected to move toward ever increasing autonomy in utilizing the supervisory process for personal and professional growth, moving eventually in the direction of peer consultation rather than supervision.

Supervisory Competence

Most professions assume that one who has been fully certified or licensed as a practitioner is prepared to take on the supervisory role. There is an implicit assumption that if you have gone through supervision you are ready to provide supervision. This assumption is somewhat incongruous given the uniqueness and complexity of the supervisory process and its critical role in the ongoing development of a profession. The quality of professional training in a given profession is directly related to the quality of the supervised experience available in practicum and internship experiences.

With a view to meeting the need for supervisors to reflect in a systematic and intentional way on the supervisory process, some professions have a formal period of introduction to the process of supervision and a rigorous program of ongoing critique and evaluation. My own professional journey in the American Association of Pastoral Counselors involved fifty hours of individual supervision of my supervision in which I presented videotaped supervisory sessions much as counselors-in-training would present counseling sessions. This was followed by a board review by regional and national committees of my application for Diplomate status.

Whatever the requirements of a given profession, the central element for us as supervisors is the opportunity to reflect critically on our work with other supervisory peers with a view to identifying our own ongoing supervisory strengths and growing edges. As part of the recertification process for supervisors of the National Association of Catholic Chaplains (NACC), initiated in 1986, the candidate presents evidence of ongoing continuing education, a paper discussing his/her theology, philosophy, and theory of supervision, and a significant work sample, preferably an audio or video tape, and meets for a two hour peer review with fellow supervisors to assess strengths and growing edges in an atmosphere of collegiality. As a member of the commission which drew up the peer review interview guidelines, I was privileged to be among the first two candidates to be recertified as a supervisor under the new process. The process of preparation required a thinking through of my concept of supervision and a careful critique of my work with one supervisee. The opportunity to have three fellow supervisors give their individual and collective attention to my written materials and to the video-taped sample was a rich opportunity. During the review of the tape helpful observations were made regarding parallel process issues which have provided me with insights regarding supervisory growing edges that I would not have arrived at alone.

C. Stage 3 (Final Phase): Concluding the Alliance

The conclusion of the supervisory relationship is usually determined by the time parameters of a given training program as, for example, the end of an academic year or the completion of a training module. Normally the approximate termination date has been set from the beginning in the learning contract. Sometimes termination occurs earlier than anticipated in terms of illness and other unforeseen extrinsic factors. A supervisee's inability to meet the expectations of the training program may also precipitate the need for an early termination, interrupting the normal flow of the supervisory process. Typically, however, both supervisor and counselor are in a position to anticipate the tasks of Stage 3 in a timely and systematic manner. These tasks include summation and termination.

Summation

As the end of the learning contract begins to near, both supervisor and counselor benefit from a review of the supervisory process. If weekly progress notes have been kept, a reflection on topics, sequence of topics and ongoing reactions to process are useful in understanding the many facets of the supervisory process. An evaluation and discussion of both strengths and growing edges brings a close to the supervisory chapter, leaving the counselor with a sense of satisfaction with what has been accomplished as well as a formulation of some of the agenda for the next supervisory chapter. It is helpful to the trainee's developing sense of professionalism to be affirmed, when performance has warranted it, as an individual who is making progress toward becoming a professional in the field. The supervisor may commend a neophyte for having laid an excellent foundation and affirm a near graduate for one's growing professional competence. An attitude of collegial affirmation from the supervisor helps counselors to firm up their growing professional identity and sense of competence and typically motivates them to higher levels of performance.

Termination

When I first began supervising, after a decade of teaching, I was not fully aware of the transference issues present in the supervisory relationship and the need to work through termination issues carefully. Over the years I have come to realize that the supervisory relationship of mentor can be more complex and equally as intense as that of psychotherapy. Working with supervisees who share similar interests and values and who are seeking to emulate one's own professional role may give rise to levels of emotion which go beyond the objective data of the supervisory contract. What will be the ongoing relationship with the supervisee after the series of compensated supervisory hours comes to an end? Adherence to the supervisory working alliance during the early and middle phases allows the supervisor to deal more clearly with issues of termination. If it is clear that the relationship has been a professional working alliance, albeit a warm, caring, empathic and supportive one, it is easier to deal with mutual expectations for the future. Issues to be addressed will vary with the intensity, depth and nuances of each given supervisory relationship. Shall the relationship continue in the future as supervisor–trainee? Will it move toward becoming professional colleagues? Is there a mutual desire to explore a relationship as friends?

Attention to termination issues by the supervisor provides excellent modeling for the counselor who typically is simultaneously involved in the process of termination with clients. I find that beginning counselors are surprised at how early I begin to raise issues of termination regarding their clients. As they begin to understand the complexity of termination for a client who is thoroughly invested in the counseling process, they typically begin to see the parallel process issues in their own supervisory termination.

Summary

In the preceding pages the core process of supervision has been described as a process of *attending leading to awareness*, of *exploring resulting in insight* and of *personalizing culminating in integration*. The typical supervisory process includes three stages in which unique supervisory issues are addressed. During each of the stages identifiable supervisory attitudes and skills facilitate the work of the respective stages.

The core process, however, is always individualized because of the uniqueness of each supervisor and trainee and their respective relationship as well as the many variables introduced into the process through the clients presented. Using the "core-process" concept as a general navigational chart does not take away the mystery inherent in every person and more pronounced in every relationship. As the sailor responds instinctively to unpredictable variations in wind direction and velocity and to the influence of currents and tides in sailing toward his destination, so the supervisor responds to the emerging challenges of the supervisory working alliance. There is an element of mystery in the supervisory relationship which allows each relationship to be new and fresh and unpredictable. It was Einstein who commented that the most beautiful thing we can experience is the mysterious. It is the source of all true art and all science. It is the hope of the authors that our attempts to explore this mystery will assist us all in appreciating its depth and breadth.

References

G. Corey, *Theory and Practice of Counseling and Psychotherapy*, 2nd ed. Monterey, California: Brooks/Cole, 1982.

C. Barnard, *The Body Machine*. New York, N.Y.: Crown, 1981.

Part 2

The Supervisory Process

3

The Supervisory Learning Contract

Starting the supervisory experience without a learning contract is like beginning a journey to an unknown destination without a map. The end result of such a venture is usually the loss of time, money and energy, a feeling of frustration and anger, and the very real probability that you will never reach your intended destination at all. The journey of the supervisory experience also needs a map. This tool takes the form of the supervisory learning contract which the supervisor and student create together at the beginning of the supervisory experience.

I. Rationale for the Supervisory Learning Contract (SLC)

The *first* rationale for the SLC is to clarify expectations for the benefit of both candidates and supervisors. Supervisors come to the learning experience with certain expectations for themselves and of their supervisees. Candidates likewise have expectations for themselves and of their supervisors. Many of these expectations will coincide but some may not. To leave these expectations unspoken will only lead to possible difficulties in the future.

To return to the analogy of the trip, if the supervisor wants to journey to New York and the candidate envisions a trip to San Francisco, there will be dire consequences if they do not clarify the destination before they begin their journey. The most productive and rewarding supervisory relationships result when both the supervisor and the candidate are striving to reach the same destination.

One area that needs particular clarification is the criteria and process of evaluation to be used in grading. Supervisees need to know how their progress will be evaluated and what criteria will be used in this evaluation. If there is an evaluation form that will be used by the candidate, and perhaps also by the student, this form needs to be discussed as a part of the contracting procedure. If the candidate has any questions or reservations about the evaluation procedure, it is best to work through this as a part of the trust-building process at the beginning, rather than have this take place at the end of the evaluation period.

The *second* rationale for the SLC is to set boundaries and parameters around the supervisory relationship. This boundary setting is in no way restrictive or limiting, because the supervisor and supervisee may set the boundary wherever it is most beneficial and appropriate. On the contrary, setting the boundaries and adhering to them gives the supervisor-supervisee relationship the freedom to live and grow so that they can meet their mutual goals without extraneous distractions.

There are many boundaries that must be set, and one of the most important of these is the boundary between therapy and supervision. If candidates have a good self-concept and high levels of emotional resources, the boundary is fairly easy to establish and maintain. If, however, the supervisee is going through some sort of personal or professional crisis, or if the candidate does not have a positive self-concept or a strong reserve of emotional resources, then he or she might try, either consciously or unconsciously, to secure some "bootleg therapy" during the supervisory time. If this happens, the supervisor needs to identify what is occurring and then process it with the candidate. If a supervisor, without being aware of it, is seduced into moving away from the supervisory relationship and into a therapeutic relationship, this movement has a tendency to grow and push aside the supervisory-learning relationship. This is why it is imperative that the supervisor be constantly alert to the possibility of this movement away from supervision. If the issue that the supervisee presents is a matter of deep severity and of a long-standing nature, it is best to refer the candidate to another professional for psychological help. This way the SLC remains clear and defined, and the candidate receives the necessary additional psychological support.

The *third* rationale for the SLC is to set a role model for candidates who someday may become supervisors themselves. One of the best models of teaching is the "living model," i.e., to exemplify and live out in behavior what the supervisor wants to teach the supervisee.

If the supervisor wants to teach mutuality and respect to the candidate, this can usually be fostered by setting an example of mutuality and respect through the contract-building process. The supervisor can communicate to the supervisee, when this is demonstrated in the contracting process, that the supervisory relationship leaves room for the supervisor to learn from the supervisee, as well as for the candidate to learn from the supervisor. This, in turn, sets the tone for the whole learning atmosphere and the future learning relationship.

Even if a candidate should never become a supervisor, this role model process is valuable because supervisees can utilize what they learn from this supervisor-supervisee relationship and apply it to the candidate-client relationship. The role modeling process then has a double benefit. It helps candidates enhance their client work, as well as further their growth toward becoming effective supervisors.

II. Areas of Concern To Be Defined in the SLC

Now that we have reflected on the rationale for the SLC, in this next section we take a brief look at some of the areas that might be included in the SLC. Every contract might not include all the following areas enumerated; likewise, there might be other items that could be added depending upon the unique circumstances of the particular situation.

One of the *first* areas to be clarified is the purpose of the supervision. In the business and financial world the primary purpose of supervision might be to increase the productivity and raise profits of that company. In the helping professions supervision has a very different purpose, i.e., the professional growth of the person being supervised and the well-being of the client served. Since this is the broad goal of the supervisory process, it needs to be stated.

Once this overview purpose is established, the supervisor and supervisee need to work out the specifics. If the candidate wants to grow in the area of marriage and family counseling, this needs to be stated. If the focus is individual counseling or group counseling this needs to be established. Sometimes a candidate might want to have a dual or multifaceted focus.

Some supervisors find it very helpful to familiarize themselves with a candidate's background prior to the first supervisory session. This can be done by reviewing a supervisee's transcripts and course work, and by looking at evaluations of previous supervisors. With this review, supervisors can explore with supervisees whether or not they want additional help in former areas of concentration, or would prefer to move on to another focus. For example, if the candidate has been concentrating on individual counseling, the supervisor would want to determine whether the supervisee prefers to continue the emphasis on one-on-one counseling or proceed to the area of marriage or group therapy.

If candidates have had no previous supervision, then the supervisor will want to take some extra time to get to know those supervisees in order to establish the most helpful and appropriate educational goals. What are their strengths? What are the areas that need to be developed? Learning candidates' strengths as well as their areas of limitations can help establish the specific purposes of the supervision.

A *second* area to be defined will be the expectations regarding clients. Who will the clients be? How will the candidate secure the clients? How many clients will the supervisee be expected to carry? Are there some clients that would be inappropriate for supervision?

If candidates work in agencies, they can counsel with clients from those agencies. If, however, if they want more variety in their client load, then other agencies or settings can be secured to expand their learning experience and further their educational goals.

I presently teach in the Master's program in Pastoral Counseling at Loyola College in Maryland, and also serve as the Director of Field Education for that program. Candidates in our two-year program are expected to counsel with at least four or five clients weekly to satisfy the clinical requirements. Candidates in the intensive full-time program are expected to carry twice that client load. If priests or ministers choose to utilize their own parishes for their clinical setting but do not have enough clients to satisfy the numerical requirements, then they must seek adjunct placements so that the minimal number of required clients can be maintained.

Are there clients that would be inappropriate for supervision? The answer to this question could be either yes or no, depending upon the goals or purposes of the supervision. If the goal of supervision is to learn to do marital therapy, then a client with severe intra-psychic difficulties would not be appropriate. If the goal was to learn to do child or play therapy, then a ten year old child would be an appropriate client.

It is generally best to have a beginning counselor work with a variety of clients—both men and women, who represent a wide span of ages. The presenting problems should be mostly neurotic and developmental. Until a candidate is more seasoned and experienced, it is usually preferable to avoid specialized counseling, i.e., child therapy, marriage/couple counseling, and family counseling.

A *third* area to be defined in the SLC would concern the relationship between the candidate and the agency. Each agency or institution has its own rules and regulations. To spell these out clearly for the supervisee is of utmost importance.

If it is against the policy of the agency to remove a client's folder from the premises, this needs to be spelled out. If the agency provides liability insurance, the terms and provisions of this policy need to be clarified. If the candidate is to collect fees from clients, how and when this is done needs to be explained. If the candidate is to receive a stipend, or percentage of fees collected, this, too, needs to be made clear. The use of office space, the billing of clients, confidentiality, cancellation policies, and restrictions on the use of the building and audio-video equipment are some of the other areas that also need clarification.

Most progressive agencies include all of these policies and procedures in a handbook or manual. When this is the case, the learning contract can simply refer to this manual and state that the policies enumerated in the handbook are to be respected and followed.

A *fourth* area to be defined in the SLC relates to the format for presentations. After the supervisor and supervisee have established the purpose or purposes of the supervision, then the mechanics and tools for accomplishing these purposes can be selected. Because this is such an important area, a significant portion of the next chapter will be devoted to this topic, entitled "Supervisory Formats and Evaluation Procedures."

A *fifth* area to be defined in the SLC relates to the schedule and timing for supervision. To designate a specific day and time for supervision is one of the best ways for the supervisor to say to the supervisee, "Supervision is very important."

Unfortunately in many agencies, supervision is not given the priority of a set day and time. It is squeezed in, when and if there is time. This says to the supervisee, "Supervision is not important."

There will, of course, be emergencies that emerge from time to time, when the supervisor must attend a conference out of town, or respond to the cry for help of a suicidal client. When this happens it will be to the advantage of everyone concerned for the supervisor to reschedule the supervisory session. This shows respect for the supervisee and the supervisory process as well.

What about the length of the supervisory session? It is common to designate an hour for supervision. This allows time to listen to a portion of a counseling session, and also time for processing it. If the cases being supervised are very critical or complicated, then an hour and a half might be preferred over the allotment of only an hour. This might be especially true in processing family or group therapy.

How much supervision is enough? Some theorists might say that you can never get enough supervision, but because we live in a world of reality and limitations decisions must be made. A rule of thumb that I have followed with candidates is an hour of supervision for every five client hours. A supervisee working with ten clients weekly would then want to have at least two hours of supervision. Ideally, this candidate would receive weekly two hours of individual supervision, plus an hour of group supervision.

How about the frequency of supervision? For beginning candidates or supervisees moving into a new form of therapy, weekly supervision is a must. For more advanced candidates, or supervisees with smaller counseling loads, every other week or even once a month would be adequate. This form of supervision takes on the features of a consultation. The candidate's training level and the need for supervision can be evaluated and taken into consideration in setting the frequency of supervision.

A *sixth* area to be defined in the SLC is the duration or time frame of the supervisory relationship. When will the supervision begin? When will the supervision end? If a candidate is involved in an academic program, then the school year is usually a reasonable time frame. The supervision would begin as soon as the candidate begins seeing clients and end at the close of the school year.

In the Loyola two year Master's Program, our candidates begin their supervision the first of September and conclude toward the end of April. If candidates decide to remain at the same agency for a second year and volunteer to continue with clients through the summer, then a summer supervisory contract will need to be negotiated. Vacation dates also need to be determined.

A *seventh* area to be defined is in regard to the location and setting of the supervision. If a candidate is counseling in an agency, then the supervision would probably be held right in the agency's supervisor's office.

If the candidate is counseling in his/her own setting, then the supervisee would generally meet at the office of the appointed supervisor. In any case, the office needs to be sufficiently private so that tapes played and the discussions about clients would not be overheard. A respect for confidentiality needs to be maintained at all times.

It is also most important that the supervision take place in a setting free from outside distractions. Phone calls need to be held until after the supervisory session and interruptions should take place only under emergency circumstances.

Taping expectations are an *eighth* area to be defined in the SLC. Most supervisors want to hear the actual interchange between the supervisee and clients. This can be accomplished through either audio or video taping.

Most agencies have regulations regarding taping procedures. It is always important to have a client's permission prior to taping any counseling sessions. In order to protect the agency, the candidate, and the supervisor from any legal difficulties, it is preferable to have the client sign a release form or a statement giving permission for the taping. This form would describe and define the manner in which the tapes will be used. It should also assure that the client's confidentiality will be protected.

The *ninth* area to be clarified in the SLC deals with evaluation. Evaluation is not what takes place at the end of a semester or another specified time frame. Evaluation is an ongoing reciprocal process that takes place between supervisor and supervisee.

It is obvious that the candidate under supervision is going to be evaluated by the supervisor. Supervisors who feel confident enough about their identity and competence will also welcome a form of evaluation feedback from the candidates that they supervise. This process will be discussed more fully in the next chapter. It is enough at this point to indicate that the tools of evaluation need to be clarified in the SLC.

The *tenth* and final item that needs to be determined is the establishment and payment schedule of the fee. In most agency settings, where the supervisors are salaried employees, the supervision is a part of their job description and no fee is involved. Even when there is no fee involved, it is good to clarify this in writing.

In other situations, where there is no exchange of service, there will be a supervisory fee involved. This fee would probably approximate the supervisor's average client fee. However, because many supervisors recognize the numerous benefits that come from supervising candidates, they will negotiate for a lesser fee in order to benefit from the stimulation, growth, and rewards that come from serving as a mentor-supervisor.

How the payment of the supervisory fee will be made must also be clarified. In most academic programs the supervisor receives payment after the written final evaluation is completed at the end of each semester. The check, in this situation, would be issued by the academic institution.

For candidates in a non-academic/degree program the payment could be paid weekly, monthly, or quarterly depending on the supervisor's preference. The check in this instance would be paid directly to the supervisor by the candidate.

III. Constructing the Supervisory Contract

As has been pointed out in previous chapters, and earlier in this chapter, the construction of the SLC is a collegial process. It is a part of Stage 1 where the focus is on building the alliance through acceptance, understanding, and trust. See Chart I in Chapter 2—The Stages of Supervision. The contract is not dictated by the supervisor nor by the supervisee, but rather the document emerges out of the supervisor-supervisee dialogue.

Candidates in their eagerness to learn may desire to focus on too many areas. A supervisor will want to foster this enthusiasm but also temper it with reality. This, then, needs to be negotiated so that attainable goals can be established.

Should the SLC be verbal or written? The answer to this question is not set in stone. I have worked with both verbal and written contracts.

The natural tendency of supervisors is to take the path of least resistance and go with the verbal contract because it is easier and takes less time. However, many supervisors prefer to take the extra time needed to complete a written contract. Those from this school believe that the written contract is preferable because there are fewer chances for confusion or ambiguity.

After I completed my basic and advanced units of C.P.E. (Clinical Pastoral Education), I moved into a year of supervisory training at Spring Grove Hospital Center in Catonsville, Maryland. It was in my first unit as a supervisor that I worked with Ned, a very flamboyant and erratic student. Because of problems, Ned was moved from his former assignment and placed in a new division in the hospital. Unfortunately, a written SLC was not drawn up, only a verbal contract. Two days into the new unit I had several calls from personnel in Ned's former assignment wanting to know why he was still there. When confronted about this, Ned pleaded ignorance and said he did not know about his placement change. If there had been a written SLC this assignment change would have been very explicit. This incident emphasized to me the importance of a written SLC to clarify expectations.

If questions or problems arise in the supervisory process, the written contract can usually clarify those problems and answer those questions. At the very least, the SLC provides viable data with which to bring resolution to those problems and answers to those questions.

In the 1970's I served as Chairman of the Department of Pastoral Theology and Director of Field Education at St. Mary's Seminary in Baltimore, Maryland. As the program there evolved, it was discovered that the written SLC eliminated many problems, and because of this, each fall all supervisor-supervisee teams were asked to complete a contract for the school year.

Although it is rare, there are occasional instances when the dynamic of the working-through process of the SLC brings to light the fact that the mutual expectations of the supervisor and the candidate are too divergent. Sometimes a destructive transference/countertransference dynamic emerges. In such instances, it would be wise for the appointed supervisor to direct the candidate to another supervisor.

For those supervisors who would like to utilize a written SLC but have not done so in the past, a sample SLC follows.

Sample Supervisor Learning Contract

In order to clarify expectations, this Supervisory Learning Contract has been discussed and negotiated between ___(supervisor)___ and ___(supervisee)___. The following provisions have been agreed upon.

1. Purpose of the Supervision:
   The overview purpose will be to promote the professional growth of the candidate. The major focus will be on marriage/couple counseling. The minor focus will concentrate on how grief impacts on couple relationships.
2. Expectations Regarding Clients:
   The candidate will see couples in his/her own parish (two each week). The candidate will also see couples in the local mental health center (three each week).
3. Expectations Regarding the Agency:
   The candidate will abide by the regulations set up by his/her parish council and senior pastor. He/she will also follow the rules and stipulations as explained in the mental health center policy manual.
4. Format for Presentations:
   The candidate will present on a weekly basis twenty minutes of one audio-taped counseling session and will prepare a write-up according to the prescribed form.
5. Establishing a Schedule:
   The candidate and supervisor will meet each Tuesday from 1 to 2 P.M.
6. Beginning and Ending Time Frame:
   Supervisory sessions will begin on the first Tuesday of September 1987 and end on the third Tuesday of April 1988. There will be a one-week vacation Thanksgiving week and Holy Week, and a two-week vacation at Christmas (starting the week prior to Christmas).
7. Location and Setting:
   The supervisory sessions will be held in the office of the supervisor at the mental health center.
8. Audio Taping Expectations:
   The candidate is expected to have all clients sign an agency release form before they can be recorded. These tapes are to be utilized only in a supervisory setting and are to be erased following the supervisory session, except with special permission. The original copy of the release form is to be placed in the client's agency file. A copy of the release form is to be kept in the supervisee's file of the client. Tapes presented are to be clear and audible.
9. Evaluation Process:
   Both the supervisor and the supervisee will complete a weekly evaluation form. These forms are contained in the Field Educa-

tion Handbook. At the end of the semester a summary evaluation will be completed by the supervisor. This will be shared with the candidate prior to returning it to the Director of Field Education.

10. Establishing a Fee:
    The supervisor will be paid at the rate of fifty dollars an hour. This will be issued by the Director of Field Education at the end of each semester after the semester evaluation has been received.

The terms of this SLC are open for renegotiation if the need should arise. Any changes will be made in writing and signed by both the supervisor and candidate.

Signed _____   (Supervisor) (Date) _____

Signed _____   (Candidate) (Date) _____

IV. Evaluation as Part of the Supervisory Learning Contract

In Chapter 1 entitled "Toward Professional Integration," it was pointed out that the third focus of supervision, besides professional growth of candidates and client welfare, is evaluation. Because this is true the process of evaluation needs to be clarified in the SLC.

Some candidates welcome evaluation because they see it as a way of affirming their areas of strength and identifying the areas that they need to strengthen. Other candidates, because of their own insecurities or experiences with previous evaluation, tend to respond to evaluation with apprehension and fear.

When a supervisor experiences a supervisee in this latter category, the skills of empathy, respect, genuineness and concreteness become extremely important. Just as a candidate with no anxiety might lack motivation, the candidate with high anxiety becomes blocked and paralyzed and this becomes an obstruction to the supervisory experience. The approach and manner of the supervisor can do much to allay candidates' anxieties. As the trust level builds between the supervisor and supervisee these anxieties will diminish and the supervision can progress.

One of the best ways to help fearful candidates relax is to help them recognize that supervision is a learning and growth process for both the supervisee and the supervisor. A few years ago I was supervising a student from the Philippine Islands. Naturally, as the semester began his anxieties were elevated. However, as the semester progressed, and he realized that he could teach me about the unique cultural aspects of the Philippine people, his anxiety leveled off and we both enjoyed and grew from our supervisory time together.

V. Negotiating Changes in the Supervisory Learning Contract

All circumstances of the supervisor-supervisee relationship cannot be foreseen at the time that the SLC is agreed upon. This is particularly true of the goals of supervision. Candidates' learning needs can change as they progress in their skills. Although one candidate might not complete all the learning goals set up in the original SLC, a second supervisee might complete those original goals and want to move on to other growth areas.

A few years ago I was working with a candidate who desired a rather broad focus at the beginning of the SLC. In the middle of the school year the supervisee was offered a position for the following fall in a drug and alcohol abuse center. Because his knowledge of drug and alcohol abuse was rather limited, we negotiated to add this emphasis to the other SLC goals, and zeroed in on these during the spring semester. This new focus helped to better prepare him for his future position after graduation.

There are also times when the reverse takes place. Rather than narrowing the goals, the goals need to be expanded. This is particularly true if the original goals are very focused. The candidate and supervisor may set as the focus the use of Transactional Analysis with depressed clients. This focus might need to be expanded to the use of behavior therapy or Rational Emotive therapy when some clients do not respond to the T.A. approach.

The emphasis of an advanced candidate might change from the focus on many clients to the concentration on one client. This might also be the case with a beginning candidate who is experiencing numerous difficulties with one particular client.

So the SLC needs to be flexible and open to negotiation as candidates grow, clients change, and circumstances are altered.

Other parts of the SLC, in addition to the purpose and emphasis of supervision, need to be changed as well. Some other examples follow. When candidates need more exposure to clients, the number of client hours can be increased. If the agency secures television equipment, the candidates could be asked to make some video tapes of client work. The supervisor might be elected to a committee that convenes at the time designated for meeting with the supervisee, so this has to be moved to another mutually satisfactory day and time. The format for presentations may not meet the candidate's needs so another learning tool would need to be selected.

When changes are negotiated and made in the original SLC it is professionally helpful to note these changes as an addendum, at the bottom of the SLC; the supervisor and supervisee can then initial and date these changes.

Summary

The rationale and purposes of the SLC are threefold:

1. To clarify expectations for both candidates and supervisors.
2. To establish boundaries and parameters around the supervisory relationship.
3. To set a role model for candidates.

Areas that might become part of the SLC are:

1. Purpose of the supervision
2. Expectations regarding clients
3. Expectations regarding the agency
4. Format for the presentations
5. Supervision schedule
6. Time frame
7. Location and setting
8. Taping expectations
9. Evaluation process
10. Fee and payment

The SLC is constructed and negotiated through a collegial process. The end result might be either a verbal or written contract. Evaluation is an integral part of the supervisor-supervisee relationship. This would include the evaluation of (1) candidates, (2) supervisors, and (3) the process. Evaluation tools and forms need to be discussed and clarified early in the supervisory process.

Occasionally the SLC needs to be altered. This might become necessary because of (1) supervisee needs, (2) client changes, or (3) the emergence of special circumstances.

4

Supervisory Formats and Evaluation Procedures

Introduction

In the previous chapter I used the analogy of a journey to illustrate the supervisory experience. I pointed out that the supervisory learning contract is like the road map that helps the supervisor and the supervisee establish the overall route of the journey after the destination has been determined.

In this chapter I would like to again draw on the analogy of the trip; however, this time I want to draw a parallel between the compass and the supervisory format. Just as drivers on an unmarked country road in unfamiliar territory need a compass to help keep them on track, so too, drivers of the supervisory vehicle need the aid of a structured format to help keep them and their supervisees moving toward the chosen learning objectives.

The purposes or functions of supervision at Loyola College are three-fold in nature: (1) the welfare of the client, (2) the professional growth of the candidate, and (3) the evaluation of the candidate. As I work with graduate candidates in supervision, I seek to emphasize all three of these areas. Sometimes, all three areas receive equal attention while at other times one area might receive more emphasis because of the particular needs of the supervisee or the clinical situation.

I. Supervisory Formats

The World Book Dictionary defines "format" as "the shape, design, plan, or arrangement of anything." So a supervisory format is that shape or plan that gives form to the supervisory process and provides the structure for the supervisory sessions. In the Loyola program we utilize a variety of formats, each with its own particular purpose. Our three basic formats are: (1) Individual Supervision, (2) the Clinical Case Seminar and (3) the Interdisciplinary Case Conference. All three of these formats involve four stages: (1) preparation and review, (2) clarification, (3) clinical presentation, and (4) evaluation.

A. *Individual Supervision*

It is a high priority for each student to receive individual supervision. In this format the individual candidate meets, one-on-one, with a supervisor to review each week some aspect of his or her clinical work.

Individual supervisors are selected to serve on the basis of their training, competence, broad experience, maturity and high level integration of all the aforementioned aspects.

1. *Rationale for Individual Supervision*

The rationale for individual supervision is that it provides the opportunity for a very special relationship to develop between the candidate and the supervisor. This relationship of trust, caring, sharing and respect allows the supervisory thrust to focus on the very special and individual learning needs of this one student, without having to take into consideration the learning needs of any other students. Succinctly stated, the advantage of the individual supervisory format is that it eliminates the demands and distractions potentially present in a group setting and allows the supervision to be highly focused.

In order to accomplish this focusing, the supervisor and the candidate need to select an appropriate presentation outline which calls for a body of written information from the supervisee. This information is prepared ahead of time in accordance with a mutually agreed-upon structure, which encourages and moves supervisees toward new learning experiences.

Before a presentation outline for supervision can be chosen, the supervisor and the supervisee need to look at all of the various relationships involved in the clinical experience. Only after they have done this can they then decide which relationship or relationships are to be emphasized.

Below is a diagram of the clinical diamond. This diagram depicts the various relationships of supervision and how they inter-relate with one another.

SUPERVISOR

AGENCY/INSTITUTION   SUPERVISEE/COUNSELOR

CLIENT/COUNSELEE

The basic relationships that might be viewed in supervision are between the:

    a. Supervisor and the Supervisee

    b. Supervisee and the Client

    c. Supervisor and the Agency
    d. Supervisee and the Agency
    e. Client and the Agency
    f. Supervisor and the Client

The major focus in supervision is usually on the relationship between the supervisee and the client. If this is the relationship that is selected for primary focus, then it must also be determined whether the concomitant focus will be on the supervisee's professional growth or the welfare of the client, or a combination of the two. It is important to clarify these factors, for in doing so the appropriate outline presentation can best be selected.

2. *Presentation Outline*

The purpose of the presentation outline is to help the candidate focus on one client in a way that will identify strengths in the student, as well as elicit those areas that need further refinement, reflection and growth. The outline would pose such questions as:

a. Who is the client? (age, sex, race, physical description, education, marital status, vocation, religion, family, mood, affect, previous counseling, medications, etc.) Was this an agency or direct referral? The identity of the client is to always remain confidential.

b. What brings this client to counseling? What are the other problems or dysfunctions that have subsequently emerged?

c. What are the goals for this client? Identify both short term and long range goals. How are the counseling goals and the pastoral goals similar? How are they different?

d. What has happened thus far in the counseling process? What are the resistance issues? Fee issues? What is happening transferentially? How is countertrance being worked through and understood?

e. What is the prognosis for the client? What is the rationale and clinical evidence for the prognosis? Explain.

f. What are the theological themes that have emerged? It is incumbent upon the pastoral counselor to develop the skill of identifying the theological themes in a case. These themes may be verbalized (guilt, hope, forgiveness, etc.) or unarticulated. Whether or not "God language" is used, supervisees are encouraged to identify the theological themes that are relevant to each client.

g. What responses, expressed through the counseling relationships with clients, were helpful? One of the most important reasons for supervision is to affirm the candidate's areas of strength and competency. This can best be done by encouraging students to identify their own areas of strength. When they are able to do this, then the supervisor can substantiate their perception. When a candidate is not able to identify a particular strength, then the supervisor can bring this to the student's awareness by asking questions about that particular area or skill.

In addition to helping students identify responses that were helpful, it is also important to help them articulate how and why they were helpful. As students develop this ability, they can then recognize strengths in future counseling sessions.

h. What responses were least helpful? In order for students to improve their counseling skills, they must learn to recognize which responses, either spoken or not verbalized, were least helpful to the client. After these are identified, then students are encouraged to verbalize alternate responses that would be more helpful. It also assists candidates in their growth when they are encouraged to give the rationale as to why this alternate response would be more helpful.

i. In what way can the supervisor be helpful in this supervisory session? Oftentimes students do not articulate clearly how they feel that the supervisor can help them in their professional growth. This question then encourages them to do this; that is, ask for what they want and need in this particular supervisory session. When this is done the learning experience becomes more intentional and rewarding for both the supervisor and the supervisee.

B. The Clinical Case Seminar

The second format for supervision in the Loyola program is the Clinical Case Seminar. This seminar, usually referred to as the small group, is composed of five or six clinical students who are at a similar place in training and experience. The group meets weekly for an hour and a quarter. The purpose of the seminar is to help the presenting supervisee to share work with one of his or her present clients for evaluation and feedback.

1. Rationale for the Clinical Case Seminar

The rationale for the small group is to give students an opportunity to share some of their clinical work with a group of peers. As I view the small group, I see four main advantages: (1) each student's clinical experience is broadened, (2) each client is seen from a variety of clinical perspectives, (3) the evaluation process is enriched by differing views, and (4) the various therapeutic approaches represented in the group can help the presenter move through or around therapeutic obstacles.

The first advantage of this format is that each student's clinical experience is broadened not only by his or her own presentations, but also through the cases presented by the other students in the group. For example, one student may be situated in an agency where teenagers are treated. When this student presents an adolescent to the small group, the other members of the case seminar learn about adolescent treatment, even though they may not have this experience first hand in their agency. The sharing of a broad spectrum of clients tends to enrich the learning experience of all the members in the small group. The second rationale of the small group is that clients are seen from as many perspectives as there are students in the class. This is especially helpful in understanding clients from differing cultures and socio-economic backgrounds. A third advantage of the small group is that members of the group can react and respond to comments made by other members of the case seminar. One student might feel that a response by the presenter was not helpful, whereas several other members of the small group might see something positive in that same response. It is not so much the purpose of the group to decide which perspective is correct, but rather to provide the presenting student with a variety of insights. A fourth rationale for the small group format is that when a student is therapeutically "stuck" with a client, there are rich resources in the group to help the supervisee to get "unstuck." For example, the presenting student may come from a more analytic approach. When this approach is not working with a client, another student in the clinical seminar, who comes from a behavioral perspective, might be able to offer some suggestions that will help to get the client "unstuck."

2. Presentation Outline for the Clinical Case Conference

The presentation outline for the small group is usually similar or identical to that used in the individual supervision format, except that in the small group, the question requesting the help of the supervisor is directed to the members of the clinical case seminar as well.

There are four stages to the small group process. In the *first* stage the small group members read the write-up prepared by the presenting supervisee. A copy of the write-up is given to each member of the small group at the beginning of the class. In the *second* stage questions generated by the written materials are raised by the group. These questions generally try to clarify any issues in the write-up that might be ambiguous. If a supervisee omits certain information in the written materials which is pertinent to the case, that information can then be filled in. No evaluation is allowed at this point in the process as this stage is only for clarification and information gathering. In the *third* stage the supervisee plays a twenty minute segment (audio or video) from a recent counseling session. The twenty minute segment is selected by the supervisee for a particular purpose. The candidate might feel that this segment shows his or her strengths, and wants to use the group as a sounding board to check this out. On the other hand, the segment chosen might reflect a specific difficulty that the supervisee is having with this client, and the group is called upon to review what is helpful and not helpful. I have found that it is important for the supervisee to identify for the group, before playing the tape, the reason or reasons for selecting this particular segment of the tape. Evaluation is the *fourth* stage. After reviewing the tape a period of evaluation and discussion follows. This feedback from both the supervisor and the members of the group incorporates both positive and negative reflections. When the presenting supervisee is able to identify the "trouble spots" in the tape, the members of the group can then share from their own experiences what responses they feel might be constructive and helpful. Special attention is given to the question, "What would you like from the group?" All the members of the small group are expected to share their perspectives, thoughts, ideas and questions in each case presented. The Clinical Case Seminar, within the Loyola program, gives each student a minimum of two opportunities to present cases within the small group setting each clinical semester.

It is recognized that candidates will have a certain level of anxiety when they present their clinical work, especially at the beginning of their training. Some anxiety can be beneficial to the learning process, but too much anxiety is destructive to learning and growth. In order to keep anxiety at a productive level, candidates in the Loyola program are involved in a peer counseling experience during the first few weeks of their first clinical semester. This builds an ideal, non-threatening environment for learning with strong supportive relationships prior to the presentation of any clinical material. It also gives time for the case load to build.

C. The Interdisciplinary Case Conference

The third format in the Loyola program is the Interdisciplinary Case Conference. Students and faculty alike usually abbreviate the title for this format to the ID Conference, or simply "Interdisciplinary." Twelve students are assigned from the various Clinical Case Seminar groups to form the ID group. At Loyola we try to achieve a good mix of age, sex, denomination and other factors as we form these groups.

1. The Rationale for the ID Case Conference

Many of the advantages found in the individual supervision and Clinical Case Seminar formats are benefits found in the ID Conference; however, there are several distinct advantages to be found in this format. These advantages are fourfold:

(a) the focus is broadened to include the overall management of the case,

(b) the leadership is given by two professors who represent differing disciplines,

(c) the presentation outline is more formal and demanding, and

(d) the time frame is expanded.

The first advantage of the ID Conference is a broadening of focus. Whereas in the clinical case seminar the focus is mainly on one segment of an individual counseling session, in the ID Conference there is greater opportunity to look at the overall management of the case. How does this one session fit into the ongoing clinical dialogue? How do the goals of this particular session fit into the other goals for this client? What kind of progress is this client making in the various therapeutic areas in the light of the total clinical picture?

The second rationale for the ID format is the broadened perspective of two helping disciplines. Instead of one leader, as in the case of the Clinical Case Seminar, the ID Conference is given leadership by two professors, who represent two different and distinct helping disciplines. This past year I co-led an ID Conference with a social worker, last year with a clinical psychologist, and the year before with a psychiatrist. The richness of this mix expands the clinical horizons of students and adds new dimensions to the various aspects of the cases presented by the candidates.

The third rationale for the ID Conference is that it gives students the opportunity to make a more formal presentation to a larger and more diverse group of peers. Whereas the small group has the advantage of a more relaxed setting where the members of the group are encouraged to present their "warts" as well as their "wings," in the ID Conference students gain the experience of presenting their clients in a more formal setting. In this setting candidates are encouraged to present their very best counseling work. The presentation outline for the ID Conference is more complete and technical than in the case seminar. Whereas the write-up for the small group might be two or three pages, in the ID Conference the written materials would probably be at least twice that length.

The fourth advantage of the ID Conference format is the extended time frame. Whereas an hour and a quarter is adequate for the small group presentations, at least two hours is devoted to the ID Conference.

2. *Presentation Outline for the ID Case Conference*

The presentation outline for the Interdisciplinary Case Conference in the Loyola Master's program in Pastoral Counseling is as follows:

Identifying Information
>   (Name, age, sex, religion, etc.)

Initial Clinical Impression
>   (Description of appearance, behavior, speech, etc.)

Chief Complaints
>   (Problems as patient sees them, and patient's thoughts as to why they are present. Recent crises, if any.)

Personal History—Background
>   (a) Childhood, Adolescence, Adulthood (succinctly!)
>   (b) Marriage? Description!
>   (c) Relations to others, e.g., interpersonal, sexual.

Mental Status
>   (a) *Symptoms*, e.g., depression, anxiety, phobias, etc., compulsions, rituals
>   (b) *Any Psychosis*. Hallucinating, delusions, ideas of reference, sensorium, memory, insight, and judgment.

Medical History
>   (a) Serious illnesses, operations, head injuries
>   (b) On medication now? What kind, dosage?
>   (c) Seeing a psychologist, psychiatrist, counselor now? in past? How often, how long?

Psychodynamic Formulation
>   (Overall statement of problems, defenses, using material at hand)

Diagnosis, Prognosis and Recommendations
>   (If counseling is recommended, what goals, how often will client be seen, what kind of counseling?)

Pastoral Perspectives
>(Reflections on theological presuppositions of client; identification of theological themes; formulation of pastoral goals.)

Requests of the Group
>In what ways can the group be helpful? Be specific.

The ID seminar follows the same basic stages as the Clinical Case Seminar process. However, some ID leaders require the write up to be handed out a week in advance, so that it can be read prior to class. This allows more time for discussion and evaluation. The ID format also allows five to eight minutes at the end of each class for the presenting supervisee to summarize the strengths and "growing edges" identified by the members of the seminar.

In the two year Loyola program, our students begin with Individual Supervision and Clinical Case Seminar Formats the first year, and then add the Interdisciplinary Case Conference Format the second year. This enables the supervisees to begin at a basic level, then proceed to a more advanced level as their knowledge, skills and confidence increase. This enables the supervisee to build one learning success upon a previous learning success.

The forms utilized in the Loyola program to evaluate the progress of beginning and more advanced counselors and the progressive expectations of candidates-in-training are described by Estadt in a chapter entitled "From Technician to Artist" in *Pastoral Counseling* (Prentice-Hall, 1983).

II. Evaluation Procedures

In the second part of this chapter I would like to describe briefly the evaluation model as it is implemented in the Loyola program. Ideally, evaluation is an ongoing process from the first supervisory session to the last, not something that takes place only at the end of the supervisory experience.

One of the main purposes of evaluation is to help both the supervisor and the supervisee to determine what is helpful and not helpful to the client, the counselor/supervisee, the supervisor, and the agency. Each point of the supervisory diamond needs to be considered.

A. *Feedback from Each Supervisory Session*

To avoid a hit-or-miss model of evaluation, supervisors are encouraged to make evaluation a part of each supervisory session. The following

questions might be asked by both the supervisor and the supervisee after
each session:

    a. What were your feelings about this supervisory session: In antic-
       ipation? During the session? During the subsequent week?
    b. What were the supervisory issues addressed? Was it helpful to ad-
       dress more than one issue?
    c. What pastoral and/or theological issues were addressed in this ses-
       sion?
    d. What further reflections do you have about this session?

The supervisor might also ask: What, in your judgment, did the student (or students) learn from this session? About clients? About the counseling process? About the supervisory process? It would also be beneficial
for the supervisee to describe the type and quality of responses from the
supervisor and ask: How were these helpful? Not helpful? How could they
have been more helpful?

These questions can be shared and discussed at the beginning of each
supervisory session. They can help both supervisor and supervisee identify their feelings and the supervisory issues addressed, and confirm what
has been learned by each. A substitution can be made for the item dealing
with pastoral/theological issues to meet the needs of other professional disciplines.

From my own experience, I have found that there are two important
reasons for investing the time necessary to follow this weekly process. The
first is to validate the learning that has taken place, and the second is to
identify when assumed learning has not taken place. The latter becomes
a natural springboard into the new supervisory session.

B. Semester Evaluation

Early in the supervisory process the supervisor will want to show and
explain the final written evaluation form. This final evaluation would contain a summary of the feedback from all the previous supervisory sessions.
It is most important to point out that nothing will be included in the final
written evaluation that has not been previously discussed. Students tend
to experience evaluation anxiety and that is to be expected. It helps to reduce or eliminate excessive anxiety for the supervisee to know from the
beginning that there will be nothing in the final written evaluation that has
not been processed earlier.

It is helpful to a student in an academic program to know that this
evaluation will be discussed by the supervisor and the supervisee prior to
sending it in to the academic institution, and that the supervisee will have

the opportunity to respond in writing, if he or she desires. This response would then be attached to the supervisor's evaluation.

C. *Coordination of Evaluations from Various Sources*

At the end of each semester I send out, as Director of Field Education, the various evaluation forms that need to be completed. These are sent to the agency supervisors and to Loyola supervisors. Loyola supervisors supplement the agency supervision and provide the individual supervision for students who use their own parishes or agencies for their clinical practicum experience.

When the semester evaluations are received from the agency and Loyola supervisors, they are then passed along to the Clinical Case Seminar supervisors, who serve as the clinical coordinators for the students involved in the experiential part of the program.

D. *Peer Consultation and Review in the Evaluation Process*

The professors leading the Clinical Case Seminars and the ID Conferences (referred to as the Core Faculty) meet monthly to evaluate and review the progress of each clinical student. Does the student have enough clients? Is the student experiencing enough of a variety of clients to have a well-rounded experience? Crisis counseling? Short term? Mid phase? Long term? Is the student getting adequate support and supervision in the agency? Are there any special concerns regarding this student? When needed, remedial help is offered to students who can benefit from this. This is also the setting where determinations are made regarding students who are not ready or suited for the program.

At the end of the semester the Core Faculty meets to determine the clinical grades of students. This is done through a collegial consensus process, taking into consideration students' self-evaluations, and the evaluations of the agency, Loyola and Clinical Case Seminar supervisors. Because the supervisors, as well as the candidates, use the same evaluation form, each category can be compared to see if the perceptions of the candidate are similar or dissimilar to the perceptions of the supervisor's evaluation.

E. *Formal Summary Feedback Session*

During the last week of the semester the small group supervisor meets individually with each member of the Clinical Case Seminar. The purpose of this meeting is to share the end of the semester evaluation with the candidate and give the student the clinical grade for the semester. After the student has received and reviewed the evaluation there is time to discuss the evaluation and the grade. If the student feels that the evaluation and/or grade are appropriate and fair, then the supervisor can talk with the candidate regarding the clinical experience of the next semester. If the student feels that the evaluation and/or the grade are either inflated or deflated, then a time period can be set for consideration and re-evaluation.

In addition, this final session is a time to review the student's clinical summary sheet which is then placed in his or her permanent file. The clinical summary sheet includes information about the number of client hours (individual, couple or family), hours of supervision (individual, small group, interdisciplinary), as well as time devoted to clinical preparations and other clinical commitments (staff meetings, intake interviews, etc.). These clinical summary forms will be useful to students later on when they apply for membership in the various certifying organizations.

F. *Evaluation of the Supervisor*

Last, but certainly not least, is the evaluation by the candidate of the supervisor. Most academic institutions require that students complete an evaluation of each professor. Other agencies and settings also find this procedure helpful in determining the effectiveness of their faculty and staff.

Because the nature of a clinical course is so different from that of an academic course, the Loyola program has devised a guideline for the evaluation of its clinical supervisors. Each clinical student is invited to evaluate his or her clinical supervisors (Excellent, Competent, or Unsatisfactory) in regard to the following fifteen areas:

_____ 1. Accepts students in a non-judgmental way.

_____ 2. Enters into the frame of reference of the student.

_____ 3. Elicits essential data from the student.

_____ 4. Assesses the strengths of the student.

_____ 5. Assesses the weaknesses and "growing edges" of the student.

_____ 6. Affirms the student in relationship to the strengths.

_____ 7. Points out weaknesses and "growing edges" in a professional manner.

_____ 8. Initiates pertinent discussion in the supervisory sessions.

_____ 9. Helps students to gain insight into transference-countertransference issues in the counseling relationship.

_____ 10. Facilitates the formulation of counseling goals.

_____ 11. Facilitates an understanding of the psychodynamics of the client.

_____ 12. Assists the student in dealing with termination and/or referral.

_____ 13. Has a sensitivity to ethical issues in the counselor-client interaction.

_____ 14. Facilitates theological reflection on the counseling experience.

_____ 15. Establishes and maintains good interprofessional relations with students.

Students are also encouraged to make written comments and to give an overall rating of the quality of supervision.

Summary

The Loyola program uses three formats for supervision: Individual Supervision, the Clinical Case Seminar and the Interdisciplinary Case Conference. The rationale behind a variety of formats for supervision has been to combine the advantages of the three different learning situations. It is recommended that the evaluation of clinical progress be ongoing and sequential. A method of evaluating each supervisory session is proposed as an aid in keeping supervision focused and identifying issues as they emerge from week to week. In the Loyola program, the formalized evaluation process takes place at the end of an academic semester in keeping with the terms of the Supervisory Learning Contract. This evaluation attempts to integrate clinical data from a variety of sources: (1) the student's self-evaluation, (2) reports from the agency supervisor(s), and (3) reports from Loyola Supervisors involved in Individual Supervision, Clinical Case Seminars and Interdisciplinary Case Conferences. The supervisor of the Clinical Case Seminar, in the Loyola system, serves as the candidate's clinical director for the semester with the responsibility of integrating the data from the various sources in dialogue with other supervisors. The final step in the evaluation process is the opportunity for candidates to evaluate their supervisors.

5

Interpretation and Resistance

The purpose of the next two chapters will be to present how a given supervisor works with students in understanding and utilizing important middle phase concepts of therapy. The first chapter begins with a brief introduction concerning the supervisory process and then focuses on the issues of interpretation and resistance and how these issues form the communication component of the therapeutic relationship. The second chapter covers the important concepts of transference and countertransference and how these comprise the relational quality of the counseling relationship. Each concept will be defined in terms of theoretical understanding and technical implications will be explored. This approach is advanced since theory without technique is useless and technique without theory is empty. Hence, there will be a constant interfacing between these two all-important topics of theory and technique.

Before going into the chapters as such, the author presents some convictions which have, through the years, infused his work with hundreds of counseling students. At the end of each section, some important psychotherapeutic implications will be summarized regarding the issues discussed.

I. Convictions

Convictions have always been a powerful motivating force in my life. Two major convictions which have informed my way of being with students and professional associates over the years are: that all behavior is a manifestation of need and that learning how to do therapy results from the supervisory process. Our behavior as supervisors says a great deal about the kind of persons we are as well as the kind of supervision we give. From an analysis of our supervisory behavior, we can deduce the person-enhancing philosophy that undergirds our unique way of being with those who are in the process of learning. Research tells us that students frequently model their behavior with clients based on the way we as supervisors relate to them. Hence, it is important that supervisors of counseling students know what motivates their work. One source of motivation that has prompted my supervisory work has been a statement I read many years ago, but the power of its message still has deep meaning. The statement is that they who wish to teach must never cease to learn. There is a reciprocal relationship between teaching and learning and nowhere is this truth more poignantly felt than in the process of supervision. Another source of motivation that has infused my work with students who are learning how to do psychotherapy is the memory I have of my own supervision and of the supervisors with whom I worked in order to develop my professional identity as a therapist, to gain theoretical understanding of important concepts and to acquire technical competence. I can attest to the fact that I have modeled my therapeutic way of being with these based on the positive and empathic way my former supervisor related to me.

Other lesser, but still important, convictions that determine my supervisory style are those elements which define the activity of supervision. One of these convictions is that the purpose of supervision is to help actualize the potential of the therapist. Another way of saying this is that through supervision we enable another less well trained person to become a more fitting instrument in order to help people in their difficulties in living. A second conviction regarding the supervisory process is that it is a teaching experience. As supervisors we educate those in training in the art of using technical knowledge in the hope that in their own person there will come together an integration of both theory and technique and that they will come to the understanding that the most effective agent in the counseling relationship is the use of the self. We can say with confidence that effective counseling is not merely the use of techniques nor theoretical understandings. It is first of all the counselor's use of self in a way that enables those who are counseled to do something constructive and creative about their lives. Lastly, my third conviction is that supervision is an active process. Supervision is not above the fray of therapeutic activity. If it is, it means that the supervisor is fearful of entering into the unchartered waters of life's mysteries. Through the supervisory process, we gain intimate knowledge of how students relate to clients in the process of counseling. We come to an appreciation of the conflicts, defenses, personality style and behavioral expression of both students and clients. Hence, supervision is a demanding responsibility, and to be active in the process requires constant attention to one's own dynamics as well as those of the student and the client. To be active in the process of supervision in no way endangers the so-called neutrality of the supervisor's position. In addition, supervision is not after the fact. If it is, it means that supervision is not fulfilling an important function and that is its predictive quality. As supervisors, we have spent thousands of hours doing therapy, have received hundreds of hours of supervision ourselves, and many of us have spent a great deal of time working in supervision with counseling students; it is my contention at least that this fund of experience should give us the ability to predict the psychotherapeutic results of our students who are working with others. After years of doing therapy, many of us have an intuitive awareness of what clients will do through the course of treatment. In like manner, the supervisor who has worked extensively with a wide variety of students who, likewise, are relating therapeutically with divergent clients obtains a sense of the "rightness of fit" between a given supervisee and a client. It is, as it were, a matter of matching supervisee level of training, expertise and personality functioning with the client's needs for insight and understanding. Being able to sense the predictive outcome of supervisory work gives the student a sense of confidence and the supervisor a sense of well-being knowing that the client is receiving competent help.

In summary, the direction of this chapter will flow from the convictions already presented that all behavior is a manifestation of need. What we do as supervisors springs forth from the depths of our being with others and important needs are answered through the process of working with students in supervision. Learning how to do therapy is best accomplished through supervision. Hence, most of us recall with gratitude those supervisors who helped us to become our best selves. The function of supervision is to help actualize the potential of another less well trained professional. It is basically an educative experience through which both supervisor and supervisee learn all the more about the psychotherapeutic process. Learning of this kind never ends, and as a result of our work our lives take on energy and purpose.

Supervision is an active process—one demanding constant attention to the multi-faceted dimension of the counselor's work with a client as well as those relational issues which develop between the supervisor and the counselor. Lastly, through the supervisory process, there should come about a predictive quality that the supervisor can learn to share with those who are supervised so that they can begin to have an intuitive grasp of how therapy will proceed with a given client. This demands that supervisors know the territory of the counseling field and likewise have a profound understanding of the supervisee's ability as well as the client's needs. This chapter and the one to follow will focus on important middle phase issues of therapy and how these are handled through the supervisory process. The issues to be discussed and explored are the following: interpretation, resistance, transference, and countertransference. It is my hope that the manner in which I teach my students to understand and work with these therapeutic concepts will be a source of help for others.

II. Interpretation: To Put into Words

On the first page of recorded history and mythology we read of the importance and need for interpretation in the lives of people. Numerous examples exist of people who sought an interpretation of what was happening to them and wanted to know the causes and reasons for their feelings, behavior, and attitudes. In mythology, we read of the ancient riddle: What animal is that which in the morning goes on four feet, at noon on two, and in the evening upon three? The Bible, too, is replete with stories of people who sought an answer to life's difficulties, struggles, and perplexities. One such example is found in the delightful story of Joseph where the pharaoh needed to know an interpretation of his dreams, and Joseph was able to translate what was unconscious in the dream work of the ruler and from this information the ruler was able to make plans for the economic safety of his people and to avoid the tragedy of famine. In many and less dramatic ways, ordinary people day after day seek an interpretation for what causes pain in their life and what keeps them from being the free people they have a right to be. The process through which such an interpretation is given is usually some form of therapy practiced by a host of people in the helping professions. By and large, a commonly accepted understanding of therapy would be that it is a human interaction and transaction. As a result of this interaction, a union is effected between the therapist and client. For the most part, therapy functions within the developmental structuring of the conscious mind through the use of verbal and non-verbal forms of communication. The fabric of therapy consists of everyday events and focuses on reactions in the lives of both therapist and client. This accumulation of attitudes, feelings, reactions and actions become the "stuff" of the therapy hour. Through the supportive framework of therapy, clients are enabled to develop an ego structure wide enough to express urgings, and a trust results from such a structure that permits the clients ultimately to respond to any stimulus insofar as it exists. In order to bring about this condition of freedom, it is necessary for the therapist to understand what is happening in the lives of clients and to communicate effectively the underlying reasons and causes of the distress and pain brought to the therapy hour. This communication is technically known as interpretation and it will be discussed in the following section.

There is much professional discussion regarding the meaning and the role interpretation plays in the process of therapy. Numerous authors define the term in keeping with its psychoanalytic heritage. Likewise, the role interpretation plays varies from being the major force in the therapy to where the therapist is encouraged not to make interpretation so as not to encourage dependency in the client's life. I consider interpretation to be an extremely important concept because therapy is primarily a process of communicating understanding. After listening and gaining an appreciation of the client's difficulties and the questions life might be asking, it is incumbent on the therapist to begin to put into words the meaning of what is happening and why it is happening to a given client. This is the work of an interpretation. Within the context of supervision, I try to help students make practical application of what they have learned about interpretation in academic classes. (While conceptual clarity may not lead to greater truth, it is important that a concept be well understood.) Accordingly, what follows will be the understanding I want students to have regarding the theory, techniques, and specific psychotherapeutic implications of the use of interpretation.

A. Theoretical Understanding

An interpretation is basically a statement. It consists of putting into clear and precise words something a client has said or done. Interpretations take on many different forms of making comments about the feelings, behavior, and attitudes of clients. At different stages in the therapy relationship, interpretations will try to explain a client's current personality functioning in terms of antecedent causes. Basically the role of interpretation is to make conscious what had been an unconscious source of motivation in one's life. After becoming conscious and aware of the motivating forces, people derive the insight to make choices in order to become free. However, just because a person has insight is no guarantee that therapy has been successful. There is still involved in the course of therapy the working-through phase. Several forms of these interpretative comments will now be discussed.

1. Reflective Interpretation

A form of interpretation that proves helpful to many people, and which comprises to a large degree the Rogerian mode of therapy, is to reflect, restate, and refocus more clearly what a client has said. This is not done well if a therapist simply uses the same words of the client. The client in this instance would be justified in asking: "Is there an echo in this room?" When a therapist reflects on a client's behavioral or verbal expression it should be literally a bending back over one's experiences in order to understand more deeply what is happening. Making reflective interpretations demands a great deal of work, practice, and skill, and what might look or sound easy is more difficult than one might expect.

2. Tentative Interpretation

It is a well known fact that confronting a client prematurely through an interpretation will only raise the level of resistance and change. In fact, I have taught students never to confront until the relationship or the working alliance has been firmly established and the client knows that there is a union existing between the therapist and the client. To avoid making what would appear to be a confrontation, I will from time to time or when the situation arises make an interpretation in as few words as possible, beginning with "I wonder." "I wonder how you look at that?" This tentative interpretation is a rich source of therapeutic energy because it has a way of helping clients to ponder more deeply on their communications. It also becomes a means to help clarify the reasons behind a person's action and feelings.

3. Facilitative Interpretations

Sometimes in the course of therapy, a client might be struggling to put into words certain important thoughts and feelings, and will get stuck. The flow of communication will become punctuated with a staccato-like string of words and clients will become frustrated by their inability to put into words what they desire to say. A cardinal rule of counseling is never to put words into a client's mouth. It is insulting to people to do so. However, through the course of therapy we come to know people so well that we can facilitate by making comments that result in the client talking more about a given situation. It is also helpful to ask clients to go more deeply into a feeling or an emotion in order to surface meaning and insight.

4. Time-Related Interpretation

Each therapy session is related to the previous session and is likewise connected to the following sessions. The function of memory is to conserve and understand the thread which continues through the various sessions. It is the responsibility of the therapist to make these connections known by means of a time-related interpretation. The therapist can compare how clients are responding to a situation "now" in light of how they responded to a similar situation in the past, and vice versa. This form of interpretation readily yields how a change in perspective can come about through distance and time. The therapist can also use a time-related interpretation to make comparisons of events, thoughts or feelings. Likewise, it is therapeutically productive to make time-related interpretations in terms of a client's developmental history by understanding how a client's chronological age differs from his/her developmental age. Therapists see people daily who are fifty years chronologically but are functioning as if they were fifteen years developmentally. After developing a good working relationship with people, I will encourage supervisees to make such time-related interpretations with a view to enabling clients to become psychologically current in their personality functioning.

5. Confrontative Interpretations

This form of interpretation is probably the most misunderstood as well as the most powerful of all the interventions between clients and therapists. Beginning therapists overuse this technique and perhaps because of their inexperience often offend clients by the intensity of feeling caused by confrontative interpretations. These interpretations can be made only when there exists between client and therapist a relationship that will convey the challenging and truthful question along with sensitivity and compassion. A confrontative interpretation is used effectively when clients avoid recognition of their own involvement in their problems. However, to use confrontative interpretations will demand great patience on the part of the therapist and a willingness on the part of clients to face the truth of their lives. Since confrontative interpretations are difficult and easily misunderstood, the recommendation is made that they be used after other forms of interpretations have been used. At this point, we turn our attention to the technique position of this chapter in order to understand when to make an interpretation as well as what to interpret.

B. Technical Issues of Interpretation

In order to make effective use of any forms of interpretation described in the previous section, it is important to ascertain when an interpretation is called for as well as what might be interpreted. Timing is a very important variable in making an interpretation. There is no hard rule which states when an interpretation is to be made. Again, this is an area where supervision plays such an important role in the professional development of the therapist. Most therapists have learned or acquired a sense of timing from the trial and error method. However, there are some guidelines as to when to make an interpretation. Ideally, an interpretation should be expressed at the crossroads of the client's receptivity to receive such information and when the therapist is well prepared to offer it. If a therapist waits too long to offer an interpretation, clients will sense incompetency because they already have come to the insight contained in the interpretation. If the interpretation is premature, clients will be preempted in coming to an insight or it may appear alien to their way of understanding. Hence, interpretations must be well timed to convey meaning and understanding.

Along with the necessity to acquire a sense of proper timing comes the demand to discern what to interpret. Therapists need to guard against saying what is already obvious to clients, or what is unnecessary to say. Basically, there are four different issues to be interpreted. It would seem that clients would be well taught through interpretations how they use certain defense mechanisms against anxiety. Hence, it is extremely valuable for supervisees to have a firm grasp on the various defense mechanisms. After identifying clients' defensive style, the deeper interpretation can be made regarding the underlying cause of the conflict. Second, within the course of therapy, interpretations can be made on the contexual defensive style of clients. In a given setting, a person tends to act in a given or predictable manner. Hence, the interpretation is made on the basis of context which alone gives understanding. Third, interpretations can focus on the unique style of the person which is learned from being with the client for any length of time. Lastly, interpretations are made in keeping with the classical categories of content and process. Content refers to what clients say while process involves how it is said. Thus far, we have presented material outlining when an interpretation should be made as well as what is interpreted. Before turning our attention to that power which blocks changes, insight, and health, we review some practical and technical implications of interpretation.

C. Practical Psychotherapeutic Implications

In the course of doing supervision with students in small group as well as individual supervision, a number of very practical and helpful hints have surfaced. A list and brief description of them follows:

1. It is important to choose words wisely and to find the right words to convey the meaning you want the interpretation to effect. Avoid using the same word over and over again. Practice different grammatical forms including questions, and expletives as well as statements. Clients remember a shorter and well placed interpretation longer and use it more productively than long drawn out discourses. A good short sentence is still the strongest means of communication. Hence, both the quality of words used to make an interpretation and the quantity of words used are very important considerations.

2. An interpretation should not go beyond the data determined

through the direction of the therapy. In the course of understanding, it is important for counselors to be current in time and parallel with the process of their clients.

3. The more a therapist shows higher levels of empathy to clients, the more deeply felt and productive will be their interpretations.

4. Confrontative interpretation should only be used after other forms have been tried.

5. In making interpretations, it is helpful to present them in a provisional form rather than as pronouncements. Through interpretation, we try to generate the reasons why clients behave, act, and feel. We invite clients and supervisees to become more reflective and insightful.

Thus far, our discussion has been on those means which further the therapeutic process. Various kinds of interpretations have been presented.

III. Resistance: The Irony of Therapy

In his book, *Psychopathology of Everyday Life*, Freud set the stage to show us how in everyday events and experiences we find examples of psychopathology. We have already noted the need for interpretations in the lives of ordinary people. It should come as no surprise that resistance also plays an important role in the lives of people. Resistance wears many masks, and the therapist's task is to invite the wearer to discard the facade and dare to face life without the protective device or defense called resistance. It should also be noted that people resist for a reason, that resistance is a form of rationalization and becomes a pattern of behavior that blocks and impedes the path toward freedom that therapy points out to clients. Isn't it ironic that people would block the very process that would enable them to become free, or to change? At first sight, it might appear so. However, it is also frightening to change, to give up former ways of thinking, feeling, and acting. It demands courage to become a different kind of person. In effect it means acknowledging that what I was before therapy was an incomplete self. After therapy, which is a difficult process of working through, of trying on different ways of being, of changing old patterns, of discarding ineffective ways of answering needs, clients become their integrated selves. Hence, the therapy process might be looked upon as change and therapists as change agents. Life invites people to change as each of us responds to the questions implicit in each developmental stage of our existence. Cardinal John Henry Newman once said that to live is to change and to be perfect is to have changed often. Perhaps we can paraphrase that understanding and say that therapy is a process inviting people to change and to become integrated as a result of psychotherapeutic implications of interpretation.

A. Resistance: Its Many Forms

Thus far, we have seen how resistance plays a part in the everyday lives of people. That we all resist certain understanding of ourselves is no surprise. That we all avoid taking certain measures, such as proper exercise, appropriate dieting, and patterns of work and recreation, indicates that we prefer what has become a patterned way of being rather than changing to a newer and more productive way of life. When clients enter into a therapeutic relationship, they take with them these accumulated and unexamined patterns of behavior, thinking, and feeling. In supervision, it becomes important for the supervisee to detect the form and feature of these resistances to the treatment process.

In the early part of the supervisory process, I encourage supervisees to read about the concept of resistance. Once they begin to do therapy, they soon learn to recognize the various kinds of resistances that get expressed in the therapy hour. Basically, as supervisors and supervisees, we deal with four major classes of resistance: resistance to change, character resistance, resistance to content and transference resistance. It is a well known fact that clients become who they are only after a long period of time. When therapy reaches the intensity of mid-phase work, it becomes necessary to realize what must be changed in a client's life. When clients resist the invitation to change, we see played out in lively form the resistance to change, and the reasons why they refuse or are unable to change further qualify the particular kind of resistance being expressed. The most easily detected form of this type of resistance is secondary gain. A useful means to surface this form of resistance is to ask the question: What is the client getting out of not changing? The answer to this question will vary from client to client as well as within the client at various times. Clients might enjoy their illness for some unconscious reason and be unwilling to change, or to do something constructive about their difficulties because they derive sympathy and pity from loved ones and friends. The manifestations of secondary gain resistance are myriad, and supervisees must learn to be attentive to delve into the underlying reason why clients resist the very process offered to them to adapt. Another modification regarding resistance to change is seen through the interpersonal relationships of clients. Often clients are reluctant to change because they fear the rejection by significant people in their lives. Perhaps this form of resistance might be called interpersonal but nevertheless it is based on fear. Clients will in effect say: What will happen to my relationship with others if I change? I usually encourage my students to tell such clients that really good and non-neurotic relationships survive therapy. That when a client changes for the better, this is an invitation for others to grow and develop new levels of intimacy and interpersonal closeness. Still other clients will say that they prefer the misery of their known ways of responding to others rather than risking the unknown. To allay that fear, supervisees can ask clients: Can you imagine how different your life might be if you changed? Are you limiting yourself to only what you know? Through the positive and encouraging mode of relating, clients are willing to try out different styles of being present to significant people in their lives as well as accepting the challenge to be different in the way they act, feel and think. A third form of resistance to change is the fear that clients have about being in therapy. Sometimes this unverbalized resistance might be expressed in these or similar words: What will my therapist think of me? Will the therapist think I'm losing my mind? Will the therapist be able to understand me? Any and all forms of this resistance which is the accumulated reservations clients have about the treatment process must be explored and understood. I encourage supervisees to say something like this: My concern is to help you overcome these fears. Let me explain once again what therapy is. You have to do your share of the work to build the relationship. I, in turn, will do my part to make this a relationship that will enable you to find solutions to your problems. Lastly, clients might resist treatment because they fear whatever progress they have made simply won't last. They fear that all their hard work will be useless and empty. The fear will even go further and take on the manifestation that they are unworthy to have changes take place in their lives. To respond to this kind of resistance, supervisees can reinforce the fact that any gain through the therapy process is the result of the client's efforts. When clients feel unworthy of the help received or distrust why it has happened to them, they can be told that these fears are simply ways that they were taught to punish themselves through the burden of guilt.

1. Character Resistance

The word character is derived from the Greek word "charassein" which means to cut deeply, mark, or form into a lasting style. In psychological terms, it takes on the added note of being a defense insofar as a person's habitual way of acting and being becomes known as character. We have colloquial expressions such as "He's a character" which usually means that such a person is funny and might be the life of a party. The expression

"That's a bad character" is usually figurative and denotes a person having many negative personality traits. After a person develops such style of relating, the term characterological is used to describe the fact that reasons for such behavior are etched into their way of being. Character resistance is expressed through various defenses. For example, a client might use a specific defense mechanism and this mode of acting becomes habitual. In the section on interpretation, supervisees were directed to know the many forms the basic defenses of the ego take. A second form that character resistance takes stems from how clients respond to life. They may be passive and dependent or active and independent. This response pattern can serve to destroy the communication process established between therapist and client. Lastly, any of the personality disorders might be used to inhibit the attainment of therapy goals.

2. Resistance to Content

After therapy has been underway for some time, resistance to content will become evident. Any and all events, experiences, situations or interpersonal difficulties that clients are reluctant to present within the therapeutic context are known as resistance to content. There are many analogous examples of resistance to content found in various kinds of interactions and living. We all have some areas of our lives that we prefer to keep to ourselves. This might be the result of conscious choice. On the unconscious level we might refrain from talking about those areas of life that are shameful, embarrassing or what has become expressed in popular usage as "the shadow." Clients might express resistance to content in these or similar words: "I know that I have not been able to talk about some of the things that are bothering me. I was afraid to do so—afraid of what you might think about me." Through the supervisory process, I encourage supervisees to work with clients to talk about anything that enters their minds. To get beyond resistance to content, supervisees might compile a list of topics that people typically try to evade while in therapy. Before termination, one unique resistance to content can be surfaced by asking a client: "What secret have you been keeping to yourself all these years?" As a result of this question, there usually has resulted a closer bonding between myself and clients because of the honestly revealed self-disclosure.

3. Transference Resistance

Transference resistance is formed as a result of the transference which is formed between client and therapist. In the following chapter, the issue of transference will be discussed. However, for the present, we can say that resistance based on transference can either be positive or negative. Poetry has a way of expressing deep layers of truth in beautiful fashion. In the poem "Ulysses," Tennyson says: "We become part of all we have met." This profound truth has immense consequences for therapy and supervision. It serves to place in bold relief the importance of modeling behavior. Whenever clients respond to therapists the way they did to previous significant people in their lives, we have examples of transference resistance. Whether the transference resistance is positive or negative, supervisees must be taught that it must be seen as a signal and whatever is signified must be uncovered, understood, and interpreted because transference resistance produces a distortion to communication patterns. Clients might express transference resistance through these or similar words: "Sometimes I find myself thinking that you seem so calm and assured just like my father. I wish I could be like you." Supervisees must be alert to any of the relational figures in the lives of clients, and other significant figures especially when comparisons are made.

B. Technical Issues of Resistance

What was primarily discussed concerning technical issues of interpretation has clinical implications for technical issues of resistance. Once again, it is important for supervisees to acquire an intuitive understanding in terms of the proper timing to identify the manifestation of resistance, and to name the resistance in such a way that clients will use the information in their interior process of change and integration.

Resistance has many forms and these were described in the previous section. Within the context of therapy, supervisees and counseling students encounter resistance from the first moments when the relationship begins. Hence, it is necessary for them to appreciate the technical aspects of the reality of resistance and how this irony gets expressed. Supervisees would be well advised to observe any irregularities surrounding the circumstance of time. To do therapy effectively, clients have to learn how to do the work of therapy. This demands that both therapist and client begin and end their work on time. When clients want to miss sessions for unrealistic reasons, this breach of the treatment contract must be interpreted as resistance. Under the rubric of time, resistance takes on many forms. What I stress with supervisees is that they remain regular and consistent regarding the arrangements of time of sessions, frequency, and whatever conditions have been established concerning vacations, or breaks from the therapeutic situation. I model this in my supervisory relationship.

Another technical manifestation of resistance is when clients curtail either the quality or quantity of communication within the therapeutic setting. Clients, struggling with ambivalent feelings of one kind or another, will restrict perhaps the quality of description that would aptly depict a certain situation. They will underplay a certain range of emotional expression perhaps to place themselves in a more positive light, or to gain the respect of the therapist. Supervisees must be alerted to keep in the background of their minds the question: Does the data described by the client aptly cover the reality of the situation? If the clinical judgment is made that there is a distance between affect and verbal expression, this qualitative restriction of communication is interpreted as resistance.

Along with qualitative restriction of emotional expression is the added construction of amount of information presented for reflection within the therapy hour. Perhaps the most difficult aspect for supervisees to learn how to handle is the resistance of silence. This resistance is all the more keenly felt by therapists working with court-referred clients. Silence, as with any of the other forms of resistance, is hardly a unitary function. It depends to a great extent on the quality of the therapeutic relationship. Even though the therapeutic alliance is positive and productive work is resulting from the interaction, silence will undoubtedly occur. Supervisees are well advised not to interpret every lapse into silence as a resistance. Silence is a resistance when clients refuse to say whatever is on their minds; when there is a momentary interruption of the verbal exchange, this is hardly a resistance. Even when clients pause in the course of their verbal productions, resistance is not expressed. Supervisees would be well directed, if they experience a great deal of silence with clients, to review the treatment contract and be sure that they are working on the questions and issues clients want to address during the treatment session.

Therapy begins with the questions that life asks of clients. The process of therapy consists in exploring with clients solutions to their problems and questions. Hence, therapy has to do with the reality of a client's life. Accordingly, when clients try to isolate what goes on in their lives from what they are experiencing through the treatment process, this can be interpreted as resistance. Supervisees can effectively deal with this resistance of isolation of therapy from life by emphasizing what is going on between them and their clients within the therapeutic context. By and large, the way a therapist responds to a client is similar to the way other people do. As agents of reality, counseling students must be aware of the connection between what is happening in the real lives of their clients and what is transpiring within the therapy hour. If clients want to separate what they are learning about themselves through therapy from the application of these insights and understandings from their lives, then supervisees must point this out to them through the medium of interpretation.

Thus far, we have described various manifestations of resistance and how the resistance is expressed within the treatment context. A form of resistance that takes place outside the therapy hour is known as acting out. This occurs when clients put into action and express through behavior the feelings and impulses they should bring into the treatment setting for reflection. In a sense, what clients do through this resistance is to withdraw from therapy what they experience as problematic in their lives by translating their feelings directly into a behavioral expression. Supervisees can become attentive to the resistance when clients run out of things to say or what originally brought clients into therapy no longer causes them problems. This happens as a result of discharging those conflictual elements by direct action. Another form of this resistance is when clients use other people as surrogate therapists and thereby dilute the intensity of their issues through talking with a number of other people about those troubling aspects of their behavior and feelings. It is necessary for supervisees to have clients bracket their verbal expression and bring the sum total of their responses and feelings to be discussed with the therapist.

During this section, we have reviewed the major indications of resistance as found in the middle phase of therapy. Supervisors can enable supervisees to detect resistance through what is expressed or what is kept out of the therapy session. The amount of communication as well as the quality of the exchange can constitute a resistance. Refusing to allow therapy to touch their lives is an important resistance as well as diluting the therapeutic dialogue by acting out on impulses rather than bringing them into the therapy for reflection. Lastly, talking about therapeutic issues with a variety of therapeutic surrogates is a resistance that breaks down the intensity that should exist between therapist and client. Now, we turn our attention to practical psychotherapeutic implications of resistance.

C. Practical Psychotherapeutic Implications

Supervisees soon learn that resistance is part and parcel of the therapeutic situation. In fact, I encourage them by telling them that when they encounter resistance with clients they can have the confidence that they are doing good work. In other words, where there is evidence that resistance has entered into the therapeutic dialogue, we can discern that we have discovered the source of a person's conflict, or what is fearful, or what is causing the level of anxiety. A list of helpful ways of dealing with resistance follows.

1. Once resistance has been identified, it must be focused upon and the sources of it must be explored. To name the resistance or to express it

in words is the task of interpretation, and I refer the reader to the list containing the various kinds of interpretation.

2. Resistance discovered early on in the therapeutic process is determined by the psychological patterns which are brought into the treatment situation. Clients can present this resistance to counselors as expressions of their unique starting point in therapy, or simply as defenses, or ineffective means unconsciously chosen to deal with anxiety.

3. Resistance that develops during the course of therapy is sometimes the result of the therapeutic relationship. Supervisees are encouraged to understand their own relational dynamics as well as those of the clients to see if there is a connection with what is happening in the treatment.

4. Resistance is a rationalization and a pattern of behavior that blocks and impedes the course of therapy. Accordingly, supervisees must be encouraged to look upon resistance as a fear and to discover with their clients what they are defending against, what is being defended, or what they are afraid to verbalize or ashamed to admit of themselves.

5. Resistance is a protective barrier and supervisees can begin to identify the resistance that is less threatening to clients, and then build through a connecting series of interpretations until the underlying reason for the resistance is found.

6. Silence is a special form of resistance and can be a source of intimidation for counseling students. Supervisees can be taught to appreciate that silence can be a productive time for clients. I encourage supervisees to ask clients: Is the silence productive for you? Are you thinking through something that would be important for us to reflect on together?

7. Not all resistance can or should be identified. However, major resistance must be worked through and removed. When clients are shown that resistance is a psychological process through which we seek to protect ourselves from hurtful truth, they can be invited to work with us in the process of obtaining freedom from fear in all its manifestations.

Conclusion

This chapter began with the understanding that supervision is a learning alliance. Both supervisor and supervisee learn a great deal about the process of therapy and about the dynamic interplay of what is going on in their lives as well as in the lives of clients. Interpretation and resistance form the communication pattern that results in the therapeutic dialogue.

Interpretation deals essentially with making statements that will bring about insight, understanding and clarity in the lives of clients. Various forms of interpretation have been presented. Resistance is a block to the communication pattern and the major forms of resistance were described. The common denominator for all resistance is basically fear. Practical psychotherapeutic implications for dealing with interpretation and resistance were offered as an aid to respond effectively to clients. In the next chapter, we discuss the relational dynamics of therapy when we explore the issues of transference and countertransference.

6

Transference and Countertransference: The Relational Dynamics of Counseling

Several years ago, a student who was just beginning the study of psychotherapy and counseling wrote in his initial self-evaluation that he had not run into problems of transference and countertransference. This student was gifted intellectually, but was somewhat rigid in his personality functioning. However, he was determined to become a first rate therapist and counselor. Through the course of his studies, he read extensively in the research of psychotherapy. Again and again he read about the importance of transference and countertransference, but in the early days of doing counseling at his clinical placement he had not experienced these relational dynamics of therapy. During the second semester, as he was beginning to relax more and feel more at home in the counseling situation, he came to the conclusion that transference and countertransference are present in all relationships, and that the focus of supervision is to point out the presence, power, source, and the means to resolve these impediments to the counseling relationship. This student was unaware in his initial self-evaluation that he had run into problems of transference and countertransference because he was so fearful in the early days of doing counseling that he risked very little of what was personal about himself in the counseling relationship. His own issue of rigidity did not permit him to respond freely and humanly to his clients. In a sense, one could say that he came close to being a robot—a replica of a human person but lacking in the ability to feel, believe, express impulses, experience the power of memories, hope and dreams. As the weeks of supervision continued, he became more and more relaxed and shared his feelings of what was preventing the establishment of a warm and effective relationship with clients. He came to the awareness that the same reality was going on in his supervisory relationship with me! The day arrived when he was able to say that he was acting like a little boy, that he had to be right all the time, that he had to be perfect. Through this insight, he was able to see what was happening in his relationships with clients. They were present in the same consulting room but there was little interaction and consequently little therapeutic progress made. He was mouthing all the words about counseling, about therapy, that he read about in books. He was able in a certain way to repeat questions and approaches he was learning in academic courses and through the supervisory experiences, but he lacked a sense of self in the therapeutic situation. In a very real and painful way, he realized that he was hiding behind a mask. His particular mask was perfectionism and an excessive sense of responsibility. As time went on, he revealed that he was an adult child of an alcoholic father. The pieces of the puzzle began to fall into place. He was acting with his clients in many of the same ways he acted with his own father and with other significant people in his life. Through a parallel process, he was acting with me in the supervisory relationship. Once the insight was gained, he freed himself of the tension to respond to clients through a wooden and stiff manner of fear and apprehension. Similarly, in the supervisory relationship, he began to trust me, and to allow himself to feel the support and encouragement as well as the challenge and confrontation that form the supervisory relationship. This example which provides an introduction to this chapter on transference and countertransference is real. At present, the fledgling therapist, who was so fearful as he began our program, is now working in an agency and has achieved membership in a number of accrediting organizations. I selected the example because I think it demonstrates the starting point of many students as they begin their clinical programs, and grapple with the relational issues of transference and countertransference. As they continue in supervision, they learn experientially the meaning of transference and countertransference. The purpose of this chapter will be to provide a theoretical understanding of transference and countertransference, to suggest technical assistance to respond to these dynamics, and lastly to offer some helpful psychotherapeutic suggestions.

To understand the concepts of transference and countertransference, I would like to paraphrase the words of Shakespeare that the players' vocation is to be a mirror on which to show each age its very form and feature. The metaphor of the mirror is powerful in its ability to reflect the meaning of a situation. Accordingly, I would like to suggest that a supervisor's primary function regarding these issues is to be a mirror to reflect to the supervisee what is going on in the real relationship established with a client as well as within the working alliance and to bring to awareness what is transpiring within the transferential and countertransferential components of the relationship. Using the metaphor of the mirror gives us a means to remove the distortions which intrude in the relationship between the therapist and the client. These distortions are typically called transferences. When the therapist responds irrationally or inappropriately to the client, these reactions are called countertransferences. Lastly, when therapists relate to supervisors the way they do with clients, we have examples of parallel process. The mirror has properties which permit its use for our therapeutic as well as supervisory effectiveness. In the first place, the mirror has the quality of emptiness or the absence of preconceptions. If we as supervisors can serve as mirrors to our supervisees, they can be free of unrealistic expectations and projections. Secondly, mirrors have the quality of acceptance. They accept everything without distortions or judgments. They reflect what is there, and there are no comments made. Mirrors have the quality of accurate distinctions. In making distinctions and giving reflections, supervisors enable students to see what is going on in their therapeutic relationships. Lastly, mirrors have the quality of non-attachment insofar as when the object is removed, there is a letting go of the subject. This quality of freedom is important in both the therapeutic as well as the supervisory relationship. The client is enabled through the therapeutic relationship to come to a sense of freedom and self-discovery without being made over into the image of the therapist. So, too, through the process of supervision, the students are encouraged to form their own unique way of relating to clients without becoming clones of the supervisors.

I. Transference

A. *Theoretical Understanding*

Perhaps one of the most important concepts which Freud has given to the clinical world is that of transference. Basically, transference refers to the client's expression of attitudes and behavior derived from prior developmental and conflictive relationships with significant others into the current relationship with the therapist; these expressions are typically distortions because they spring forth or are stimulated from outside the immediate therapeutic context. Within the accepting and non-judgmental environment of therapy, clients have typically, but through covert means, tried to relive earlier conflictive relationships. It may be said that what happens in therapy is simply a new edition of an old concept expressed through the everyday experiences and events recalled by the client. Through the talking cure of therapy, clients review their past, and the power found in this retelling enables them to work through present issues by placing in proper perspective what was problematic for them during an earlier time in their history. This concept gives understanding to the idea that we cannot go backward in time to undo what we did at an earlier moment in life, or that we cannot make up for what we lacked at a prior developmental period. What does get expressed is that by living more effectively in the present we put to rest what was disturbing in our lives at a previous time. Through the therapeutic dialogue, the concept of transference emerges from week to week and becomes known and visible, and the analogy I would use to describe this reality is that of a photostatic plate. To see transference expressed is to watch a person who might be fifty years old chronologically act like a fifteen-year-old developmentally. What gets expressed are the thoughts, feelings, behaviors and conflicts representative of adolescent personality functioning but reflected through the person of an adult. When these experiences are projected onto the therapist within the context of therapy, the reality of transference becomes evident.

Within the supervisory relationship, I frequently ask therapists to project onto an imaginary screen what the actual experience between them and their client would look like. The reasons this is done is to demonstrate the observations Freud made regarding transference. An insight gleaned from doing therapy for a number of years is that many people have an enduring set of relationship patterns that recur throughout life. Once the pattern is detected, it becomes a key which helps us to unlock and to understand both conscious and unconscious forms of behavior. This insight is consistent with Freud's observation regarding the number of transference patterns. It appears at least that Freud thought each client had one transference pattern. This transference pattern might also be expressed through a constant theme which becomes a "golden thread" woven through the fabric of therapy. A certain client of mine epitomizes this one transference pattern through which she expresses hostile and angry reactions with males as a partial retaliation attempt directed at her all-powerfully perceived father. It would appear that all males simply take the place of her father in one way or another. This transference pattern is consolidated in the context of the themes expressed which occur around her relationships at work with males, her inability to find an enduring love relationship with a man (no male has yet proven himself equal to her father), and her unwillingness to acknowledge that she is just like her father. She will deny anger, and refrain from expressing anger, because then she would be just like her father.

Since each client is a unique person, it comes as no surprise that Freud's second observation regarding transference is the uniqueness of the transference patterns. This uniqueness of the transference pattern becomes expressed through the main wishes of the client. I will help to tease out this transference pattern through various questions and through the use of a quotation: "If horses could fly, beggars could ride for free." Accordingly, I would ask clients what they really would like to do or to be if they were totally free. Many times, the answer comes that they would be fearless, free, emotionally close to someone, in control and responsible, experience peace and happiness, and be seen as a great person.

Through the transference pattern, a client also expresses the erotic basis of the conflict. This pattern is begun in childhood and perdures through ensuing developmental periods. Since we are sexual from at least six weeks after conception, it is understandable that our transference pattern would have an erotic basis. Sexuality here is understood as a person's way of being in the world, and how that person establishes closeness and maintains distance from others. Freud's third observation on the erotic basis of transference patterns enables us to understand the subtle and covert ways that clients will attempt to transform the working alliance into something sexual. This fact is well illustrated when a woman client will attempt to dress up for her therapist. Likewise, hysterical male clients will attempt to seduce a woman therapist either directly through invitation to a sexual encounter or indirectly through the explicitation of his previous sexual exploits. Within the therapeutic setting, this original erotic basis is expressed through new illustrations of the old conflict between seduction and responsible closeness.

The basic rule of therapy is to make the unconscious conscious. The cardinal rule of therapy applies likewise to transference. This insight of Freud is in keeping with his topographical concept of the preconscious, unconscious, and conscious. Accordingly, there are parts of the transference pattern that are unconscious and other parts which are conscious. This insight into transference enables us to understand the ambivalent acting pattern of some clients. They are conscious of the pattern and this awareness gives them freedom to change. At the same time, there are aspects of their patterns which are unconscious and this tension produces the state of ambivalence. Therapists are encouraged not to enter into this tug-of-war when clients say "Part of me wants to do this—while part of me wants to do that." I try to help clients understand that they are the one and same person having conflicts trying to resolve whatever the wish that is being voiced.

Another observation Freud made regarding transference is that there is a consistency in the transference pattern through time. He stated that the pattern is repeated and in a sense made new through the experiences and events in a client's life. This insight is validated in many of my case studies, and even the dream material of clients will reveal this consistency.

Along with consistency, there is the phenomenon of change in the transference pattern. The hypothesis could well be formulated that as a person progresses in the pursuit of freedom and in the process of self-discovery, there should be a concomitant change in the nature of the transference pattern. I would suggest further that the person's behavior outside of therapy is becoming more grounded in reality and that relationships are more in keeping with what is possible.

For many years, the remark has been made that therapy is a microcosm of the larger world. What a client does within the therapy situation is a replication of what happens or occurs outside the context of therapy. Freud's observation of this phenomenon is called the transference pattern in relation to the therapist. Basically, what this means is that the client treats people outside the therapy situation in a fashion similar to the way the therapist is treated. Using the metaphor of the mirror, we could obtain a still life image of the client's personality functioning outside the therapy setting simply by videotaping a client's response in therapy around important and conflictual persons or situations. This insight of Freud gives added meaning and significance to the statement that the only important stimulus in therapy is the therapist. Likewise, it underscores the importance of the therapist's role in the management of the treatment contract.

Early memories also become a source in the formulation of a transference pattern. It is shown in case studies that clients treat others in much the same way they were treated by authority or parental figures. Freud called this the early origin of the transference pattern. Frequently I will ask clients to recall their earliest memories, and the memory recalled will provide the separate piece which when glued together through the means of interpretation will become the mosaic, pattern, or internalized script which becomes the clients' characteristic way of responding.

Lastly, Freud made the comment that it was not a fact that transference emerges with greater intensity and lack of restraint during psychoanalysis than outside it. Stated positively, transference is evident both inside and outside of therapy, the data of everyday experience confirming the truth of Freud's insight. In fact, we could marshal empirical evidence to support this assertion. We have all seen grown men, who were intimidated by angry and punitive fathers, relate in the here and now to authority figures through subservient and ingratiating means.

While listening to therapy tapes with counseling students, these nine observations of Freud provide a focus for discussion and case review. Students gain an insight into transference which enables them to understand and respect the power which the past has on the lives of clients. Likewise, an appreciation is revealed when clients through insight are freed from having to repeat unconsciously either thought or behavioral patterns of an earlier age or context which might be inappropriate in the present. Attention now is turned to an understanding of the technical issues of transference.

B. Technical Issues

The central technical issue regarding transference is to remember Freud's original instruction that as long as the person continues to utter without hindrance the thoughts, feelings, ideas rising to awareness, the theme of the transference should be left untouched. He goes on to say that when transference becomes resistance it should be dealt with. From what we have gained from looking once again at Freud's basic observations on transference, it should be understood why he would be reluctant to identify fleeting images of transference. It must be clearly expressed within the therapeutic context, and well established as a recurring pattern of thought, feeling, action and behavior to have the therapist interpret the meaning of the transference. With this overview in mind regarding transference, we can next explore under what conditions transference can be encouraged or the conditions set to produce transference reactions.

Keeping in mind that transference is a revivification of past emotions, feelings, thoughts, and behavior projected onto the therapist in the current relationship, there are a number of ways through which transference can be manipulated. Perhaps the clearest way to induce transference is to divert attention away from the current life situation of the client in the here and now functioning of life and to consider in large part only past experiences. In this approach, through transference, we can see how clients' present behavior is determined by the past. Asking clients to relive or narrate their experiences with parents and other authority figures and therapists responding similarly as the parent is another way to enhance a transference reaction. For some reasons, therapists might decide to be passive and withdrawn in the therapeutic dialogue, refraining from answering questions, and these responses too can effect transference. Encouraging a stream of consciousness approach and inviting clients to do free association is conducive to the development of transference. Doing an exploration of dreams, musings, and images is another means to highlight transference reactions. Time is likewise a factor in the production of transference, and it is axiomatically true that the greater frequency of sessions per week will increase transference, while decreasing the frequency of sessions will reduce the manifestations of transference. Lastly, when therapists abstain from dealing with unrealistic expectations of clients and these build up over time, transference reactions will develop in proportion to the fantasies engendered.

When, for a variety of reasons, transference should be contained, there are conditions which will prevent the production of its manifestation. Many of these conditions will be the flip-side of the previous discussion. To reduce transference, therapists can restrict the dialogue to present relationships and what is happening in the here and now of the client's life. Rejecting the use of dream interpretation, fantasy, and musing reduces the possibility of transference to arise. Reducing the number of sessions per week has already been mentioned. Not allowing unrealistic expectations to be voiced or reinforced and focusing attention on the working alliance and problem solving reduces considerably the formulation of transference. Becoming more interactional in response to clients and insisting on maintaining the role of therapist are powerful deterrents to the establishment of transference. Now we turn our attention to some practical psychotherapeutic suggestions regarding the treatment of transference.

C. Psychotherapeutic Suggestions

What will follow is a list of suggestions and reflections regarding the treatment of transference. The presence of transference in practically all relationships should be kept firmly in mind. Its manifestations are subtle and sometimes fleeting.

1. Supervisors would be well advised to cultivate a deep appreciation of a client's past. Since the past is the best predictor of the future, knowing well a client's past gives us an index of what to anticipate in terms of transference possibilities. Included in this suggestion would be a knowledge of a client's relationships with parental and authority figures.

2. Since I place a great deal of emphasis on the successful accomplishment of developmental tasks, knowing a client's developmental lags or fixation points is another way to pinpoint where a possible transference manifestation might surface.

3. Understanding and charting what a client is dealing with in therapy and having a knowledge of the data generated in previous sessions is a necessary condition to detect transference. What is non-contextual in terms of reaction patterns, feelings, or behavior can be seen as transference indications.

4. Supervisors would be well advised to know the ego defense mechanisms of projection in terms of transference and practice in the immediate situation of therapy to understand what and why a client is projecting. Are the projections realistic or unrealistic? Are the expectations in keeping with the treatment contract?

5. Knowing a client's needs is another way to understand the development of transference. For example, when a client has high needs for affection and nurturance, he/she might seek praise or excessive assurances of help from the therapist; clients might also seek for other signs of affec-

tion by having several changes in appointment times or possibly a change in the location for the therapeutic hour.

6. Attitudes play an important part in our psychological functioning, and they reveal a great deal about us. Accordingly, knowing and detecting attitudinal patterns of clients toward the therapist gives us clues in the observations of transference. Many times, the attitude of "I want to be like you" is a familiar manifestation of transference. Supervisors would be well advised to discover through what means clients are trying to identify with them or to be like them.

7. Reviewing the therapeutic contract to see how well or poorly its terms are being followed in the therapy is another potent source in the detection of transference. Are clients demanding more time, more attention outside the context of treatment? Are clients trying to manipulate or change the terms of the treatment contract? What is so important to remember is that therapy focuses on reality factors, and the goal of the therapeutic alliance is to identify and work toward adequate solutions to real problems.

8. Supervisors should respect the individuality of clients and know that certain kinds of treatment groups are not conducive to the development of transference. It is not advisable to induce transference reactions in the borderline client, those clients who are psychotic, those who have psychophysiologic reactions and those who are obsessive-compulsive.

Thus far, we have reviewed the relational dynamics of transference as a powerful ingredient in the counseling process. Freud's original observation regarding transference provided us with the theoretical insight to understand the presence, power, and source of transference in our clients. Likewise, his instructions that transference should be left untouched until it becomes a resistance to the therapy gives us an overview to appreciate some important technical aspects in the treatment of transference. Lastly, a list of psychotherapeutic suggestions was given to serve as guidelines to counseling students. At this time, the relational dynamic of countertransference becomes the focus of our discussion.

II. Countertransference

A. *Theoretical Understanding*

Countertransference is a concept which has practical relevance for anyone who does counseling. Through the years, however, the term has had different interpretations depending on the various schools of thought. For one school, the reaction or response of a therapist might be seen as a breakthrough into a new frontier of therapeutic effectiveness. Another school might interpret the same experience as being an intense form of countertransference which distorts the relational dynamic between therapist and client as well as impedes the therapeutic effectiveness. To highlight this confusion, two examples are offered which may help to identify why this term has such a wide variety of interpretations.

Recently, a therapist brought to supervision this scenario and wanted to reflect on the significance of the experience. On Easter Sunday, the son of a client calls the therapist to say that the family has something for him and could they bring it over? The therapist is delighted with this gesture of friendship and answers affirmatively. Once the family arrives, consisting of mother, father, and two sons who give the therapist an Easter basket filled with an assortment of foods and candies, the therapist invites the family for snacks and soft drinks. Next, the therapist, since he knows the city well, invites them to sightsee some unusual places. The therapist felt that he had to do something to repay the family for its kindness with some act of hospitality on his part.

Another therapist brought this scenario to supervision: a young unmarried woman, who is described as being timid, fearful, lacking in differentiation and wanting to return home to live with her parents, announces to her therapist that she is pregnant. They explore her feelings regarding this event and she is overwhelmed with the challenge and responsibility that this unwanted pregnancy has caused her. The therapist in an effort to be empathetic and self-disclosing tells her that many years ago his wife and he were in the same position and how together they overcame the obstacle of parents, unemployment, living arrangements, and his own immaturity, and says that things have a way of working out.

Regarding the first example, the therapist came to supervision and wanted to delve into the meaning of the transaction. He felt that there was countertransference present, and wanted to know what was happening. For a very productive hour, the full meaning of his response to the family became known. His excessive concern for this family, his desire to keep the mother and father together, and his fondness for the sons prompted his unusual and extraordinary response of hospitality. The therapist was open to learn from the experience, and came to a greater appreciation of his own needs.

On the other hand, the second therapist wanted to conceal from me that he told the client about his own life experience. Only after direct questioning did he tell me the truth of the matter, and he offered a supporting argument that he wanted to be empathetic and self-disclosing. He knew that I would be negatively disposed toward his behavior within the therapeutic setting.

These two examples illustrate well the difficulty in understanding the full meaning of countertransference. In the first example, we have a therapist who uses the material to understand his own need and motivation more clearly. He openly acknowledges the presence of countertransference and his reluctance simply to defer the gift but at the same time remain courteous and gracious. With the help of supervision, he reviewed the experience, and came to a more profound appreciation of the family's dynamics and in particular the interaction of the husband and wife. Since the student is doing a great deal of family and marital counseling, the suggestion was made that he could experiment more fully with the limits of the counseling contract but that he be aware and conscious of his own motivations. The second therapist presents more serious problems insofar as he wanted to withhold what he actually told the young woman. It is evident in the experience that by talking about himself he was trying to remove the guilt and negative feelings of the client through his expression that other people have done this, and their lives turned out just fine. Rather than deal with the feelings of the client, he inappropriately inserted himself into the therapeutic dialogue.

Depending on one's theoretical orientation, other features of countertransference might become evident on the supervisory mirror. Nevertheless, what is clear is that countertransference can either be conscious or unconscious. Likewise, countertransference can be rational and yet at the same time be seen as irrational. It is at times appropriate and inappropriate depending on one's viewpoint. Countertransference can be viewed to include all of the counselor's thoughts, feelings and behaviors. This approach makes manifestations of countertransference almost meaningless and unspecific. The approach I would like to advance is that countertransference is anything that distorts or damages the neutrality of the therapeutic contract. When the therapist's response, feelings, behaviors are non-contextual, then this too is an expression of countertransference. Thus far we have seen how the term countertransference lacks conceptual clarity. What is evident, however, is the presence of countertransference in some form or manifestation, and that when it distorts the therapeutic effectiveness of the working alliance it must be removed. At this time, we will consider some technical issues relative to our discussion of countertransference.

B. Technical Issues

Unlike transference, which Freud said should not be interpreted until it becomes a resistance, countertransference must be acknowledged and worked through. Freud went on to say what calls for a very sensitive reflection in the lives of all therapists, that therapy does not go beyond the complexes and internal resistance of the therapist. Hence, we again see how terribly important is the presence of the therapist both as a real person and as a symbol of reality. The therapist becomes the instrument through which insight and freedom come to the client. Accordingly, we must explore those conditions which cause the presence of countertransference. Basically, there are many ways that countertransference might be observed. However, I would like to suggest four windows through which this phenomenon becomes visible.

1. Window of Excessive Caring

Through our reading of philosophy, we realize that caring is what is constitutive of the human person. Therapists, in particular, are people who care a great deal. However, when this case becomes excessive, the presence of countertransference may be the cause. Questions may help us to identify countertransference manifestations. Do I worry excessively about my client? Do I consider my clients to be fragile? Do I cushion my observations unnecessarily? Am I apologetic in my remarks? Do I attempt to shield my clients from hurt, anxiety, or grief? Does my relationship with my client have overtones of that existing between parent and child? Is there a conspiracy between my client and myself against other people?

2. Window of Inappropriate Attitudes

As was true of transference in the lives of clients, attitudes play an important part in our lives as therapists. Am I fearful of a client's anger? What will be my reaction to an angry client? Am I afraid to risk my own genuine feelings in the counseling relationship? Do I try to keep the relationship on an even keel? Is there a great deal of idle chit-chat in my therapeutic dialogue? Am I overly disclosing with clients?

3. Window of Excessive Distance

This form of countertransference is the direct opposite of caring. It might be used by fearful therapists who are afraid of being seen as warm, interested, and caring people. The young therapist, as was illustrated in original examples of the chapter, epitomizes this form of countertransference. He was wooden and stiff and had no problem with countertransference! Questions which might help us to identify this form are: Am I aloof and cool in my relationships with clients? Am I unwilling to accept my clients when they are needy and dependent? Am I opposed to working through step-by-step when a client is deeply involved in a different decision-making process? Am I overly blunt in my responses? Do I show boredom or a lack of interest in what my clients say? Do I abandon clients emotionally when their issues begin to impinge on my own? Do I suggest early and premature termination because I dislike the client? Do I refuse through silence to answer appropriate questions of the client?

C. Psychotherapeutic Suggestions

The three windows which were used to cluster possible countertransference behaviors and attitudes were offered as a means to identify this reality. They are only representative, and what will follow are some further practical suggestions.

1. Those who do counseling or therapy should be in some kind of ongoing professional relationship. This might include formal supervision, personal therapy, or consultation.

2. The defense mechanism of identification should be thoroughly understood by those who do therapy in order to identify where the patterns of convergence are between client and therapist.

3. Since the research is clear that therapists treat clients over time in much the same way that other people treat the client outside of therapy, supervisors would be well advised to observe the rule of internal consistency by noting any changes in the reaction pattern which might foster either excessive caring or rejection.

4. Remaining aware of one's attitudes and needs is likewise a powerful aid in recognizing possible countertransference.

5. Observing any treatment group which is either desired or rejected is another means to detect possible countertransference.

Conclusion

This chapter began with an example of a young and inexperienced therapist who did not encounter problems with transference and countertransference. As experience dictates, they are present as relational dynamics in every therapeutic situation. Both theoretical and technical issues were reviewed so that the concept of transference and countertransference might be understood. This is in keeping with the axiom that theory without technique is useless and technique without theory is empty. Lastly, a list of psychotherapeutic suggestions was given to serve as a means of reflection to be incorporated in the supervisory process.

Melvin C. Blanchette, Ph.D.

7

Termination: The Creative Summing Up of the Counseling Relationship and the Learning Alliance

Courses in the theory and practice of counseling and psychotherapy give a great deal of deserved attention to the importance of beginning the therapeutic relationship. Counselors, starting their clinical placements, have high levels of anxiety and apprehension as to how the process of counseling is begun. Counselors want to know the theory which supports the relationship as well as the practical skills which give a sense of competence and self-confidence. They will ask what questions should be used to begin the helping relationship. Some are worried about how they will present themselves to clients, should they use first names, and how to answer questions about credentials. Others are anxious about the possibility of silence, and what to say if clients become withdrawn and unable to initiate a therapeutic dialogue. These questions and underlying concerns are clearly real and were experienced by just about all of us as we began our clinical work. What does not get adequate coverage in many counseling courses, however, is the issue of termination. The concept of termination warrants more careful attention, and the process of termination could well be reviewed since the ending of the therapeutic relationship is so essential and necessary in order to preserve what was acquired through the hard work of therapy.

Counselors are well directed by supervisors to ascertain how self-reliant their clients are becoming and how well they are practicing the coping skills learned through the counseling relationship so as to transfer this learning to their life situation. When these skills and insights are accomplished and are translated into action, the termination process can begin.

Beginnings and endings are paradigmatic of the human condition, and therapists are expected to know how to do the human thing well. Accordingly, since we have explored in previous chapters the communication components and the relational dynamics of the counseling relationship, the focus of this chapter will be to highlight the significance of termination and to understand that through the process of ending a helping relationship, a sense of wholeness can result for clients, and counselors can derive the satisfaction that comes with doing effective work. Ending the supervisory or Learning Alliance is likewise reviewed in order to bring about a resolution of the therapeutic work done by counselors and supervisors.

I. Significance of Termination

Counseling has been described as a process involving communication and resulting in understanding. Communication theory underscores the importance of beginnings and endings. Through various experiments, researchers have defined the positions of primacy and recency. In the primacy position, what a person says at the beginning of a speech or presentation is deemed more influential in affecting behavior or influencing decisions. What is said at the ending is likewise noteworthy and this is known as the recency effect. Research confirms what human experience has known for years: that at endings and terminations people cherish the most what they have heard, felt, touched at the very end. This understanding is realized whenever we hear a farewell speech, bid a sad goodbye to a dear friend, or reflect on a souvenir given to us from a dying parent. These are all opportunities of leave-taking and occasions of farewell. Hence, they are moments to say what is truly most important as we bring closure to a variety of personal and professional relationships. However, since beginnings are so intricately related to endings, the next part of this chapter will be a reflection on some of the more important tasks facing a counselor at the initial stages of the counseling relationship. This is not meant to be a comprehensive account but to serve as a bridge from the midphase issues already discussed and linking with the discussion on termination.

A. Beginning Counseling

When counselors begin a counseling relationship invariably they begin it with eager anticipation. They are unsure about many issues affecting the therapeutic relationship. For the most part, when counselors begin a counseling relationship, they are either in a supervisory relationship or about to begin such an experience. Likewise, they might be unclear about the supervisory relationship. When evaluation of the clinical work is also a component of the supervisory relationship, the experience becomes even more emotionally sensitive. What has been found common through the years is that counselors want to do their very best, and this tension has a way of escalating performance anxiety to an even higher pitch. What has proven helpful is the insight to be clear about beginnings, to understand what are the expectations of supervisors as well as for the counselors to know what clients are feeling when they call for help and want to receive counseling. Accordingly, supervision can be seen as existing in a tri-personal field insofar as the supervisor needs to be aware of the issues with the supervisee, between the supervisee and client and between the client and the supervisor. Supervision is certainly a complex series of relationships, and supervisors are well advised to be clear about the beginnings of the supervisory relationship as counselors are encouraged to be certain about the beginnings of the counseling relationship.

Beginning a relationship with anyone is difficult because we don't know all the many issues facing a person, and we certainly don't know the host of personality variables that contribute to the complexity of the human person. However, each helping relationship has certain well-defined functions or tasks which must be known and skills acquired if the relationship is to accomplish a therapeutic and effective purpose.

In the early stages of the counseling relationship, I encourage counselors to learn how to establish rapport. This is probably one of the most simplistic statements ever written, but one that requires much thought and reflection. Reading statements in a textbook is far different from the knowing the responsibility, that when I close the door to the consulting room and I am alone with the person who has called for help, knowledge must be expressed through a caring and helpful relationship. Rapport is experienced through the human interaction when counselors face test situations appropriately. Test situations would include issues of competence, credentials, and what counseling or therapy is all about. As a supervisor, I encourage counselors to memorize at the beginning of their therapeutic work a short recommendation to therapy speech. This response is given to clients either after the initial interview, or after four initial interviews designed to determine whether counselor and client have the capacity to form a therapeutic relationship. Hopefully, it will be sensitive and effective in letting people know what they have a right to expect from the monetary or personal investment they are making.

This brief recommendation to counseling also reminds counselors about the importance of beginning a new therapeutic relationship. They will be reminded of the importance of establishing a warm, accepting, and uncritical relationship. This mode of communication is felt when counselors have understanding attitudes and are unafraid to stand below the person, to use a metaphoric expression, in order to gain a perspective on the fears and anxieties that clients have in the early phases of counseling.

Knowing what needs to be accomplished in the initial interview and reviewing with clients what therapy is has a useful effect in reducing defensiveness in counselors because they sense the uncertainty and ambiguity of clients. Through the supervisory process, counselors are alerted to how difficult it is for a person to ask for help. Aristotle is supposed to have said that the superior person gives help while the inferior has to receive. Hence, it is important to realize that people might feel inadequate because they can't cope with certain problems.

This very inadequacy can give rise to defensiveness, resistance, and fear. When counselors develop a genuine helping attitude and acknowledge the fear and anxiety present in clients, a good beginning is made. After the initial interview with clients, counselors continue to help clients with the reduction of fear associated with the counseling relationship, and this reduction increases the level of rapport. Counselors are invited to enter into the lives of clients through effective communication. Basically, I encourage supervisees to be clear about the words they use. Language is so important to the process of creating understanding, and when clients are upset, they can't handle long and involved questions and comments. As the counseling relationship continues, counselors and clients develop their own unique mode of communication. However, at the beginning, counselors have two primary tasks. The first is to establish the relationship using all the interpersonal skills and talent they have in terms of being a warm and genuine caring person. Secondly, they have the responsibility to communicate clearly and effectively what counseling can do for a person. This involves a description of the structure of counseling and what is expected of a person who wants to gain insight and to develop understanding, as well as to develop attitudinal or behavioral change. When this kind of communication pattern is accomplished, clients' fears are reduced, and they are encouraged to continue the counseling process to find solutions to their problems in living.

Counselors can gain a sense of competence that comes in knowing the unique starting point of their clients and the questions that life is asking of them. Through this beginning phase of treatment, counselors must determine whether or not they and the clients have the capacity to develop a therapeutic relationship which will enable them to negotiate the midphases of the work. If the decision is made that they don't have this capacity, then the counselor's responsibility is to transfer this client to another therapist. This inability to form a therapeutic relationship is a rare occurrence, but it is helpful to acknowledge that as therapists we are not obligated to work with everyone therapeutically. After the establishment of the counseling relationship, the process of reflection, interpretation, and insight continues as both counselor and client contribute to the therapeutic dialogue through the relational dynamics of transference and countertransference. Good beginnings make for good endings, and this brief review of the beginning phases of counseling leads us to the discussion of termination.

B. *The Termination Phase*

While moving through the mid-phase issues of counseling to the termination phase, counselors must remain alert to detect signals that indicate the readiness or desire of clients to end the counseling relationship. Various modalities of counseling handle termination in different ways. In time-limited counseling, the end point is clearly established through the contractual arrangements. However, in long term or open-ended therapy, counselors must observe through the spoken word or through behavior the readiness or desire of a client to end therapy. Some clients, when they feel ready and when certain accomplishments have enabled them to live life more freely and effectively, will raise the issue of termination verbally. At this point, termination is seen as part of the treatment process, and it is a distinctive stage. This stage can be effectively accomplished when counselors can refer to their process notes begun at the very beginning of the treatment. Counselors who are just beginning might also find it helpful to keep for review the actual tape of the initial interview, and use it as part of the termination process. Whether or not counselors feel inclined to keep tapes for a long period of time, it is insightful to reflect on an initial interview transcript to discern the movement, integration and freedom clients have accomplished. Process notes, however, contain much of the same material, presenting the problem and how this initial problem or questions in living changed or became more nuanced as the relationship developed. When the work of therapy has been successful, counselors and clients sense that termination is near.

There are other indications of termination, and they might be expressed through various forms. The clearest signal is when clients reduce the seriousness of purpose which motivated them to enter therapy in the first place. Time is a very important indicator and any change regarding time must be understood. Some clients will begin coming late for sessions. Others will want to change the time reserved for sessions. Some will even forget appointments. Accordingly, all these manifestations must be carefully and fully explored, to distinguish signals of termination from resistance.

In addition to time considerations, what clients do in therapy can be seen as an indicator that they want to terminate. Some will lessen the quality of the dialogue through joking and treating issues on a superficial level.

They will refuse to reflect on the multi-levels of reality involved in their actions, attitudes, thoughts and feelings. They could just be tired of therapy, however, and simply need a break. Counselors should be sensitive to discern the needs of clients for a vacation from therapy or an unspoken desire to terminate. What clients say in an hour might also reveal their intention to terminate. For instance, some clients will anticipate termination with the counselor by talking about ending a relationship with a friend, spouse, or significant other. Other clients will express their feelings of loss and abandonment in words. If the relationship has become meaningful, then not to have feelings of regret and loss clearly indicates the presence of other therapeutic issues.

Along with time-related issues and what clients say within the counseling session is the very important factor of what they do outside the session. It is axiomatically true that actions speak louder than words. When clients regress to less mature forms of acting and when they lose motivation to change or to move to more adaptive levels of functioning, counselors are encouraged to interpret this behavior as a possible sign of termination. Any one of these four indicators is important, and a full discussion with clients is necessary. If the decision to terminate is made, then counselors and clients enter into the process of termination. When the data gathered evidences the approach of termination, two important tasks remain to be resolved. Through the supervisory relationship, counselors should review the readiness of their client to terminate, and share in this decision-making process. Secondly, counselors must recognize clients' feelings about the decision. When clients have progressed through the various stages of the counseling process, they will give evidence of the many gains achieved while in counseling. Still, there will remain an uncertainty whether or not they can get along on their own. As counseling comes to an end, they begin to feel much better about their situation, and also realize that not all their problems and conficts have been solved or will be completely eliminated. This is a good sign. Through the strength derived from the counseling, clients obtain renewed confidence in their ability to cope. This confidence is felt when clients receive the conviction that counselors believe in their ability and power to cope. Counselors enable clients when they recognize their desire to get along on their own strength even while some doubts and fears persist. Clients become reliant on counselors, and grow accustomed to the nurturance and encouragement received through regular and consistent sessions. When the decision to terminate has been mutually made, both counselor and client are invited to reflect on the work they have done together.

Reflecting on the work accomplished through the counseling relationship constitutes the major focus of the termination process. A minor thread woven through the process is the resolution of feelings related to counseling. These two tasks serve as point and counterpoint through this stage. There are several criteria that guide counselors and clients as they discern the ending of a counseling relationship. Perhaps the most obvious is to what extent the problems and conflicts have decreased or been worked through. Have clients been enabled to answer more effectively the questions life asks of them? Has the antecedent stress that motivated the clients' entrance into therapy been removed or channeled in such a way that clients have learned to deal more realistically with stress and anxiety? In an age which has been called anxious, stress will never be completely eliminated, but clients can develop more adequate coping skills to deal with the demands and challenges of life. Are these coping skills refined to a degree where clients can encounter life on their own? Since counseling consists of communication and results in understanding, in what ways have clients increased their level of self-understanding. Do they know and have insight into the tendrils of their problems, and have the solutions found through the counseling process permitted them flexibility and satisfaction?

Life is a series of intricately connected relationships which help people answer their needs. Through the termination process, counselors ascertain the quality of their clients' relationships. Are these sustaining and supportive of clients' self-esteem and self-worth? Are the all-important questions being answered through these relationships? Am I loved and do I have the capacity to love another? Work is a necessary part of all our lives, and when problems in living are experienced, our work suffers. Are clients engaged in satisfying work, and does the responsibility that comes with work well done permit them the integrity they deserve? The abilities to play, to be renewed, to recreate, merit review and examination. Have clients learned to become happy? Has the lesson that happiness consists in liking what we do rather than what we want been realized in our clients? Freud reduced all these criteria to two simple questions: What is the quality of my loving? What is the quality of my working? Counselors are well directed to review these guidelines as they begin to bring closure to the counseling relationship.

Some of the above guidelines have been incorporated in the evaluation instrument which follows. This instrument is intended to facilitate the dialogue between counselor and client as they review what has been accomplished through the counseling relationship. It will also serve as a point of discussion between counselor and supervisor as they discern the readiness of a client to terminate. Since it is in the form of a before-and-after design, counselors and supervisors can detect the change and movement in clients based on their own self-perception. What is recommended is to have clients, counselors, and supervisors complete this instrument so that an inter-rating index might be obtained from the three people most directly involved in the counseling process. The instrument attempts to ascertain the change and progress in important aspects of the counseling work. It attempts to measure salient features from basic behavioral functioning to the extent that clients have increased their level of insight and understanding. There is also room for clients to write about the value and effectiveness of their counseling. When this instrument is used in the process of termination, it serves as an important function in bringing together the data upon which an enlightened decision to terminate can be determined.

II. Counseling Termination Guide

Name of Client:_____ Date:_____

In order to determine your readiness to terminate counseling as well as to gain an index of our counseling effectiveness, would you give your best judgment on the following categories. If you are not sure, please offer your best guess. These answers will enable us in our counseling relationship, and will give you an awareness of your change and progress, or its lack thereof.

Please read each category carefully, and place a check mark on that alternative which measures most accurately what applied to you at both the beginning of counseling (B) and after the counseling (A).

1. The degree to which I had disabling or incapacitating symptoms (such as headaches, depression, physical discomfort and nervousness): (B) (A)
   a. Extremely severe ____ ____
   b. Severe ____ ____
   c. Fairly marked ____ ____
   d. Moderate ____ ____
   e. Only mild ____ ____
   f. Seldom, and mild ____ ____
   g. None ____ ____

2. The degree to which I suffered from anxiety/stress:
   a. Extremely severe ____ ____
   b. Severe ____ ____
   c. Fairly marked ____ ____
   d. Moderate ____ ____
   e. Only mild ____ ____
   f. Seldom, and mild ____ ____

3. Difficulties I had in getting along with people (such as shyness, inability to maintain friendships, inability to relate, etc.):

(B)   (A)

   a. Extremely severe ___ ___
   b. Severe ___ ___
   c. Fairly marked ___ ___
   d. Moderate ___ ___
   e. Only mild ___ ___
   f. Seldom, and mild ___ ___
   g. None ___ ___

4. The amount of insight or understanding I have had about myself and my condition:

   a. None or very, very little ___ ___
   b. Very little ___ ___
   c. Just a little ___ ___
   d. A fair amount ___ ___
   e. Better than fair ___ ___
   f. Quite good ___ ___
   g. Excellent ___ ___

5. The degree to which I was able to function well or effectively in most situations:

   a. Extremely bad ___ ___
   b. Very badly ___ ___
   c. Badly ___ ___
   d. Only fairly well ___ ___
   e. At least reasonably well ___ ___
   f. Quite well ___ ___
   g. Exceptionally well ___ ___

6. The following best describes my general adjustment or general well-being before (B) and after (A) counseling:

   a. Extremely bad ___ ___
   b. Very bad ___ ___
   c. Only fairly good ___ ___
   d. At least reasonably good ___ ___
   e. Quite good ___ ___
   f. Exceptionally good ___ ___
   g. Bad ___ ___

7. If you like, you may write below and continue on the
    reverse any other general remarks which would
    indicate how you feel about the value and
    effectiveness of your counseling.

When the decision to terminate has been made based either on the data gathered from the Counseling Termination Guide or through some other procedure, counselors and clients need to establish how many sessions will be needed to bring an end to the counseling relationship. One cardinal rule, however, to be observed is never to terminate during the session that termination is first talked about or presented as a possibility. Some supervisors suggest that the process of termination constitute one-sixth of the entire counseling process. This might be appropriate for in-depth analytical work and open-ended therapy, but for the most part the recommendation is made that termination of the counseling relationship requires an additional four sessions. During these, counselors become more active and interactional in the process. They will want to understand how clients will live without their supportive presence. Likewise, they will need to know the plans and expectations that clients have about their future.

When clients terminate with me, I use the metaphor of the diving board. When persons dive into the water, they must have consciously chosen how they are to accomplish the complex series of behaviors expressed through the graceful gesture of diving. Likewise clients must decide how they are to re-enter into the world of everyday life without the supports and challenge of counseling. Sometimes they will be fearful that what they have accomplished will be lost, and they will need reassurance that whatever we have accomplished as a therapeutic team will always be there and no one can ever take it away from them.

When feelings have become particularly intense, counselors might want to institute a gradual schedule of termination sessions, going from weekly sessions to bi-weekly, then monthly to every other month, until the final session. In my practice, I encourage clients to enter a monitoring schedule which permits them a session six months after counseling has ended. This session permits me the opportunity to review with clients their unique response to life, and it gives them the sense of being connected with someone who knows them very well. Beginning counselors will need to grapple with how they want to tailor the termination process. Some will end the relationship through a rather formal process which will be professional and effective. Others will involve more of their own humanity and will offer clients advice and encouragement, and will even celebrate the ending with a small token or gift. When the gesture is done, the suggestion is made that the gift be symbolic, or a metaphor of what has been worked through the counseling process.

In turn, counselors must also resolve their feelings about receiving gifts from clients. When I ended therapy many years ago, my therapist was honored to receive a wood carving from me of the Man of La Mancha, the Knight of The Woeful Countenance. The gift was given because he enabled me to dream impossible dreams and to understand that without a vision incorporating the whole of life, dreams fade into insignificance. Accordingly, any gift should have meaning for the counselor and client, and be seen as a medium through which important feelings and information are shared and resolved. When these are discussed in the termination interview, the two people, who have become one functioning unit through the therapeutic dialogue, can once again reclaim their individuality and the process of therapy be brought to a productive ending.

As counselors guide their clients through the termination process, supervisors must be aware that a similar process is going on within the learning alliance between themselves and their supervisees. Bringing the counseling relationship to closure is similar to bringing the learning alliance to the final point of leave taking or termination. Supervisors need to understand what is going within their supervisees. Do they need additional support during this time? Perhaps they want to review what has happened to them through the supervisory relationship. Compton has written about this important dimension in his chapter on the supervisory learning contract. Have candidates acquired what they expected to accomplish through the supervision? As counselors end the therapeutic relationship with clients, supervisors are encouraged to bring closure to the learning relationship in similar fashion. They may choose to review the work done with a single client, attempting to understand the change and integration obtained through their collective efforts. Perhaps the focus might be to discern more deeply through some kind of evaluative procedure the competence and advanced level learning the supervisee gained through reflection, practice, and greater skill acquisition. Whatever form is chosen is open to mutual dialogue and discussion between supervisor and supervisee.

What remains the central issue in bringing the supervisory relationship to termination is whether or not the terms of the working arrangement have been fulfilled. In addition, when the work of supervision has gone on for a long period of time, supervisors must be aware of the feelings of supervisees as this mentoring relationship is ended. Hence, it is important for supervisors to know how counselors will continue to grow professionally. Will they enter into some kind of ongoing group experience of supervision? Should the recommendation be made for additional supervision with a supervisor of a differing philosophy or mode of therapeutic interaction which will bring about greater growth and integration within the candidate? When the supervisory relationship is in the process of termination, both supervisor and supervisee are encouraged to review their beginnings and to acknowledge the progress and depth obtained. When supervision has been done well, it is a source of learning for both parties, and this fact demands recognition and attention.

Conclusion

In summary, this chapter has highlighted the significance of termination as a time of tremendous importance for the client. It is also a time for counselors to learn more deeply what has been accomplished through their efforts while working with clients. In addition, the suggestion was made that feelings must be more cherished than ever while clients are preparing to end what for most people is a life-giving and restorative relationship. Supervisors are encouraged to review the therapeutic work done by counselors so that they will derive a greater sense of competence and professionalism. Concomitantly, supervisors accept and work through any unresolved feelings that supervisees have developed toward them. When there is such a recognition of work well done and feelings explored, the situation exists in much the same way when Freud ended his analysis with Little Hans. The professor was happy and Little Hans and his parents were happy. When the termination process between client and counselor and between supervisor and supervisee is a creative summing up of the counseling relationship and the learning alliance where the work is brought to completion and feelings are accepted and understood, clients are happy, counselors are happy, and supervisors, too, are happy for work well done.

Part 3

Supervision and the
Variety of Helping Modalities

8

Short Term Counseling

The effective supervision of counselors who are providing short term coun-séling is directly analogous to the effective supervision of counselors engaged in any method of counseling. However, although the supervisory principles are coterminous, there are some particular issues of which supervisors should be more cognizant if they are supervising counselors who are providing short term counseling.

Before beginning the discussion of the psychotherapeutic supervisory issues in short term counseling, it is essential to emphasize that the paradigm of supervision as a working alliance and the general facilitative supervisory skills as presented in other chapters of this book form the basis for the discussion that follows. There is no attempt here to impose a different model or separate skills, but rather to supplement supervisory methodology in relation to short term counseling.

Short term counseling is a relative term that implies that there is long term counseling. It also implies to some supervisors and counselors that short term counseling is less intense, more behavior oriented, and perhaps truncated counseling for those with less severe problems or for those clients who are unable to face their real therapeutic issues. While in general short term counseling deals often with behavior, current problems, and situation distress, short term counseling has been some of the most exciting, dynamic and truly insightful experience that I have witnessed, facilitated and participated in. A review of related literature and clinical studies, indicated that authors recognize short term counseling as thorough, active, economical and frequently the therapy of choice (Bellak, 1986; Wolberg, 1980). In these cases the counseling was extremely intense, affectively oriented, and pivotal for the clients in terms of their personal development. In addition, I was cognizant of not only the readiness of the clients to effect change but also of the economic reality that short term counseling costs less for the client. Therefore, lest the prejudices build against short term counseling as pseudotherapy, consider that truly well orchestrated short term counseling will be well organized, intensive, goal oriented, aimed at behavior change, and cost effective.

For the purpose of this discussion, an arbitrary guideline of one to twelve sessions will be defined as short term counseling. This is not to imply that the thirteenth session immediately indicates that the therapeutic experience has become long term counseling. This guideline is proposed as a common denominator from which to approach discussion. If you as counselor and supervisor consider short term counseling as many more than twelve, then the discussion is still appropriate.

Familiar examples of short term interventions abound. Crisis intervention, most behavioral interventions, biofeedback, cognitive therapy, hypnosis, career counseling, grief counseling, and communications assessment and change are stereotypical of short term counseling. However, as proposed previously, very intense, affective oriented subjects can be appropriate for short term counseling. In addition, short term counseling can become long term counseling as various therapeutic issues develop. Similarly the client who is perceived as the long term client can become a short term client. Therefore, getting a firm, enduring grasp on a definitive description of short term counseling, how short term counseling is performed, how to diagnose the need for short term versus long term counseling, and components of short term counseling are difficult if not impossible subjects to address with dogmatic principles. However, guidelines for supervisors to consider as they facilitate counselors performance are apropos and useful.

It is important for supervisors not only to instill a respect and knowledge of the assets of short term counseling, but also to address when short term counseling is appropriate, how to structure short term counseling goals and what happens when short term counseling does not produce results. Therefore, the following issues will be discussed in hopes that supervisors may glean helpful suggestions and information: major aims of short term counseling; assisting supervisees in assessing appropriateness of short term counseling versus long term; setting short term therapeutic goals; increasing the timeliness of supervisory and intervention activities; aiding counselors in assessing the clients' need to lengthen their time in counseling; handling termination issues for counselor and client.

I. Major Aims of Short Term Counseling

There are three major aims of short term counseling. The first aim is to modify or remove symptoms. Second, counselors would aim to influence the client to correct or modify his/her behavior. The final aim of counseling is to initiate essential changes in personality.

A. Assisting Supervisees in Assessing the Appropriateness of Short Term Counseling Versus Long Term Counseling

As the supervisor of counselors, the ability to communicate essential client assessment skills is presumed. As a part of those assessment activities, a discussion between counselor and supervisor will invariably arise as to the appropriate length of a client's counseling. During initial sessions most clients will raise the question as to the number of sessions that will be required to alleviate the presenting problem. Most counselors will hedge on answering the question when it is raised by clients, and most supervisors will encourage their counselor supervisees to avoid making any firm commitment as to a prescribed number of sessions. Although it is difficult to predict the exact number of sessions needed, there are some guidelines for assessing whether a client will be in need of short term or long term therapy. Here is a list of systems that I look for:

1. Behavior Problem Versus Affective Problem

Clients who wish to change their behavior will usually identify a specific action that they wish to alter. For example, the client will identify a need to lose weight, stop smoking, relax, eliminate a phobia, etc. Clients who wish to change their affective state will identify a feeling state, usually depression, frustration, or anxiety. As a supervisor, it is important that you assist your supervisees in distinguishing between those clients who are presenting behavior changes as their counseling goals and those clients who present an affective problem.

There are some clear-cut cases which fall into one of the above two categories, but most clients fall somewhere in between or present a mixture of problems and symptomatology. Your job as supervisor will be to assist the counselor in assessing whether the presenting problem is more of a behavior issue or a psychological one. The more the presenting problem leans toward being a behavior issue, the more probability that the counseling will be short term.

An example of short term behavior oriented counseling follows. Freda presented herself to me for counseling to cease her self-defeating behavior of nail biting. She was a fashion model and needed her hands to look better in order to be versatile in her career. After performing an intake, I learned of no serious family problems, no severe pathology, and a sincere desire to change her behavior. Within four sessions Freda had learned how to change her nail biting behavior, had practiced it and had noticed improvement. The fact that her hands began to look better to her was immediately reinforcing. After eight sessions, we terminated her counseling. A follow-up session revealed that her nail biting behavior had been extinguished.

This same scenario is applicable to smokers, over-eaters, and phobics. If a behavior change is the client's prime reason for entering counseling, then the time in counseling can be shorter than if the counseling is directed toward an affective change that has grown out of a psychological dysfunction (Sifneos, 1972). As a supervisor, assist the counselor in looking for the following:

Does the client indicate a behavior that needs changing?
Does the client express frustration at not being able to change the behavior?
Does the client describe himself/herself as healthy and competent to handle most problems that arise?
Does the client feel positive about his or her support system?
Has the client handled past behavior problems with success?
Is the client free of drug addiction?
Is the client in good physical health?

If the answers to the above are affirmative then most likely the client is describing a self-defeating behavior that has reinforcing properties.

In conclusion, the supervisory issue is one of prudent and reflective probing of the supervisee to assure that the counselor did not overlook any symptomatology that could be indicative of a more serious problem.

2. Desire for Change

Clients who are self-referred, who are highly motivated, and who are in a great deal of pain tend to cut through the defensiveness and get down to the business of changing more quickly than a client who is court-referred, unmotivated and uses defenses effectively to keep conscious pain at a manageable level (Malan, 1963). Highly motivated, motile clients can make counselors look good and feel good about their intervention. These clients usually hunger for their sessions, glean all they can from the counselor and then work very hard away from the sessions. They usually make rapid progress that counselors can see as too rapid at times. The counselor can feel not in control of the counseling and can be tempted to try to slow the progress. The supervisor's role is one of monitoring the counselor's feelings more than the clients' feelings.

These clients take a counselor by storm. If the supervisor can assist the counselor in understanding the intense motivation of a client, then the counselor can allow the client the freedom to progress. Counselors who are in touch with their own feelings will sometimes feel that they are not doing anything for the client and are superfluous to the progress. Nothing is further from the truth. Supervisors must reinforce the idea that if this client was not in need of the counseling relationship to make progress, then the client would have been able to change on his or her own. The fact that counseling is sought and is ongoing speaks clearly that these clients need the counselor to facilitate their growth. If the counselor can relax and enjoy the client's growth, then this client will teach as well as learn in the psychotherapeutic relationship.

3. Support Systems

If a client has a strong healthy support system to assist with the growth and change, then the probability is that the client will need less time with the counselor (Sifneos, 1972). It is important for the supervisor to remind the counselor that clients will spend approximately 167 hours outside of the counseling relationship for every hour they spend in counseling. If the counselor can take advantage of the support system, then a client's work in therapy can be reinforced at home or work.

4. Chronic Problem Versus Situational Distress

This area requires careful exploration by the counselor and the supervisor needs to be cognizant of how well the counselor has probed into the possibility of the chronic nature of the client's problem. Too often a counselor ignores the past clues which yield repetitive type manifestations of problematic areas. A client who has had chronic type problems will be much more resistant to change than the client who is experiencing a situational stress. When the counselor is determining the degree of assistance a client may need, it is imperative that the counselor probe into the history of the symptomatology of the client to look for similar repetitive type problems. This journey into the past is viewed by some as extraneous and not "here and now" centered, but, in my opinion, this type of probing is essential in grasping the degree of strength with which a client repeats problems and behavior. Clinical findings support the assertion that severe pathology and chronicity are factors which should be considered before contemplating short term counseling (Malen, 1963).

The supervisor's responsibility is to remind the counselor that a presenting problem with all of its symptomatology may or may not be *the* problem. Sleuthing out clues to behavior and forming a hypothesis about why and how the client is reacting to current stressors will yield invaluable information as to whether counseling will be short or long.

5. *Appropriateness of Emotional Response*

Clients who are exhibiting appropriate emotional response or who have a history of such are more apt to be suitable for short term counseling (Sifneos, 1972). These clients are usually able to exhibit flexibility in their emotive states, manifest early transference symtoms and interpret their actions and symptoms (Malar, 1963).

6. *Conclusion*

If a client exhibits a problem that is behavior oriented, is highly motivated to change, has a positive support system, manifests appropriate emotional response, and is experiencing a situational problem, then this client is more likely to be a candidate for short term counseling.

As a supervisor, if you will facilitate the counselor's targeting the behavior change, utilizing the client's motivation, encouraging the support system's activity, interpreting transference issues, and dealing in the here and now, then the short term therapy will be dynamic, change oriented, and complete.

The more the client's problems and environment vary from the above paragraph's description, the more time will be needed to meet the major aims of counseling. Counselors can often miss important clues that due to the proximity of the counselor-client relationship are obscured. Supervisors have an objective and distant view that can often assist counselors in seeing the proverbial forest instead of the trees. As a supervisor facilitating the work of another, the above five yardsticks can assist you in helping the counselor assess the relative length of the counseling needed by each client.

B. *Setting Short Term Therapeutic Goals*

Goal setting is probably one of the most under-utilized and over-emphasized tools in counseling. Many counselors find that goal setting is a relatively simple process, but establishing the action steps to reach the goal and then implementing those action steps are very difficult tasks. Therefore, the whole process is often ignored. However, in short term counseling, goal setting is more than desirable; it is crucial.

Once a client has been assessed as a candidate for short term counseling, the next step is for the counselor and client to agree on the outcome or goal of the counseling process. Then, the counselor and client should agree on a plan of action. The client's suggestions are extremely important in developing the objectives and action steps, for these are the activities in which the client will be invested. Be careful that the objectives and action steps really do lead to the therapeutic goal and not to avoiding the goal or the real issues. A timetable is also useful for implementation and adds credence not only to the short term nature of the counseling but also to the contract nature of the counseling.

Below is an example of a goal that was realized by a previous client. I have provided here an excerpt from her goal setting contract.

Client: Estelle was nineteen years old, living at home due to financial constraints, and a clerk typist at a local business. Estelle was frustrated and unhappy because she knew that she needed to act grown up and independent but could not make this move financially. Living at home caused Estelle to fall into very dependent type behavior patterns that were childlike. She depended on her parents for everything including morning wake-up calls. Estelle and her parents agreed that she needed more independence but after trying to establish new ground rules found themselves reverting to previous behavior. Estelle appeared healthy and motivated to change. She had a great deal of love and respect for her parents. Estelle's parents were very supportive. The following Goal, Objectives and Action Plans were set by Estelle.

Goal: To become more independent of family and accountable for own life.
   Objective 1: To be physically independent of parents' time keeping.
      Action Plans: 1. Purchase an alarm clock and set it each night.
                          2. Get up in morning when alarm goes off.
                          3. Set own bedtime hour and adhere to it.
                          4. Tell parents to refrain from awakening me even if I am oversleeping.
   Objective 2: To be independent of parents for social life.
      Action Plans: 1. Let parents know where I am going and when I will be home as a courtesy to those I am living with.
                          2. Do not ask parents for approval of social activities.
                          3. Plan at least one social activity each week without parents.

Other objectives called for Estelle to pay her parents a small amount for rent and for saving money for a security deposit on an apartment. Counseling lasted about ten sessions, and follow-up revealed that within six months Estelle had established an independent life style and had moved out of her parents' home to share an apartment with a friend.

C. Increasing the Timeliness of Supervisory Intervention Activities

For the supervisor, one of the key issues in supervising a counselor who is involved with short term counseling is the timeliness of monitoring counseling activities and intervention. Because the counseling will only last a few sessions, the input from the supervisor should be immediate. I liken the difference between long term therapy and short term therapy to the difference between steering a battleship and steering a speedboat. The speedboat is very responsive to the touch, and turning the speedboat yields a more immediate response than turning a battleship. Supervisors need to be available and immediate in their response for assistance when dealing with counselors who are engaged in short term counseling.

When the counselor informs the supervisor of a short term case which may need the supervisor's attention, the supervisor and counselor should go over the case as soon as possible and outline the necessary strategy and goal definitions. In this way, the counselor and supervisor can be more proactive than reactive. This strategy is appropriate for all cases that counselors and supervisors are conferring on, but it is more essential for cases that are short term in nature.

D. Aiding Counselors in Assessing the Client's Need To Lengthen His/ Her Time in Therapy

Perhaps the most common reason that the number of short term counseling sessions are increased is that the client feels the need to complete some perceived unfinished business. As the client and counselor approach the end of their contract, the client will sometimes state that there is another therapeutic issue to be discussed. Sometimes this is a ploy to avoid termination (see termination issues later in this chapter), but more often it is a sign that the client feels comfortable with the counselor and wishes to discuss another problem area. The supervisor can assist the counselor in ascertaining the legitimacy of the new presenting problem and further assist the counselor in setting new goals.

Another reason for the lengthening of therapy is that the goals set down were not reached. A multitude of reasons can account for the lack of goal attainment. Among them are interruptions, crises that the client unexpectedly experiences, the timetable for the goals was too short, the client did not fulfill his end of the contract, the counselor allowed the sessions to get sidetracked, and other problem areas surfaced during the counseling. For each of the above reasons, the counselor could consult the supervisor for assistance. Together, the counselor and supervisor would have to assess the reason and decide whether the client had sabotaged the counseling, whether the counselor sidetracked the progress, whether the reasons were beyond anyone's control, or whether the deviation was in fact a healthy response to a caring and helping relationship. If the client sabotaged the goal, then serious consideration should be given to termination. I remember one client I was working with who set his own homework assignment and then did not follow through. When I asked why he had not completed his task, he shrugged and said, "I didn't feel like it." My response was that I felt that he was wasting his time in counseling if he was not going to work, and I suggested that he wanted to terminate. He was so shocked that I had confronted him that he began to work diligently at his counseling. Later, he confessed that all his life people had let him get away with non-performance because he was charming and could win them over with a smile. He said that his shock at someone actually holding him accountable was more therapeutic than the rest of the counseling. The supervisor may need to remind the counselor that the counselor's time is valuable and clients who do not work can be a waste of time that could be spent with clients who are in need and who are motivated.

If there is a commitment on the part of both the counselor and client to continue the counseling beyond the contracted goal, then another time frame should be established and further goals should be agreed upon. No matter what the need, short term counseling necessitates a concise contractual goal arrangement that both counselor and client can agree to in order to accomplish what needs to be accomplished is a limited time span.

E. Handling Termination Issues for Counselor and Client

Short term counseling often yields the same type of termination issues that long term therapy does. However, short term counseling can feel incomplete to some clients because of the brevity. Even if clients meet their therapeutic goals in counseling there can be a residual feeling of incompleteness. Another feeling that short term clients have expressed to me is one of grieving over the loss of a potential significant other. After several sessions clients report that they have begun to feel really close to their counselor when it was time to terminate. Clients indicate that they resist termination because they want to get to know their counselor better. I seldom hear this after a client has been seen for six months to a year. The termination issue for long term clients seems to be centered around the grieving over the loss of a close relationship, whereas the termination issue for short term clients is centered more around the loss of a newly created close relationship that the client wants to develop further.

This comparison is not to indicate that short term counseling does not yield a close relationship between client and counselor but that usually the termination issue after long term counseling brings with it a greater sense of loss of a significant other while the termination issue after short term counseling brings with it a sense of loss of a significant beginning relationship.

One way a supervisor can assist the counselor in understanding the client's point of view is to have the counselor examine his or her own feeling regarding clients who terminate after less than twelve sessions. Often the feeling of lack of closure that the client has are replicated by the counselor. Both counselor and client may feel that they want to prolong the counseling so as to develop the relationship more fully. I assist my own clients and supervisees during this time by suggesting that counseling is a process, and that although we may be finished for this time, there may be another time when help may be needed. In other words, the door is left open. This assuages the client's feeling of being "terminated" and the counselor's feeling that perhaps they should be talking of other issues. The client also understands that the relationship can continue in the future if needed, and this is a comforting thought for the client.

Another technique that I use or recommend that my supervisees use is the follow-up session. During long term counseling, I usually taper off the sessions which helps with the separation grief. However, for short term clients, I terminate after the client has completed the prescribed goal. The follow-up session is usually held six months later and is financially free to the client. Through this session, my supervisees and I are assisted in gathering useful data. This follow-up session gives the short term client a sense of continuance and accountability to work beyond the sessions. Finally the follow-up session assuages the abruptness of termination.

At the follow-up session most clients feel proud of their accomplishments since termination and are ready to end their therapeutic contract. A few decide to re-enter counseling for the purpose of working on another problem. A very few have completely regressed to the pre-counseling problem state. Negotiation on re-entry or termination occurs with each client according to need.

Another technique I use to aid in termination is a newsletter. I write about what is happening in the agency, general mental health tips, upcoming groups, seminars, workshops offered and any other interesting piece of information. This newsletter helps the clients stay in touch, gives them other options and ideas for their own growth, and fortifies the idea that the agency is not just problem centered. As a side note, clients are asked if they wish to receive the newsletter. Not all want this piece of mail as a reminder of a painful time in their lives.

Conclusion

Short term therapy is usually less than twelve sessions, more behavior oriented, more situational problematic than chronic, more cost effective for the client, and deals with current time frames rather than past. Because of the nature of short term therapy, it is crucial that goals, objectives and action plans be established and adhered to, that a timetable be implemented, that the counselor be prepared to lengthen the counseling if a need arises, and that termination issues be addressed in a slightly different fashion than for long term counseling.

Good supervisory skills plus a more proactive, timely and immediately responsive attitude toward the counselor will enhance the counselor's view of short term counseling and give the support necessary to assure successful outcomes of clients who are in need of this type of counseling.

References

K.A. Adler, "Techniques That Shorten Psychotherapy: Illustrated with 5 Cases." *Journal of Individual Psychotherapy* 28 (21): 155–168, 1972.

F. Alexander and T.M. French, *Psychoanalytic Therapy*. N.Y.: Ronald Press, 1946.

Leopold Bellak, "Brief & Emergency Psychotherapy," *The Harvard Medical School Mental Health Letter*, Vol. 2, No. 8, February 1986.

L. Bellak and L. Small, *Emergency Psychotherapy & Brief Psychotherapy*. N.Y.: Grune & Stratten, 1965.

D.H. Malan, *A Study of Brief Psychotherapy*. N.Y.: Plenum, 1976.

J. Mann, *Time-Limited Psychotherapy*. Cambridge: Harvard University Press, 1973.

O. Rank, *Will Therapy*. N.Y.: Knopf, 1936.

A.J. Rush, ed., *Short Term Therapies for Depression*. N.Y.: The Guilford Press, 1982.

P.E. Sifneos, *Short-Term Psychotherapy & Emotional Crisis*. Cambridge: Harvard University Press, 1972.

W. Stekel, *Conditions of Nervous Anxiety*, N.Y.: Liveright, 1950.

Lewis R. Wolberg, *Handbook of Shorter Psychotherapy*. N.Y.: Threme-Stratton, 1980.

9

Supervision in
Long Term Psychotherapy

Long term psychotherapy is one in which a person has experienced over
seventy hours of work, at least once a week, but preferably twice a week.
This is an arbitrary definition, but in my experience anything less than seventy hours would be considered as preparatory for long term psychological
work. In the ensuing discussion regarding the supervision of long term
work, I hope that this definition becomes sensible when looking at the
process of psychotherapy.

Long term psychotherapy also means a process of steady uncovering
of a person's inner experience. This is effective in those persons suffering
anxiety neuroses or characterological dysfunction. The borderline and psychotic processes which require long term work fit more appropriately in a
discussion of supportive or chronic treatment relationships. This discussion is an essay about those psychotherapeutic efforts with persons who
have moved beyond the seventieth hour of work in a process of uncovering
insight-oriented psychotherapy.

Supervision is understood as a learning process based on a relationship between supervisor and supervisee. This process is primarily designed to assist the supervisee develop therapeutic skills derived from
understanding the psychodynamics of the person in therapy. This process
also includes knowledge based on observation of the person in the relationship with the therapist and the therapist's observation of the supervisee's own behavior and feelings. Three specific dimensions are identified
in supervision and become foci of attention during the course of the supervisory relationship. These are intervention and interpretation skills, a
sense of professional identity and a clarity of personal integrity. These
processes are essential for the supervisee to learn the utilization of self in
the therapeutic relationship.

The process of supervision is foremost a relationship between the supervisor and supervisee. This relationship is the medium of learning and

STAGES AND DIMENSIONS OF LONG TERM PSYCHOTHERAPY SUPERVISION

STAGES:	I. INITIAL (1–13)	II. SETTLING IN (14–70)	III. WORKING THROUGH (2–7 YEARS)	IV. TERMINATION (6–12 MONTHS)
DIMENSIONS				
SKILLS	1. Genuine interest 2. Non-anxious presence 3. Ego defense recog./inter. 4. Assessment/diagnosis 5. Recog. phases in shaping working therapeutic relationships	1. Recog. cyclical process 2. Diff. between content & process 3. Interpret resistance/neg. transference 4. Mang. of transference 5. Direct/simple interpretation 6. Recog. core issues	1. Capacity to move w/ rhythm from center to boundary & back 2. Patience & faith in client to do own work 3. Interpret resistance and defense 4. Recog. core content exp. for working through 5. Manage regression & intensification of transference 6. Affirm insight	1. Separation and grief process 2. Recapitulation & regression 3. Interpretation of the termination 4. Letting go/dependence & counter-depend. 5. Differential between resistance & resolution
PROFESSIONAL IDENTITY	1. Open interest 2. Confidence 3. Consistent/reliable 4. Authentic	1. Patience 2. Non-threatened 3. Observant/accurate 4. Receive emergent intimacy without fear & violation of person	1. Maintain non-anxious, non-threatened presence under impact of intense exp. of client 2. Trustworthy 3. Confidentiality 4. Intimacy without intrusion or transgression	1. Affirm without possesssion 2. Non-threatened 3. Sharing without self disclosure
PERSONAL INTEGRITY	1. Genuine/trustworthy 2. Recog. own dynamics 3. Unthreatened 4. Clear boundary between self and others	1. Capacity of intimacy 2. Recog. countertransference 3. Non-revelatory of own issues 4. Personal anxiety kept separate	1. Maintain clear boundary between self and other 2. Arena for working through own countertransference	1. Handle grief and separation pain without projection on client 2. Letting go; exper. own pain 3. Trustworthy and authentic

within it are poured the self-reflective experiences of the supervisee as therapist, the conceptual understanding of therapeutic relationship development and the anxieties and struggles of self as the experience unfolds. The supervisor's role is to enter the relationship, to formulate understanding of the supervisee's level and capacity for learning, to familiarize the supervisee with the essential understanding of the therapeutic relationship, and to offer timely observations and interpretations of the supervisee's functioning.

To facilitate the discussion of supervision of long term psychotherapy, the accompanying chart is offered so that the interactions between the stages of long term work, the dimensions of supervision process, and the learning tasks may be more clearly visualized.

I. Understanding Long Term Psychotherapy

Long term psychotherapy needs to be considered in at least four stages. The first stage is the initial phase of the relationship. This stage covers the first thirteen sessions. The second stage is the settling in period and includes sessions fourteen through seventy. The third stage is in-depth uncovering and working through psychological conflicts. This stage forms the bulk of the long term work, usually from two to seven years. The fourth stage is termination which may be from two to twelve months.

A. *Initial Phase*

In stage one, the initial phase, the therapist and client experience the beginning quality and shape of the relationship including the initial anxieties, resistances, transference, counter-transference and commitment. In the first thirteen sessions, the initial awareness of the feelings moves quite rapidly. This movement may be grouped into segments of three sessions each.

In sessions 1–3, the client presents the initial anxieties and defenses which function for that person similar to any initial contact with a new relationship. The specific anxieties which prompted that person to seek therapy are intensely highlighted but are often quickly relieved by the simple act of talking with someone who the person believes will help. The observant therapist, however, notes the patterns and defenses of the client in these first sessions, gaining a sense of the "front line" ego defense structure of the client. If that defense structure primarily relies on projection, introjection and denial, this client is not a good risk for intensive long term psychotherapy, at least in the initial phases of the work. On the other hand, if the person shows well integrated intellectualization, reaction for-mation and to a lesser extent rationalization, this person may be available for long term psychotherapy. This initial assessment of the functioning of the client is crucial in the early diagnosis and treatment decisions. These may be, and often are, modified later as the person gains in ego strength.

The second segment of this first stage, sessions 4–6, usually is marked by initial resistance to the relationship. Heightened anxiety is often re-lieved and weakened defenses are more functional, allowing for realistic coping with that which felt threatening. The therapist responds to the re-sistance and ambivalence by interpreting it and allowing a sense of free-dom to establish itself in the client. In this segment, terminations frequently occur, signaled by missed appointments, lateness, cancella-tions, and worry about payment. In shaping the long term relationship, the therapist and client experience the initial problems of transferential feeling and begin to work out boundaries which support the right of the client to maintain a sense of separateness and trust in their individuality.

In the third segment of the first stage, sessions 7–9, the predomi-nant feature is the awareness on the part of the client that the therapist is becoming a significant figure in daily life. Feelings of affection, fear, conflict and anger creep into the awareness of the client, usually stirring confusion as to what is happening. Ambivalence begins to reign again. The therapist however has the first reliable glimpse of the direction of the budding transference as well as identification of initial counter-trans-ference issues.

The first stage climaxes in sessions 10–13. In this segment the deci-sion is made, consciously and unconsciously, that the relationship will con-tinue. The ambivalence comes to a head in that the person is able to identify that therapy will be beneficial but also painful and demanding upon the psyche. This awareness is interpreted by the therapist, the am-bivalence is recorded and a decision is made to enter into a therapeutic relationship. At this stage, many terminations occur, for a person may choose that the demands are more than desirable and so commitment is withdrawn. The benefits of the process to this point are noted and the per-son leaves.

For long term psychotherapy, this first stage is very critical in that the initial shape and quality of the relationship are set. For long term therapy, trust and confidence of the relationship is initially experienced allowing the person to proceed despite difficult resistance and insecurity with the deeper levels of psychic uncovering. In supervising therapists in long term psychotherapy, attention to the dynamics and flow of this initial phase is absolutely necessary for dealing with what is to come in the latter phases of the work.

B. Settling In

While the first stage is the initiation into the quality of the therapeutic relationship, the second stage is the settling in the relationship. This stage lasts approximately until the seventieth session, each ten sessions cycling specific unfolding psychic contents of the client. Consequently, sessions 20, 30, and 40 become transition sessions. Sessions 55 and 70, functioning in a fifteen cycle block, complete this stage. From these latter two cycles the transferences become stablized and the deeper and more profound levels of the personality begin to come into consciousness.

Sessions 14 through 40 may be experienced in three repetitive cycles. Each cycle follows a dynamic pattern. The pattern is this: scanning of felt inner conflicts, selection of conflicts to explore more thoroughly, sensing when that conflict is not to be explored further, and arousal of feelings of resistance and ambivalence with some anger and discontent with therapy.

The first cycle will be five or seven sessions, depending upon the transition from stage one. Following the session in which a commitment was made to proceed with therapy (session 13) a person will scan areas of conflict to explore, for example feelings about a parent, sibling, spouse or child. Usually it will relate to the initial complaint which brought the person to therapy three months before. Session 14 will usually represent a specific selection of the general complaint and raise it to the therapist in hope that the therapist will shed light on the felt conflict. As therapist and client relate to this complaint usually for the next three sessions, the client is catching on again that the therapist will explore but not solve the conflict. The transference is interpreted by the therapist leaving the client with the feelings of hurt and anger toward the therapist. This sets in motion feelings of disappointment and anger toward the therapist. The therapeutic conflict generated is often experienced around sessions 18 to 19 in which the negative feelings surface with greater intensity than at the end of stage one. Session 20 often is a painfully difficult one, for anger is received as part of the therapeutic relationship in hope that a sense of freedom to experience anger will be part of the experience between therapist and client. This round of ambivalence and the first serious negative transference will have been lived through, allowing for session 21 to re-enter the cycle again. This cycle then moves for approximately the next ten sessions through scanning, selection, exploration, resistance, ambivalence and clarification.

Session 30 is another transition in the cycle, repeating again for the next ten sessions leading to session 40. The important matter to note is that the therapist moves with the client through these dynamic cycles, responding and interpreting, exploring and interacting in the service of establishing the relationship for the very difficult material yet to come in stage 3. Understanding, trust, change, insight and confidence emerge in the experience between therapist and client through these cycles of the relationship.

After session 40, the cycles begin to stretch out a bit, usually in segments of fifteen sessions. This is due to the ability of the client to reach more depth and intensity as specific life conflicts are explored. The ego can regress with less threat, enabling the client to live more confidently with pain and anxiety.

The transition from stage 2 to stage 3 occurs around the seventieth session. The mark of the transition is that the client signals readiness to reengage at a deeper and more significant level conflicts already explored.

The issues calling for supervisory attention in the second stage are to help the therapist identify the flow of dynamics of each of the cycles. The temptation is to expect the client to resolve the specific conflict or feeling which becomes the focus of each cycle. The client likewise expects to have finished an issue simply because it has been in consciousness for a series of sessions. In this second stage, such issues are identified for exploratory purposes. Pain and anxiety are experienced by the client in these explorations of experiences and memories. Such pain is suffered for the sake of integrating the experience into the personality in a more full way. However, the process of the second state is still preparatory and exploratory, allowing the client to touch a wider and deeper awareness of what constitutes life and its conflicts. For the therapist, this stage allows for a more profound acquaintance with the client's personality functioning and an identification of the more severe aspects of the client's anxieties and characterological patterns.

The impact on the relationship between supervisor and supervisee is also significant. Here the transferential focus and solidification become the key ingredient. The transference formation is the primary medium of work for the therapist, and its management and maintenance are the fundamental learnings. In this, however, counter-transference dynamics will arise and often appear during the supervisory sessions. The supervisor is alert for these issues as they appear in the review of clinical sessions and in the direct relationship with the supervisor.

The supervisee learns to experience openly the counter-transference feelings in the supervision, not for therapeutic intervention, but for identification and assessment as to the management, viability and utilization of the data from the counter-transference.

By the end of the second stage, somewhere between a year and a year and a half, the therapy has evolved a working relationship of experience between therapist and client. The therapist has experienced the variety of behaviors and defensive patterns of the client, allowing for a fairly accurate understanding of the core neurotic development in the personality. The client has gained sufficient self-understanding to maintain motivation for long term work and to comprehend in some fashion the depth of difficulty, and has experienced sufficient transferential awareness to contain neurotic feelings and behaviors in relationship to the therapist. Patterns of acting out the neurotic anxiety and behavior are diminshed, allowing more intense focus for exploration and change within the therapeutic relationship itself. The therapy moves into the third stage.

C. *Working Through*

The third stage is the in-depth uncovering and working through processes of therapy. In this stage, constancy of therapist behavior is essential. The client struggles session after session with defenses that have served well in neurotic adaptation but which now resist the change which the therapeutic relationship is enabling to happen. Interpretation of defenses, resistances, and transference become the major therapeutic intervention by the therapist. The focus is to maintain the person in the process of uncovering work, enduring its pain and confirming the insights.

This stage of therapy moves in cycles as the first two stages, but the cycles are determined by their own content patterns. The cycles are usually triggered by significant unconscious fragments breaking through into consciousness, either through dreams or "breakthrough" sessions.

Breakthrough sessions are those in which new psychic discoveries are made by the client or significant memories emerge which connect with current struggles or psychic pain. Such sessions set the core agenda to be worked through the cycle. Depending on the significance and impact of the unconscious material, the cycle allows for a confrontation of the feelings, insight, and dreams and the sorting through the feelings and thoughts. Those aspects of the material which are desired and are integrated into conscious experiences and those aspects which are no long wanted or needed are let go.

An example may help. A young man in the course of therapy reported increased feelings of guilt, particularly in relationship to a woman he was dating. In the course of therapy, the guilt became very intense with little apparent external reason. Anxiety and pain created by the guilt stirred high agitation to the point where he could hardly remain in the therapy session. These feelings gradually began to surface a memory in which he at age six had an erection while being bathed by his mother. He remembered his mother giving him the washrag and telling him to finish his bath, and she left, never to bathe him again. Feelings of ambivalence, anger, hurt, abandonment and guilt flooded around this memory. This session had been preceded by working through feelings of competence in successfully completing his professional education and being hired for his first position by a prestigious company. This success produced memories of anger and affection toward his father, accompanied by sexual feelings toward him. While this was occurring, he had some experiences of loss of erection in the sexual relationship with his woman friend.

The memory of his mother's withdrawal from bathing him introduced the next cycle in the working through phase of therapy. Feelings of self-punishment, secret phantasies of oral sex, anger at women, longing for father and terror in anticipation of vaginal entry in sexual intercourse came into focus. Fear, distrust and ambivalence to the therapist emerged as well as high anxiety between the sessions. Bit by bit through the next twenty sessions, he lived through a variety of feelings, identifying their long-standing nature throughout his life, including fear of abandonment for having sexual aggressive feelings. Bit by bit he experienced the inner freedom to maintain his sexual aggressive feelings regardless of the anticipation of responses he had from significant figures, especially his mother.

This example represents the emergence of specific contents which are available to insight and change in the process of the therapeutic relationship. As the therapist was experienced as the abandoning mother, he was able to work through his memory and integrate his sexual/aggressive feelings while gradually letting go of the feeling of abandonment. His ego consequently became more enhanced by working through this very painful aspect of his unconscious life.

In long term psychotherapy, these cycles come as repressed unconscious aspects of the personality emerge for working through. In the supervision of a therapist working with such persons, the primary process to observe is the therapist's ability to stay sufficiently out of the way of the client's process so that the client has the freedom to experience such working through. The therapist may have a tendency to lose patience and want to intervene too quickly or interpret too hastily. In the example cited above, the therapist who was experienced as the abandoning mother by the client could have the need to reassure the client that he was not abandoned in the therapy. While this is true, the experience of abandonment by the therapist in the transference is absolutely essential for the client to work through the internal situation. As the client discovers that the therapist was with him through the process and did not abandon him, this discovery may be confirmed by the therapist.

The therapist in the working through phase learns the timing of interventions and interpretations which allow the client to do the work with a minimum of interference. Yet the therapist is watchful for resistances and defenses which need interpreting in order to keep the process productive for insight. The role of the supervisor is to help the therapist to intervene in a timely way by interpreting resistances and defenses, while at the same time keeping sufficiently out of the center of the client's process to allow the client to do the work.

In the working through cycles, the therapist is prone to counter-transference process. The supervisor needs to remain alert to such process in the therapist, teaching the ability to detect such counter-transference and to learn from it. Counter-transference may have a negative effect on the therapy in that the therapist relates from such issues rather than what is actually happening to the client. In this way, counter-transference distorts the therapeutic relations. Counter-transference may have a helpful impact on the therapy in that the therapist may learn vital things about the client through the observation of such process. For instance, if the therapist knows one's own vulnerability to take care of people, the emergence of such feelings and behaviors which are quite beyond the usual range point to the client's intensity of feeling infantile dependency. Such indication can be checked out by the therapist and shifts in the therapeutic relationship may occur if this intensification causes interference in the therapy. Learning how to observe and understand counter-transference process is an essential part of supervision of long term psychotherapy.

D. *Termination*

The fourth stage of long term psychotherapy is termination. This stage lasts from six to twelve months. It is signaled by an awareness in the client of working through many of the felt conflicts and a sense of resolution of the transference with the therapist. Often, termination themes appear in dreams, slips of tongue, or images of separation. In the supervision of this stage, the supervisor helps the therapist to be alert to these urges toward termination and distinguish them from avoidance of new painful psychic contents. Often termination comes as a very painful experience to be avoided with persons who have high difficulty with separation anxiety. This leads to protracted therapeutic process leading to unproductive work. Avoidance of termination may become a new resistance to the necessary termination of therapy. This then is a therapeutic issue to be confronted by the client.

The major supervisory issue in termination is the process of recapitulation of the course of therapy in a shortened period of time. This is a natural process in which the memories and feelings dealt with in the therapy return for review and recognition. This appears as a regression which is understood as a vital ingredient of this stage. Such regression is welcomed, for it relates to integration and incorporation of the therapeutic experience by the client. This process is essential if the client leaves the therapist with realistic grief and sufficient resolution to provide emotional authenticity and satisfaction in the work accomplished.

The termination stage also has its own cyclical pattern, but the cycle is the recapitulation of the stages of the therapy itself. Memories of feelings in the first and second stages come back for discussion. The emotional pain and satisfaction of the psychic material of stage three is felt once again. The final step of termination is the recognition that not all is resolved, that life is not perfect, and that the journey continues. What is changed is that the client is able to embrace the ambivalent situation and to welcome the recognition of survival and venture as a constant quality of living.

For the therapist, the anxiety is often felt that the client needs to be "finished" with all psychic issues. This is clearly a therapist's anxiety and is to be confronted in supervision. This is the doorway to the therapist's capacity to let go of the client and experience the ambivalence and satisfaction in the work done in the therapeutic relationship. Grief is experienced in the separation, especially in the long term therapies. Deep emotional roots have been laid in the therapeutic relationship which are to be given up by the therapist. The supervisor helps the supervisee to understand and accept this natural process and to recognize with the therapist the fundamental humanity which has been experienced by both client and therapist through the years of work together. Transferential material, by both client and therapist, is resolved in a way that allows the reality to appear, lifting the clouds of projection.

II. Understanding the Supervisory Process

Three specific dimensions of the supervisory process have been identified which become the foci of attention during the supervisory relationship. These are intervention and interpretation skills, a sense of professional identity, and a clarity of personal integrity. The supervisor is interested in helping the supervisee to gain specific skills and the psychological knowledge which supports these skills. However, these skills are part of a larger awareness, namely the utilization of self as the primary medium of therapeutic work. A clear sense of professional identity and personal integrity are essential for this utilization to take place.

In the supervision of long term psychotherapy, the balance of these dimensions offers the opportunity to help the supervisee refine both skill and identity in the intensive work with a person. The major stance that helps to blend and balance these processes is that of participant observer. The therapist participates in and observes the process of the therapy. The therapist is both subjectively a part of the therapeutic relationship as well as objectively observing it. In long term psychotherapy, each stage of therapeutic work demands different aspects of a therapist's skill and identity. These form the teaching agenda of the supervisor.

In the first stage, the primary teaching agenda in supervision is the indentification of the sub-group sessions as the relationship is shaped. Early in the assessment, a decision needs to be tentatively reached that the person could or could not benefit from long term psychotherapy. This means that the assessment of the initial complaint, ego defense structure, depth of personality conflict, motivation, capability to change and psychological-mindedness needs to be made. The skill is to gather this information for assessment while at the same time to manage the relational subtleties of the experience of the first stage. The teaching agenda is to help the supervisee with these skills. The therapist's skills then have to do with applying an understanding of the data being observed, both content and process, of the initial stage. A professional stance is maintained to allow confidence and trust to emerge. The therapist's personal integrity is shown as transference and counter-transference dynamics are surfaced. Skill, identity and integrity work together to allow the client to experience all the phases of the first stage and to allow for trust and confidence to develop in the relationship. Above all, the therapist provides a trustworthy, reliable and non-anxious environment.

The primary teaching agenda in the second stage of therapy is to help the therapist to recognize the cyclical pattern as it evolves in the experience of the client. This pattern is scanning, content selection, exploration, resistance, ambivalence and clarification. The skill of the therapist is to recognize the movement of the cycle, to provide helpful interpretation as the client experiences resistance, and to manage the emergence of anger and negative transference.

In addition to these skills, the identity issues are the learning patience and trust of the process in which the client is now engaged. Consistency, reliability, accurate observation of feelings and receiving the emerging intimacy in the transference without violation and misunderstanding by the client are professional and personal qualities needed in the behavior of the therapist.

The primary teaching agenda of the third stage is the capacity of the therapist to learn the rhythm of the content cycles as experienced by the client. This rhythm is the movement of the position of the therapist from the center work to the periphery to allow the client to engage the primary work itself. Resistance and defense which interfere with the client's own process, are interpreted by the therapist. At times the transference pulls the therapist to the center of the client's work. This needs to be interpreted, freeing the client to continue the work of therapy. In this stage, the skill to allow the client to regress into early feelings and experience is needed. Such regression calls upon the therapist to help the client trust the pain which surfaces as the past is experienced.

The therapist learns to maintain the non-anxious presence while intense pain and anguish are experienced by the client. As part of this, the therapist is open and receptive to the anger and negative transference. Under the impact of the intense experience of the client, the therapist learns to maintain a clear differentiation between the client issues and the personal issues of the therapist. Many internal issues of the therapist may be felt in the counter-transference. Learning to utilize this data in the understanding of the client is important. The therapist is advised to seek consultation and/or supervision to manage one's own feelings which may create excessive anxiety and pain.

The primary teaching agenda in the fourth stage is the skill to understand the recapitulation which occurs in termination. Regression, unresolved issues of the transference, intensification of dependence and counter-dependence on the therapist all occur during termination. Handling the grief and the process of letting go is the skill needed in this phase. Managing one's own grief and loss in the termination is an identity issue to be reviewed in the supervision. The capacity to affirm without intrusion, to let go without possession, is a personality skill important to the therapist.

Many of the issues between therapist and client occur as a parallel process between supervisor and supervisee. The primary ones are those dealing with authority and intimacy. Both dynamics are intensified in the nature of long term work. As in the relationship between therapist and client, the supervisor/supervisee relationship yields to mutuality, consultation, negotiation and affection. As the supervisor/supervisee can identify this in their relationship, then it can be more openly recognized and identified as it happens in the therapy. The interplay between the two processes is important to keep present during the course of supervision. This allows the monitoring of transference and counter-transference more closely by the supervisor and allows the supervisee to assume more responsibility for the management of these dynamics in the therapy.

Long term psychotherapy is a learning situation which calls for intense awareness by the therapist of one's own dynamics and the interplay in the therapeutic relationship. The supervision of this process is constantly rich in new discovery and maturing of therapeutic skills and maturation of self.

Conclusion

An understanding of the stages of long term psychotherapy and the dimensions of supervisory process form the bulk of supervisory work. Each stage has its own internal structure calling upon the skills, identity and integrity of the therapist in different ways. The discussion in this essay identifies major portions of the learning opportunities for doing long term psychotherapy. Above all, the supervisor teaches that each client is unique, calling for the therapist to develop the capacity to learn from one's own experience with a particular person. This sets a major cornerstone for the commitment by the therapist to be vigilant and open to new understanding and fresh information about each person engaged in psychotherapy.

10

Counseling with Couples

I had no early models for supervising work with couples. My most significant supervisor and mentor had a clear and unequivocal approach to working with couples: he did not tolerate it.

His approach to working with couples, influenced, I think, largely by psychoanalytic perspectives, was to accept one spouse as a client, refer the other, and let the husband and wife work out their relational issues after they resolved their own with separate therapists. I have had moments of frustration when I was almost ready to agree. In any case, I was provided with no theory or method for working with couples and no model for supervising marriage counseling. I had to apply theory and skills developed for working with individuals to relationship counseling. My supervisees do the same.

Working with couples can be frustrating and defeating even to seasoned clinicians. The beginner is faced with the double task of learning basic clinical skills and exploring particular applications to work with couples. Supervision of work with couples keeps both tasks in focus.

At the same time, I find working with couples particularly rewarding. Enabling others to work effectively with couples can be doubly rewarding. Successful relationships are essential for successful living. Most pathology is somehow interwoven with relational difficulties. Any definition of "wholeness" needs to include satisfying relationships. To help others build or enrich their most important relationship touches close to the heart of human yearning and fulfillment. People are both wise and courageous to seek relationship counseling—and counselors need to be prepared to respond however challenging or frustrating the effort may be.

I. Supervision

Supervision of work with couples includes the stages and processes of supervision in general described by Barry Estadt in an earlier chapter. At the same time supervision with couples has its own unique dimensions and emphases. In order to clarify such similarities and differences, I need first to outline some of my underlying perspectives on supervision in general. Briefly and simply, here are four of my working assumptions.

A. *Supervision is primarily the work of the supervisee.*

The first task of the supervisee is to learn to use supervision. For some this requires unlearning methods and procedures from other educational settings. Making good use of supervision requires thoughtful preparation and active participation. As supervisees become seasoned the process increasingly takes the form of profession consultation. The supervisee learns to identify what is wanted and needed from supervision and to take responsibility for achieving it. Such a supervisory stance seems essential to me if supervisees are to build confidence, learn to trust their own competence, use outside resources thoughtfully and well, and take reponsibility for their own professional and personal growth.

Many if not most supervisees, at least early on, often outside of awareness, try a variety of ploys to shift the work and responsibility to me. They may give lengthy unfocused reports on their work in general. They may ask what I want them to do. They may try to impress me or seek my approval. They may suggest topics or problems for me to discuss or solve for them. My task is to continually shift the responsibility back to the supervisee. Although I may never use them explicitly in sessions, I keep questions such as those listed below in my mind to keep the responsibility on the supervisee.

What do you want to deal with today?

What do you need to say (background data) or do (tapes, etc.) so that we can deal with it?

What specific questions or problems do you want to explore?

What have you thought or done about this before now?

How can I be helpful to you?

Are you getting what you want from this session?

What can we learn from the process of our working together that can throw light on the issue we are discussing, i.e., transference and countertransference, parallel process, resistance, etc.

Thus the supervisee provides the agenda, issues, specific questions, work sample and an appropriate share of the "work" of supervision. The subject matter of supervision is both content provided and the "here and now" process, and my task is to respond at both levels. The supervisor needs to attend to what is brought in and what is omitted, what is dealt with and what is avoided, what the supervisee says and how the supervisee relates. Attending to process is often more productive than dealing with content.

Occasionally I allow myself to be seduced by my own ego needs or an aggressively passive supervisee into taking more than my share of the work and responsibility of supervision. The results are uniformly unsatisfactory. Allowing a supervisee to shift the work to me tends to reinforce unhealthy dependence, perpetuate self-doubt or insecurity, and support neediness and confusion, and results in unproductive exhaustion for me. Generally, in my experience, supervisees mostly act as competently and resourcefully as I expect. My caring, affirmation, respect and insistence on their taking charge of their professional growth may be as important as my response to their work.

At the same time, this must be balanced by the reality that I have a responsibility for the welfare of my supervisee's clients, the expectations and standards of the placement agency, if any, and the well-being of the supervisee. The role of "supervisor-consultant" needs to be balanced by the task of the "supervisor-evaluator."

B. Supervision provides a safe climate for growth.

Naive supervisees tend to view supervision as the unsophisticated public sees counseling: the supervisee talks and the supervisor says what is wrong. I suppose, insofar as the supervisor may contribute to an evaluation or grading process which impacts on the survivial of the supervisor in the profession, such an attitude is not only understandable but partly warranted.

Such a performance/evaluation approach seems to me unproductive for the helping professions. Supervisees are likely to be defensive, guarded, presenting their best work rather than dealing with issues where real help is needed. Supervisees will tend to assess the success of their work more by the approval of the supervisor than by their own professional and clinical growth. Most seriously, such a climate rewards supervisees for hiding work which most needs the attention of the supervisor, even, or especially, when ethical issues or the well-being of a client is at stake.

A mutual exploration process, in which the "performance" of the supervisee and the evaluation by the supervisor is minimized, seems more productive. Such a climate is open, accepting, relatively free from the kind of evaluative responses likely to stir contesting, defensiveness or overadapting. The supervisee is relatively free to show the worst as well as the best, to ask the "stupid" question, to disclose craziness and to look for help as well as for affirmation.

Such a safe, accepting climate is needed for exploring transference and countertransference issues, resistance and other dynamics surfacing in the supervisory relationship that shed light on clinical work. At the same time the supervisor needs to be open and straightforward about formal evaluations that may be required. The supervisee takes a risk exposing weaknesses potentially detrimental in evaluations. I assess such willingness to risk self-revelation as an asset and rate such supervisees higher in their ability to use supervision. Yet the safety of the supervisory setting is never fully assured and the risk of self-revelation never fully removed. The supervisor provides what safety is possible even as the supervisee learns to live with the risk.

C. Supervision deals with the person and the professional, the theoretic and clinical, the content and the process.

As stated, the early-on task of the supervisee whether working with couples or with other client types is to learn to use supervision productively toward chosen goals. Thus the supervisee takes responsibility for identifying issues, setting the agenda and establishing procedures to get what is needed. I pay close attention to what the supervisee brings, taking his or her agenda fully into account, and thus reinforce intentionality and initiative. At the same time I attend to what the supervisee may not be willing or able to bring to a session. I need to pay attention to what the supervisee is not seeing or is avoiding.

For example, if a supervisee fails to raise issues, suggest procedure, or take responsibility for making our sessions productive, I might explore personal issues of passivity, overdependence or possible lack of investment. If a supervisee deals almost exclusively with professional function, I might look for the person hiding behind the role. If a supervisee focuses almost exclusively on the theoretic, I might want to examine the clinical implications. When supervision seems limited to cognitive discussion, I might shift attention to the process. If a supervisee talks in generalities, I get interested in the details. If a supervisee keeps the discussion at a safe "there and then," I might bring issues to the "here and now." In each of the examples above I could add a "vice versa."

Supervision as a method of learning uniquely enables growth in self-understanding and insight which might otherwise remain outside of awareness. At the same time, care is taken not to allow supervision to become therapy although the process may well lead the supervisee to seek such help. The blind spots, avoidances, passivity and other behaviors that limit effectiveness in supervision are likely to impact on work with clients as well.

D. *The primary task of supervision is to identify strengths.*

Although hearing and responding to feedback is the responsibility of the supervisee, evaluative responses need to be given in ways least likely to produce overadapting or defensiveness. Supervisees need to develop an open, receptive, relatively non-defensive stance not only for supervision but also for effective clinical work. Supervisees must not be treated as fragile, unable to deal with reality. At the same time, supervisors need to be aware that the way evaluative feedback is given influences how it is likely to be received. Skills are needed for giving negative feedback that reduce the probability of defensive or overadaptive responses. Such skills cannot be described in detail in this chapter, but, briefly stated, a supervisor needs to build a climate of trust, give priority to affirming strengths, emphasize the positive, check for readiness, speak conditionally and leave room for whatever change and growth seems possible. A supervisor that sees no significant positive qualities or potential in the supervisee probably cannot help very much. A supervisor is likely to be most helpful when he or she sees possibilities, is genuinely hopeful that both positive and negative feedback can provide growth, and believes in the supervisee as a person and a professional—and is able to convey this perspective.

II. Supervising Work with Couples

The essential dynamics of supervision do not change, it seems to me, with the change of client type. The following perspectives on supervision of work with couples need to be couched in the more general considerations outlined above and presented elsewhere in this volume. At the same time, working with couples requires its own kind of personal experience, theoretic insight, procedural skills and clinical competence which color and shape supervisory issues. Questions such as the following can help bring this uniqueness into focus.

A. *What is the supervisee's readiness for working with couples?*

Supervisees bring an assortment of life experiences, interests, fears and fantasies, successes and failures, joys and pain from their own relationships. Assessment of such background experiences helps clarify values and attitudes which may impact on working with couples. For example, a supervisee might bring a bias in favor of or negative to men or women in the spousal relationship, perhaps seeing one a tyrant and the other as a victim. Or a supervisee might hold an idealized image of love and marriage few couples are likely to achieve; others may bring a hopelessness or futility about marital relationships. Some supervisees may tend toward wanting to "save" marriages or to rescue people from them.

Thus I am interested in the supervisee's own relationships. A counselor who works with couples, it seems to me, would do well to have had at least one close relationship and, at least to some extent, to have enjoyed it. A counselor can hardly model skills not possessed. Supervisees themselves need to be able to work cooperatively, deal with conflict creatively, provide emotional support as needed, and tolerate if not enjoy a close level of intimacy.

B. What theory, training and experience for working with couples does the supervisee bring?

The theory and practice for working with couples is not well established. Marriage counselors tend to adapt perspectives and methods developed for working with individuals to couples therapy. The supervisory process clarifies preferred modalities, counseling methods and client definitions that the supervisee applies to working with couples. Practical considerations can be explored; for example, a psychodynamically oriented supervisee might have reason to see partners separately while a behaviorist may only see couples together.

The supervisee's definition of the client seems particularly important to me. Does the counselor work with two individuals simultaneously? Work as a threesome? Is the client not a person at all but an entity called a "relationship"? More about that issue later.

My own theoretical and clinical practice with couples is highly eclectic with respect to modalities. I deal with the relationship rather than the individuals, distinguishing relational from personal issues. My supervisees are aware of my own methods but are free to follow their own. My task is to help them develop their own theory and methods and apply them effectively.

C. How can the supervisee's preferred theoretical modality be applied to working with couples?

Whatever the chosen theoretical or clinical modality of the supervisee, some alternations in accent and application are likely to be required for working with couples. The psychoanalytically trained supervisee, for example, may not immediately be aware of countertransference issues enmeshed in the dynamics of the couple relationship until he becomes aware of playing the "white knight" protecting virtuous "fair maidens" from "dirty dragons" or she becomes aware of transferring hositility toward such a controlling husband to husbands in general. Behaviorists may not see the more subtle payoffs reinforcing disruptive behavior patterns in a battering relationship. The client-centered therapist may fail to deal effectively with the competition and hostility that frequently emerge from a competitive partner when empathic support and unconditional favorable regard is offered to the other. Such applications become particularly challenging when the client is seen to be the relationship itself rather than persons in the relationship.

D. *What biases or hidden agendas motivate the supervisee?*

Couples seek counseling for a variety of reasons, overt and covert, of which they may only be partly aware. Some may come simply to decide about their relationship before making further commitment, others to stage a guilt-free separation, still others to fix or change a partner, still others merely to fix blame. Supervisees need to work with couples using such motives and goals as leverage to enable couples to work through dysfunctions to resolution. Supervisees determined to "fix" or "save" marriages or, less often, to end them are generally less helpful and can be harmful. Supervision needs to explore and clarify such motives and goals and the probable impact on the counseling process.

E. *What life experiences and other practical resources does the supervisee possess or need for working with couples?*

Working with couples tends to be more directive than individual counseling and may include more structuring of the process as well as elements of coaching, behavioral assignments and exercises. Similarly, supervision of such work tends to become somewhat more directive as procedures and interventions are explored for helping troubled relationships.

Counseling couples also tends to become more cognitive than working with individuals, at least for me. Troubled couples often seek and need basic information and skills for healthy relating. In parallel, supervision also tends to become more cognitive including teaching, theoretical exploration and relationship analysis.

III. Who or What Is the Client?

Perhaps the most significant difference between working with individuals and with couples is the shift of focus from counselor-client to the marital relationship. If what heals in individual therapy is the quality of the counseling relationship, what heals in marriage counseling is largely in the spousal relationship. Individual counseling supervision involves three relationships: the client-supervisee, the supervisee-supervisor and the supervisor-client. Supervision of work with couples becomes considerably more complex including six relationships impacting on both supervision and counseling:

The spousal relationship
Counselor-husband
Counselor-wife
Counselor-supervisor
Supervisor-husband
Supervisor-wife

Each of these relationships needs to be differentiated and viewed as impacting on both the counseling and supervisory processes. The relationship of the spouses to each other is central. The relationship of the supervisee to each partner impacts his or her perspective, diagnosis and choice of interventions. The relationship of the supervisor and the counselor influences their responses to each other and to the client couple. The relationship of the supervisor to each partner impacts his or her assessments and responses both to the counselor and the client couple.

The impact of each of these relationships on the counseling process can be pictured by imagining both the supervisor and the counselor to be males and present, as in a real sense they are, in the counseling room with the couple. The result: three men and one woman. Most women would be understandably uncomfortable under such circumstances.

Supervision of work with couples also needs to clarify the dynamics of the process with particular attention to interaction of the counselor with the client couple. Frequently my supervisees assume, usually outside of their awareness, one or more of the following stances: simultaneous individual counseling, "fixing" the problem spouse, the triangle, and identifying the relationship as the client.

A. Simultaneous individual counseling.

Some supervisees apply theory and skills learned for working with individuals to each partner. Interaction in sessions flows between the counselor and each partner while there is almost none between the partners. Spouses are frequently seen separately. In effect the counselor is giving individual counseling on an alternating schedule while the other partner looks on. Such a dynamic provides a couple with an opportunity for partners to change or grow with the participation and perhaps support from a spouse. However, such an approach often results in partners competing for the support and vindication of the counselor while blaming the spouse. The unwary supervisee is cast in the role of judge or jury and may be tempted to render a verdict which, if given, is generally appealed to a higher court.

B. *"Fixing" the problem spouse.*

Often a reluctant spouse is brought to the counseling room by a desperate partner with expectations that, with the counselor as an ally, the problem spouse can be changed. Unwary supervisees can be persuaded sometimes by a highly motivated, well-intentioned, personally-affirming and fee paying spouse whose assessment of the marital problem seems fairly accurate. The basic problem of allying with one partner to change the other is simply that it will not work over the long haul. This two-against-one approach applies maximum therapeutic pressure at the point of maximum resistance. The "problem" partner is likely to harden, retreat or withdraw from the process altogether. The allying partner is likely to feel frustrated and disappointed with the counselor. Supervision is often needed to surface such a dynamic which can be subtle, outside of the awareness of the supervisee and the partners.

C. *The triangle.*

The "triangle" is a three handed approach in which the counselor works with a couple as individuals and the partners interact with each other in the presence of and perhaps at the invitation of the counselor. All work with couples inevitably includes elements of the triangle. On the positive side such an approach offers the competent counselor a wide variety of theoretic perspectives and clinical interventions. At the same time, the human triangle has built-in problems; "three's a crowd." A competitive partner may become triumphant or resentful when the counselor seems to side with or against him or her. If the counselor accepts the role of referee or conflict manager, he or she may end up "odd man out." The effort to deal with individual and relational issues simultaneously may tend to muddy the focus and offer unrealistic expectations.

D. *The relationship as the client.*

When the relationship is the client, the supervisee distinguishes relational issues from personal ones. Each partner is encouraged to deal with individual issues in some appropriate way while keeping the primary focus on the relationship. Individual issues, of course, become relevant when impacting on the relationship. Such a stance defines the uniqueness of working with couples, sets limits and helps raise pertinent questions about the care and feeding of human relationships. Supervisees employing this approach may need to find new tools or additional resources with focused application on relationships.

In summary, supervision of work with couples brings to awareness the stance of the supervisee and explores the appropriateness of a chosen process. Of course such dynamics for working with couples are never unambiguous. The supervisee will employ a mixture of processes depending on the client couple, the need of the moment and his or her own intuitive reflexes. Nevertheless the supervisory process lifts the stance of the supervisee to awareness and invites the testing of the process against desired results.

IV. When the Client Is the Relationship

When the relationship is identified as the focus, supervisees need to be able to assess what is happening—or not happening—in the couple's interaction that contributes to the problem. What is working or not working? What is missing? What is needed to build or enrich the relationship?

Supervisees are encouraged to reflect on what they have learned from their own experiences and to develop a theoretical model for measuring a troubled relationship against a healthy one. Such a theoretical construct can help a supervisee listen with more insight, understand with more depth and respond more practically.

To provide a model to stimulate their own exploration, I may offer my own theoretical construct of what seems to be needed for a satisfying relationship. I identify four qualities as follow:

Cooperation
Compatibility
Personal Support
Intimacy

Behavioral scientists would not agree on this brief list. Neither do all of my supervisees. My goal is not to offer a correct set of systems but to stimulate curiosity in the supervisee to build such a perspective on relationship theory useful for assessment and therapeutic direction.

A. Cooperation

If the supervisee seems interested and I think it might be helpful, I might diagnose the relationship of a client couple in terms of the four components. Cooperation is fundamental because a minimal level is essential for the counseling process itself.

When assessing problems of cooperation, the supervisee and I look for patterns of competition that turn partners against each other. The most casual conversation, for example, can become a hassle when partners compete for who is right, who wins the argument, what is fair, or even who gets to define the problem. The most frequently encountered pattern of competition is sometimes called the "blaming game." Supervisees learn to detect blaming even in its more subtle forms as spouses come to define their relational problems in terms of the partner's behavior. Solutions to problems defined in this way are clear: the partner needs to change in some way. Almost all partners play the blaming game in their heads, while most covertly and some overtly express their blaming. Some supervisees are seduced into playing the blaming game by a winsome "innocent" partner. Supervision is often needed to bring this to awareness. Blaming is almost never helpful either to the couple's relationship or to the supervisory process.

Underlying most destructive competition is a desire to come out on top or at least to avoid being the underdog. Supervisees need to be aware that in human relationships the effort to win or to avoid losing is the pursuit of an illusion. "Losers" will find a variety of ways to express their resentment in brief moments of triumph. "Winners" tend to have brief, lonely victories and may not find much satisfaction in being married to a "loser." The reality is that couples have only two possibilities: both win or both lose. Successful relationships keep finding ways for both to win. Supervision uncovers the subtle ways that supervisees may be entering into the competition rather than enabling a couple to overcome it.

When problems with cooperation are identified as an issue, the supervisee and I might explore procedures and interventions to enable a couple to deal with conflict more creatively. Supervisees often have their own resources. I share some of mine, i.e. role reversal, Gestalt exercises, exaggeration for awareness, exploration of costs and payoffs, early childhood patterns of competition, and practical methods of problem solving.

The supervisory relationship itself is a "lab" for exploring such issues. The supervisee and I explore how competition comes to expression between us and how we deal with it.

Supervisees need to be aware of the profound sadness, sometimes bordering on despair, that can accompany the resolution of competition in a marriage. Cooperation requires an acceptance of the partner "as is." Such an acceptance means giving up on the nagging, demanding, judging and other pressures employed to produce the idealized relationship desired. Such acceptance means living with the partner in a relationship

short of the yearned for ideal. Dreams have to die. Yearnings go unfulfilled. Sadness for such a loss is often lost or avoided in resentment. Yet
couples need to grieve the loss of what they do not have in order to make
the most of what they do have. Supervision helps uncover this sadness and
find ways for its expression and resolution.

B. Compatibility

Issues of compatibility are probably the most obvious consideration
when assessing a relationship. Supervisees are likely to exaggerate the
imprtance of similarities while overlooking some subtle advantages of differences in life-style preferences. Opposites attract.

Supervision of work with couples encourages listening for metaphors,
mental images and other clues each partner brings indicating values and
preferences important to the ideal marriage. Conflicting models of marriage, often held without awareness, contribute to compatibility problems.

Supervisees are encouraged to learn from their own experiences the
inevitable costs and payoffs when building a shared life-style with another
person. Spouses come from different families, different histories, each
with fixed attitudes, opinions and values about every dimension of human
life. A lack of experience can blind young couples to the inevitable struggle. Maturity increases awareness and understanding but may reduce flexibility.

The naive supervisee might assume that the more similar the family
background is the better the relationship. Such a perspective fails to see
the oppressive boredom of some excessively "compatible" relationships.
Nor are marriages of dissimilar partners necessarily troubled. Differences
can help maintain excitement and create romance and a determination to
"make it work." Supervisees can learn to enable couples to assess their
own compatibility issues, find strength and stability in similarity and creativity and excitement in differences.

Attention may need to be given to the supervisee's own values and
life-style preference with respect to the ideal marriage. Such preferences,
especially if outside of awareness, can produce unhelpful alliances and conflicts into the counseling and confuse the supervisory process. The supervisee—along with the supervisor—needs to bracket personal compatibility
preferences in order to deal effectively with client issues.

C. Personal Support

Rarely do couples bring a deficiency of personal or emotional support
as a presenting problem. Most spouses seem unaware of such needs or
discount emotional support as unimportant or inappropriate.

Similarly supervisees often fail to detect the yearning for personal support that often comes disguised behind a variety of other complaints. An extramarital affair, for example, usually has more to do with emotional support than sexual promiscuity. The clues are obvious: "She understands me." "He listens to my needs." The supervisory process probing the underlying causes of infidelity is likely to discover a failure to give or receive adequate emotional support.

Supervisees assessing the quality of emotional support in a relationship learn to be particularly attentive to critical life situations in which such support is likely to break down. Spouses that confuse the warmth of nurturance with a sexual invitation tend to undermine both emotional support and sexual relating. Spouses in transition tend to threaten their partners at a time when additional understanding and support is needed. The naive supervisee may respond to the hurt and anger without detecting the yearning for nurturing support.

At the same time, supervision can reflect on the quality of emotional support in its own process and the ability of the supervisee to give and receive such support while counseling, in supervision or in other relationships. Supervisees not in touch with their own needs, unable to ask for what they want or to accept what they need, will have difficulty helping others work through such blocks. Similarly, supervisees who fail to provide such support in favor of reassuring, analyzing or trying to "fix" things are not likely to help spouses provide the kind of support that is genuinely helpful. Supervisees need to listen, convey empathy, provide emotional support and affirm the competence of clients if they are to help couples provide such support to each other.

D. Intimacy

The issue of intimacy in a couple's relationship may have little to do with sexual relations. A relationship can be sexual without intimacy and intimate without sex. Intimacy is that quality of closeness that tends to make a relationship special, often characterized by mutual self-revelation, emotional spontaneity, and here and now interaction in a climate free from pressures, demands or defensiveness.

The supervisory process builds sensitivity to clues indicating intimacy problems such as jealousy, loneliness, boredom or isolation. The supervisee learns to look for patterns of hiding or withholding creating a vacuum likely to be filled by jealous imagination, or for the loneliness resulting from an unfulfilled yearning for closeness, a feeling that one is living with a stranger.

The supervisee learns to explore patterns of intimacy of at least four types: conversational, emotional, physical and sexual. The needs of each partner are assessed separately. What is too distant for one spouse may seem too close to the other. This difference in the desire for and tolerance of intimacy is often a key to intimacy problems. Some partners have a life-long pattern of intimacy avoidance, hiding their inner world of thoughts and feelings even from those closest to them.

The supervisory process may well probe the expression or avoidance of intimacy in the life and work of the supervisee. Fears, blocks, preferences and family background patterns in the supervisee are likely to impact on the perspective and response to such issues in the client couple.

Summary

Supervising work with couples involves the same dynamics as that of work with other client types in most respects. Accented here: responsibility of the supervisee for content and process initiatives; a climate safe for risk and growth; attention to both the cognitive and the clinical, the personal and the professional; negative feedback given in a context of authentic positive affirmation.

At the same time, supervision of work with couples includes some unique dimensions and emphases, including: an assessment of the supervisee's own life experiences with significant relationships; history of training and practice working with couples; additional emphasis on the cognitive or teaching side of supervision; an exploration of the applicability of the supervisee's preferred modality to various approaches to working with couples; attention to the inner agenda or value system the supervisee brings to the process.

Supervision of work with couples doubles the number of relationships to explore for such dynamics as transference and countertransference, parallel process and projections.

Supervising work with couples relates the clinical approach to the supervisee's definition of the client. Does the supervisee work with two people simultaneously? Do the three work in a kind of triangle? Does the supervisee ally with one partner to work on the other? Is the relationship itself the client? The supervisory process explores the implications of such definitions and relates them to clinical practice.

Finally, if the relationship itself is seen to be the client, the supervisory process explores essential components of a relationship and is sensitive to clues for assessing each in a client couple. The process includes an exploration of the supervisee's own awareness and capacity with respect to each component in a relationship and a possible impact of his or her relational issues on the counseling process.

Rachel Callahan, Ph.D.
Robert F. Davenport, D.Min.

11

Group Counseling: A Model for Teaching and Supervision

The supervision of group psychotherapy has problems and possibilities which are different from those of other therapeutic modalities. How can the novice therapist's work be observed unobtrusively? Audio tapes are not appropriate and video taping can be awkward and expensive. The inherent inequality of a novice who is learning by being a co-therapist with a senior therapist is obvious, but an approach which is reasonable and necessary.

In this chapter we will describe a teaching and supervisory modality we have developed through eight years of work in the Loyola Pastoral Counseling graduate program which we believe overcomes some of the problems. This approach could be readily adapted to other academic settings and other training centers.

It was our conviction from the outset that for our group training program to be effective it needed to provide *experience, observation,* and *theory: experience* as both client and leader in a group, *observation* of live groups with both professional and novice leadership, and careful command of *theory* through both reading and process comments on observed work. To this end we designed a two-semester elective course co-led by female and male therapists. In this chapter we will describe the course designed to incorporate these three components, look at some of the issues that emerged in this learning experience, and provide illustrative material.

I. Teaching Group Psychotherapy—A Brief Overview

A. *Fostering Awareness of Self and Other*

In the first semester, students are divided into groups of equal size with as near a balance as the population allows with regard to gender, age, and other heterogeneous factors, e.g. religious denomination. The course meets weekly for two hours and the groups meet in "fishbowl" each week, alternating which group functions as therapists or clients. In a given class period group A meets for fifty minutes with the two faculty serving as co-therapists and group B observing the meeting in the outer circle. At the end of that meeting, group B spends ten minutes commenting on the processes they have observed. Then, after a brief break, the two groups switch functions and the experience is repeated. Students are all expected to read *The Principles and Practice of Group Psychotherapy* by Irving Yalom. The students are given the following guidelines to use in writing process observation notes.

> Write a 2–3 page narrative of what you have observed in today's group. Include a reflection on the following areas:
>
> *Your own feelings:* How were you feeling going into this group observation? How did this change? What do your own feelings tell you about what is happening?
>
> *What do you see?:* Notice seating arrangement; who initiates conversation; who talks to whom; non-verbal communications—posture, yawns, foot-tapping, etc.
>
> How do the leaders facilitate "in the room" activity—e.g. making the abstract more concrete, the general more specific?
>
> What "curative factors" (à la Yalom) do you observe and what transactions helped make them happen?
>
> If you were leading today's group now might you have done it differently? Why?

These questions are intended to focus awareness in two directions: (a) self-awareness—an understanding of the power of one's own feeling to color perception and to impact one's own capacity for participation; (b) other awareness—the sharpening of the process-observational skills which are critical to the effectiveness as a group leader.

What will follow is an actual description of one student's observations regarding self-awareness and group participation and interaction. It is the eleventh session, and only one more session remains for the group.

Going into the observation of this particular session, my feelings were quite mixed. I felt a bit of urgency, as well as a sense of loss and regret that we were so near the end of our time together in these groups. It seemed we had barely begun, and termination was near. I also felt some curiosity as to where the group would move, and some relief that I could be an observer on this particular day, before being a participant. My emotions were quite close to the surface, being in the middle of a week in which that seemed to be true much of the time. I experienced some relief as the group began and there was much laughter and use of humor, although I also felt the need for movement, because of the sense that time was short. I was more aware of some feelings of sadness and loss as the group unfolded, especially as D. touched on that theme in relationship to his father. I became increasingly pensive as the group moved toward its ending time; this was not a negative feeling, but a positive sense of engagement and presence.

F. initiated the conversation soon after the group settled in and was very active throughout, both in doing his own work and in dealing with others. H. was also quite active, with quite a bit of interaction taking place between her and F. but with others as well. The two leaders, Bob and Rachel, were very active and engaged, Bob particularly with F. D. was drawn into the verbal interaction, and seemed very involved, even when the focus was elsewhere; G. also entered in, especially in the short time she became the focus, although participation seemed a bit marginal and not quite flowing with the group. P. spoke once, perhaps, and E. and N. not at all. One member, L., came in quite late and was acknowledged by Bob; it seemed difficult for him to get involved as the group was already so deeply into the session.

A great deal seemed to be going on during the hour, both interactionally and internally. Everyone appeared to be engaged—at least, not noticeably "absent"—although I wondered what was going on with E. and N. particularly. N. sat very quietly, with a bit of a smile, with little movement or change of expression. E's posture suggested wanting to be more involved, and not being quite sure how to move in.

Both leaders brought the "out there" into the room. For example, Bob enabled F. to do that as he was talking about his father and intimacy and then the Loyola community, with the question about what he would wish he had said, if this were the last day. This facilitated some significant interaction with G. Rachel's invitation to F. to be with his feelings of the moment,

at one point, helped him to move from "out there." Her interaction with D. about his feelings toward her, in her affirmation
of his gentle side, helped him to move from relationship with
parents to relationship in the room.

Both leaders have consistently modeled honest interaction,
caring, sensitivity, vulnerability, with the freedom to take risks,
make mistakes, and admit them. I saw Rachel model that honesty
and vulnerability with D.; this invited his honest and vulnerable
response. I saw Bob being quite active with F. particularly, in a
very caring, supportive way—drawing out that person who
wanted to "tell you who I am but not tell you who I am."

Some therapeutic factors which I observed in this session
were similar to what I have noticed in other sessions, and yet
unique in their manifestation. There was instillation of hope in a
number of individual responses particularly to F. and D. His response to F. as to how she perceived him was only one example.
Universality was very evident throughout, but particularly in the
experience of different members with significant persons, especially family members, not being who they needed them to be.
(G. made that feeling—and theme—explicit, by naming it.) So-
cializing techniques were being further developed in the gentle
confrontation with G. by F., and then picked up on by H. and
Rachel—the feedback to G. about her tendency to be always affirming, uncritically so. There was some catharsis going on for D.
as he again dealt with the pain in his childhood, which he had
done in greater depth in an earlier session. I was glad it surfaced
again; I sense there is a great deal there. I felt that in his interaction with Bob, there was perhaps some corrective recapitulation of the primary family group. (I'm not quite sure when to
actually name it that.)

I have already mentioned the modeling done by both leaders; the therapeutic factor of imitative behavior was certainly evident in different group members at various points; the risk-
taking in confronting G., the rather summarizing statements by
F. about various group members, the sensitivity and caring manifest at many points in drawing others out, F. and D. in particular. His spontaneity of expression and honesty is another
example. That has been very facilitative in the group, generally.

Some themes that I observed in this session were intimacy
and keeping distance, anger and forgiveness, loss and grieving,
and letting go of illusions that people will always be who you
need them to be. I wondered, as G. referred to that last one, if

it was also something about this group. As F. spoke to tears, and the imminent loss of the Loyola community, I intuited it was also about the termination of this group. There was a lot of humor used at the beginning of the session, which I also felt might have been related to termination and some reluctance to move on into one of the last sessions. There were longer silences than usual near the end, which I experienced as pensive, though that may have been projection on my part. Bob's "It's time to stop" came out of one of those silences. I would characterize the session as very reflective, revealing the fact that members were feeling the imminence of termination. I experienced it as a very good session, with some fine work being done.

This detailed account signals what was going on inside this student, and the process of the group was diagrammed around the guidelines already presented.

B. Enabling Student Response

When this course was first suggested to the faculty as an elective in the Master's program there were a number of issues raised for discussion. Some felt that there would be little or no interest in the course and that few would elect to take it. Others felt that while some might elect the course, nothing of substance would be shared in the groups. The latter were not opposed to offering the course; they simply doubted that it would become a vital educational or therapeutic experience.

On the afternoon of our first meeting in the fall of 1980, twenty-five students had signed up for the course. That number obviously justified recruiting a second teacher which, in turn, led to the realization of the ideal—a male and female, co-teacher, co-therapist team. Since the first awkward and numerically overwhelming beginning, the course has typically attracted twenty to twenty-five students in the first semester each year and ten to fifteen in the second. The attrition is due to varied situations. Some students find the process uncomfortable and do not elect to continue. Others choose another elective simply to expand their educational experience. Still others choose to reduce their course-load in the second semester when most students are writing a reflection paper due before the end of the term. However, the number of students who subscribe to this experience affirm the validity of the experiment.

The second issue about the viability of the course design was likewise removed, and this has been a surprise to even those of us who were teaching. Many students over the years have told us that their experience in the course was one of the high points in their graduate school experience. For many it is a first experience in group interactional therapy and they find it surprisingly powerful. Others are involved in their own personal therapy, which the faculty strongly encourages, and find the group experience not only a useful adjunct, but in many cases a place to try out or try on the gains in individual work in a somewhat larger but still "safe" environment.

The fact is that the reputation of the course as a useful personal and vital learning experience has been widely shared by students, so that, as the years have gone by, students come to it with high expectations and motivation to make full use of the opportunities the course affords. The cohesion fostered by the experience of mutual self-disclosure and self- and other-acceptance has served to enrich the whole graduate experience.

C. Encouraging Sharing

Thus, we faculty-therapists are often pleasantly surprised at the depth of sharing that some students pursue. That sharing usually starts with "out of the room" issues. Those issues may be current, either school or work-placement related, or historical, then often tangentially or unconsciously related to the group. When we call attention to this fact, students begin to focus on "in the room issues" and use the group as a therapeutic modality. For example, usually one or two of our students in the course are either foreign nationals or Roman Catholic sisters or priests who have been working abroad, often in very difficult circumstances. These students are often encountering culture-shock, the coming to or returning to this country, complicated by the adjustment of being students again after years of solitary ministry, and the strangeness of a new professional vocabulary. A student will share that "person without a country" discomfort and the group will respond. Sometimes that is the extent of the disclosure. At other times that sharing will encourage others to disclose their equivalent or similar sense of displacement. We move into the room when one or more students is enabled to talk about the displacement inherent in being in the group. As therapists, we encourage ever increased specificity in the service of putting points of tension and resistance on the table, and in the service of making use of potential transference issues. Hence, we might ask, "Whom in the group are you uncomfortable with?" When someone is identified we seek to enable the students to work with one another to some point of "closure for now" with that issue. Often, of course, this process can be the beginning of turning point from a potentially negative blocking phenomenon to become an occasion for ongoing work between people who may become important to one another.

Another point of beginning "outside the room" might be a story from someone's past which the present situation of being back in school or being in the group has surfaced as incompletely resolved. So a student might tell us about a time when an elementary teacher was demanding beyond the child's sense of his or her own competency and the resulting sense of humiliation or experience of failure. Again, if that scene is not specifically related to the anxiety of "not making it" in the group, it is at least likely related to overall anxiety about being in school again. Such a story activates in other members of the group their own memories of failures or fears, which they are encouraged to share for their curative influence. The universality of these feelings gives evidence to the shared commonality of the human condition.

As the group develops cohesion and begins to have a history of its own, the work on a given day might start "in the room" with something unresolved from a previous meeting. Then the therapists serve to help students, first to be respectful of that circumstance, and then to address its resolution. At times the leaders are the focus of such issues, but even when we are not, the transference potential of the issue is always worth exploring.

D. Exploring Personality

To try out different personality styles is another opportunity which the group offers its members. We look for congruence between an historical circumstance and a current "out of the room" issue, and the sort of experience that the student is having in the group. That can start with a report of some difficulty in a current relationship. Another group member might respond that his or her relation with the presenting member is not dissimilar to the difficulty being reported. As they work through that situation in the room to some satisfaction, a therapist might ask a question to seek to identify the possible historical precedent for a relational issue which has character-style implications. When such a precedent can be identified, the potential is high for working through and deep insight is made available.

Working at this level, inevitable rivalries which are fostered by the "fishbowl" process observation/reporting and other interpersonal conflicts which emerge in the course of the two groups' work are always treated as therapeutic issues, "grist for the therapeutic mill." We seek to teach students to discover opportunity in conflict and that conflict has its own function. We receive complaints about our academic program in a spirit of openness, and as teacher/therapists we are not defensive when we make mistakes, trying to illustrate that a leader's mistakes create potential for growth in the group, the members, and ourselves. This latter modeling can be very important for our students who tend to be quite critical of themselves and to be defensively involved in the quest of the illusive "one right way" to do therapy.

Among the points of potential conflict, or at least mildly alienating influences, are the variables of gender, denominational differences, lay, professed religious and ordained, age disparity from mid-twenties to sixties, and a wide range of theological and sociopolitical orientations. The instances of stereotyping and resulting negative transference are opportunities for significant social and psychological learning and we make use of those when they arise and try to ferret them out when they are implied.

Among the issues we signal in the effort to move students beyond the defensive safety of conversing in the stylized language of counseling skills and techniques, is the need for direct, clear, intimate, and self-disclosing language. We discourage the use of jargon. "Psychobabble" is our word for such responses, and we consistently, and often humorously, confront students with the options of direct and intimate responses. It is our conviction that *engagement* at that level is healing, and that much of what is passed off as "professional" encourages, in fact, evasive, distancing, defensive, and self- and other-discounting conversation.

E. Experience–Observation–Application

Depending on the calendar in a given year the groups will meet eleven to thirteen times in the first semester. During that time students have the opportunity (1) to *experience* the impact, potentialities, and limits of group work as a client or patient, (2) to *observe* a group in its formative stages moving toward the establishment of cohesion in which mid-stage interactional work is possible, and (3) through reading to apply Yalom's theory to what they are experiencing and observing. In the last session of the first semester we provide some time for the two groups to meet as one. This meeting honors the fact that our division into two groups is a contrivance for the sake of learning, and that, in fact, all of us have been in one room at the same time with a design which obviated the expression of thoughts and feelings across group lines. In that brief time there is some closure around issues of *appreciation* ("thank you"), *resentment* ("I wish you had . . ." or "I wish you hadn't . . .") and *regret* ("I wish I had . . ." or "I wish I hadn't . . ."). This is especially important for cohesiveness in the groups for the second semester as membership invariably changes.

In the second semester students have the opportunity to rotate leadership. Because of membership changes and unfinished business from the first semester the faculty co-therapists lead the first two or three sessions. There are usually issues of cohesiveness to be resolved from the first semester. Competition often develops between the two groups together with the more potentially divisive tension stemming from their having made process observations of one another. These implicit or explicit critiques of one another's work are often experienced as a challenge to "me" or "my group." When only one group is formed in the second semester there is therapeutic work to be done to resolve old griefs and grievances. Additionally, the presence of new members requires some work at inclusion. The new member is aware of the existence of a history that he or she does not share and must accommodate to that and the other realities of being "the new kid on the block." The group needs to deal with whatever change to its cohesion a new member represents and must work through that in order to include the person(s). The very experience of feeling alienated from new members and resenting their intrusion reinforces their awareness of the power of group membership and the importance of cohesion to a group's effectiveness. In the service of respecting all of these issues, at the beginning of the second semester the co-therapists lead the group for a few sessions before the students assume leadership.

When the needs for inclusion and re-establishment of cohesion have at least been addressed, although hardly resolved, since some very primitive transference phenomena are at work, students assume the leadership among themselves as we move to the outside of the group and become the process observers. As observers, we combine the use of a verbatim together with the process observation guidelines included earlier. At the end of the group process each week the student leaders are asked to reflect upon their experience of the group and then we make our process observation for the class.

II. Some of the Issues Dealt With

A. *Self-Disclosure*

From the very first class meeting it is clear to the students that this is not a typical academic course and that they will be expected to participate in ways that are not customary. We tell them that a major part of the experience will be their willingness to disclose personally to one another and to respond personally (not as pseudo-therapists) to the disclosures of others. We then invite anyone who does not wish to participate in this kind of an experience to drop the course. Certainly this description and invitation does not fully inform the students of what is to come nor does it fully describe the surprising power generated in a group therapy experience. But it does set the stage and gives the first sign that self-disclosure in a group of peers is a vehicle for healing and that we are not simply going to talk about that but that we are going to do it.

B. Confidentiality

We also address clearly the issue of confidentiality. For ourselves, we pledge that nothing which takes place in that room will ever be a topic of conversation with other faculty outside the room and that nothing we hear, see, or experience will ever become a part of any evaluation. This pledge is important because the students know that among our programmatic approaches to quality control are regular faculty meetings in which the students' clinical progress is assessed and evaluated. We do reserve the right as therapists and teachers to talk to each other about the group and to seek consultation outside the faculty should we feel a need for that. Students are urged to respect the confidentiality rule as well.

C. Evaluation

The issue of grades could easily contaminate this kind of a learning experience. During the first semester students will be given a "B" for regular attendance and participation, and should they desire a higher grade they submit a paper. This contract takes the pressure off both us and the students, reduces competition, and frees us for our experiental, observational, and theorizing work. During the second semester students are evaluated on the quality of the leadership of the group.

D. Process vs. Content

In making verbal process observations the students are encouraged to avoid "content" and to focus on the "process" of what is going on. That becomes an important and often difficult learning. Hopefully it informs all of their clinical work as they learn to attend to what is going on relationally and structurally as well as to what is being said by clients and between clients and therapists. As the students become more steeped in the theory their observational skills become more refined. When an observation risks becoming explanatory by focusing on content we will redirect a process question to the observer. We invite the observers early on to critique our own work as leaders with questions like: "If you had been leading the group at this moment how might you have done it differently?" or "Of all the things that a therapist might have focused on at a given moment, what would you have chosen and why?" Our aim is to model for students that there is no single "right way" and some of our most potent moments of learning have come out of making mistakes and being able to process these with the class.

E. The Potency of Group Therapy

Because the student's preparation until this point has been almost exclusively in one-to-one counseling, we are constantly reflecting upon the process of the group as a potentially powerful healing medium or as a destructive medium if used irresponsibly. When strong transference issues are being exposed and worked out between members or between a member and one or both therapists, we work with that and try to maximize the transferential variety that a group experience can provide. We help students see the family-like setting a group provides and the dynamics that accrue to this which can be very useful in resolving old issues with parents and siblings. When strong positive or negative transference or countertransference issues are working between a member and either one of us, the other therapist observes the response of the group for potential follow-up interventions and/or facilitates the work between a partner and a member. While we do not discourage such transference work between student and teacher/therapist, in our conduct in the room we are careful to model the solidarity of our bond to one another which the students can safely and usefully test because they cannot break it.

The second semester provides the students a chance to rotate leadership and to continue to experience the potency of the group. Rotating group leadership does not allow the student the same kind of training experience that longer range leadership would provide. But it does illustrate the potency of the group process itself as a healing medium. This is probably where the real potency resides, not in the interventions of the leaders however brilliant and well-timed these might be.

Other issues that emerge include the tracking of themes—e.g. death, loss, failure, success—facilitating the curative factor that members experience in recognizing the universality of different experiences. If members are bringing an overbalance of "out of the room" material to the detriment of here and now "in the room" interactional work, we become curious about this and try to explore what this means.

As therapists, we attend to our own needs and take time for processing issues between us. We try to model non-hierarchical leadership, male-female cooperation and division of labor. It has been important for women students to have the model of a female professional working equally with a male, and it has been equally important for male students, many of whom come out of a hierarchical setting, to see and, at times, be subject to a woman exercising her authority with the respect of her male partner.

In summary, our model is one of learning by doing and using the process of *in vivo* observation as the means of supervision. It represents only a beginning but hopefully a valid and useful one for our students.

Richard W. Voss, A.C.S.W., M.T.S.

12

Crisis Intervention: Critical Issues in Supervision

I. The Need for Critical Reflection about Crisis Intervention Supervision

It has already been documented that people who have good supportive supervisory experiences are less likely to be candidates for "burnout stress syndrome" as it has become identified in the literature (Paine, 1982; Maslach, 1982; Munson, 1983). It has also been documented that practitioners engaged in high stress areas of professional practice do not generally view supervision as being helpful to them in coping with the distress they experience in their work (Munson, 1983). Unfortunately, line staff report that supervision is likely to intensify their already existing distress rather than help dissipate or resolve it (Edelwich and Brodsky, 1980).

The growing concern about the role and impact of supervision, whether positive or negative, upon professional practitioners and, in the long run, upon the delivery of helping services in high stress fields of practice comes as a kind of post mortem for many who have already left the field of human services or function in a chronic state of "burn out"—ineffective helpers walking on the treadmill in ineffective organizations. It is not simply a matter of changing administrators whose own "burn out" has become an unfortunate "role model" for younger "burn out" victims; no, we need to look at the big picture. Recent cut-backs in human services across the boards, along with the push for tighter cost-effectiveness, while maintaining quality services, increasing staff turnover problems, and fluctuating community expectations, have forced human service practitioners to take a long hard look at what we are doing, and what we have done. Professional survival is a compelling reason for self-scrutiny. With fewer and fewer resources available, those of us in the helping professions can no longer take the "what, how, and why" of what we do for granted.

Largely ignored in professional literature, the topic of supervising crisis intervention counseling is seldom an issue for reflection. This lacuna is particularly alarming in the face of mounting data concerning the incidence of "burnout stress syndrome." How does one learn how to supervise crisis intervention counseling services? Is it merely the application of general supervisory method? Or is there a unique dimension to the supervisory relationship in this unique mode of "short term" counseling? Obviously the supervision of crisis intervention counseling will utilize general supervisory principles of building the supervisory alliance based upon foundational skills developed in the earlier chapters. The unique dimension to crisis intervention supervision is that the processes are often telescoped in both time and emotional energy. While there are similarities in the generic practice of supervisory skills, processes, and issues, this topic involves a number of unique elements which are not as concentrated as in other types of supervisory practice.

I do not believe that supervisors, especially those engaged in high stress services, can continue to assume the "do unto others . . . as was done unto thee" model of supervision. The statistics on "burn out" do not give full credibility to this approach. Even the most noble, most esteemed, most honored, even the most rigid models of professional supervision must undergo the honest eye of self-evaluation and professional critique. The growing data regarding the occurrence of "burnout stress syndrome" among colleagues, counselors, and among supervisors ourselves should prompt us to raise critical questions concerning the nature, role, method, and professional and/or organizational context of supervision of crisis intervention counseling services.

This chapter will focus on some of the critical issues which I have come to recognize in supervising professional counselors who provide "crisis intervention" counseling. My emphasis will be on the supervisory issues which are likely to arise in the process of crisis intervention supervision and not on a detailed explication of the concept of "crisis," "crisis theory," or "crisis intervention" as a distinct mode of counseling intervention. It is assumed that the reader is already familiar with or even has practical experience either in doing crisis intervention counseling or in supervising this professional service area in an organizational setting, i.e., within some kind of professional (bureaucratic) structure where there are lines of professional boundaries and accountability. While I will briefly review a few basic concepts about crisis theory and crisis intervention to establish the key epistemological points of reference, the reader who is not familiar with this mode of counseling is encouraged to review Sharon Cheston's chapter on short term counseling which enumerates many of the specific practice issues in short Term Counseling, provides a generic background for crisis intervention counseling, and discusses most of the underlying assumptions of brief counseling theory and practice. Another helpful reading is "The Ministry of Crisis Intervention" by Rachel Callahan in *Pastoral Counseling* (Estadt, 1983), along with the recent article, "Crisis Intervention and Problem Solving," by David K. Switzer in *Clinical Handbook of Pastoral Counseling* (Wicks, 1985).

My underlying professional bias stems from my primary professional discipline of social work, and thus my viewpoint in understanding supervision is a blending and integration of the model developed by Alfred Kadushin in *Supervision in Social Work*. My "parallel" professional discipline of theology prompts me to assume a dialectic method of understanding experience, and I will build upon the notion of the "supervisory alliance" developed within this book by seeing supervision of crisis intervention counseling as largely a "dialectical dialogue" among counselor-supervisor-administrator. It is from the dialectical interplay among these three "helpers" in the "helping system" that I see the task of the supervisory alliance taking place or impeded.

II. Brief Overview of "Crisis Intervention Theory and Practice"

Even the most experienced and skilled counselor is likely to discover a quickening pulse rate when "sitting with" a client who is in the throes of an acute personal crisis. The practiced counselor quickly assesses the "crisis" situation, uncovers the precipitating event, and is deeply aware and sensitive to the unique treatment opportunity which presents itself to the counselor.

> Client: "I don't know what to do . . . I know I'm not giving the kids all the attention they need . . . I am so upset all the time. I feel like I'm going crazy . . . can you believe it? Do you think I'm going crazy? I mean, do I make sense? Why do I feel so helpless . . . ? I used to do fine. I think I must be going crazy . . ."

> Counselor: "Tell me, what has happened to upset you so much? Try to be as specific as you can. Maybe if you understood what had happened to upset you, you would feel that you at least have a handle on what's going on within you."

> Client: "Well, I thought I would be able to handle it, but I can't. Jim divorced me last year, and I thought I was over it, but now I'm seeing someone else . . . and I feel the same way . . . I can't

worry about him and take care of the kids at the same time . . .
I wonder when he's going to call me . . . I sit by the phone waiting . . . and when he doesn't call I wonder if I'll ever feel worthwhile again. Sam is nice, I like him a lot . . . but he doesn't seem
to need me the way I need him . . . I really want somebody to
need me . . ."

Counselor: "You are feeling torn in different directions. You
thought you had settled your feelings of loss about your divorce,
but your feelings about Sam, your first boyfriend since your divorce came through, have touched on something for you, something which is still very upsetting. Sometimes when this happens
we might feel we are going crazy—the upset can be so strong
. . ."

Client: "Yes, I can't stand feeling this way. I've never felt so out
of control of myself. Sam does upset me. I feel so different. I'm
always available for him. I got a babysitter just so I could be with
him last Sunday. Sometimes I wonder if Sam is afraid of getting
involved with a divorcee . . . I don't think he wants to 'get involved' with someone who has four kids."

This client, the custodial parent of four young children, ages three to
nine, is experiencing the onset of a major life crisis. She is experiencing
the psychological end of her marriage of fourteen years which she had "legally" ended upon completion of the divorce process last year. For all practical purposes the divorce is only now "sinking in" and the client is
experiencing a life identity crisis of "who she is" as a divorced woman who
is mother of four children. While she had adjusted to the actual physical
divorce and settlement, the strained and "unbalanced" relationship with
her friend Sam, whom she views as a "potential companion/spouse," has
thrown this young woman into a crisis. Until her recent feeling of rejection
by Sam, the client had been able to cope with the support of family and
friends, her usual defense holding up for her. The current perceived rejection by Sam, however, was not anticipated by the client, and it aroused
the trauma of the past divorce which has left her the primary custodial
parent of her children. The client feels herself as "disposable," "unlova-
ble," and "cheap." These intense feelings are incongruent with her previous experience of self as a "faithful wife" and "loving mother."
  The client's usual modes of support do not console her now. She is
facing an experience totally new and terribly frightening to her. She needs
to know that she is not going crazy as she fears, but is experiencing some-

thing very normal—a crisis, which has a distinct beginning, a certain process of upset and disequilibrium, and an ending. Crisis intervention counseling will help her "through the tunnel" as I often visualize it with clients by helping them to believe that, while they may not see it right now, and understandably so, there is light at the end, and that like other people who have struggled with similar upsets, she will see the light—building a sense of competence and offering the prospect of hope!

Such is the setting for crisis intervention counseling, which begins with the counselor's helping the client to identify and to "name the whirlwind" that is happening to her and to help her regain a sense of balance and control of her situation in a directive fashion as soon as possible. The overall goal is to enhance the growth potential in the experience of unbalance while minimizing the possibility of further deterioration which in the case of the above client would not only greatly affect her, but the well-being of her four children who are dependent upon her in a significant way. One easily senses the complexity of the crisis intervention situation—all telescoped within a very short period of time, powerpacked with intense emotion, expressed oftentimes by feelings of "going crazy, going over the brink, falling apart," etc. which in the crisis intervention scenario are all "normal" and "expected" reactions to the unbalancing which is part and parcel of the crisis situation.

A. Unique Elements of Crisis Intervention Counseling: A Contrast

Unlike the more extended, client-centered, and non-directive modes of counseling practice, crisis intervention counseling is grounded upon carefully determined and timed, directive counseling interventions, including the provision of material assistance as an integral part of the service. The crisis intervention is usually completed within a specific, time-limited course of counseling which will not exceed three months (Sifneos, 1980). There may be situations where the counseling intervention may shift to "longer term" counseling where the resolution of the crisis experience has introduced the client to the "helping system," and the counselor will need to assess this on a "case by case" basis with the supervisor as discussed in detail by Cheston. Our purpose here is to recognize that the crisis experience will not go on interminably. It will draw to a close one way or another, in which case the client will have either improved, maintained the status quo or deteriorated further. Frequently, in view of the telescoped time dimension, there is little or no time for the supervisee to seek exhaustive consultation with one's supervisor beforehand. And in light of the press for "clinical time" by supervisory staff, the supervisor who also provides direct counseling services himself or herself may not be "immediately" available to the counselor when he or she may feel in need of consultation, sometimes precipitating a "crisis-like" experience within the helping professionals themselves (Catalano, 1985). Ideally, the crisis intervention supervisor should be "immediately" available to his or her supervisee—this reality can be appropriately addressed in the supervisor's "job description," one of the most valuable tools in management. When this availability is not feasible, care must be taken to appreciate the effects this added stressor will likely have upon the "helping system."

What may otherwise develop over weeks, months, and possibly years in longer term counseling modalities is telescoped within weeks, days, and, in the crisis intervention mode of counseling, even hours. There is a sense of heightened possibility experienced by both client and counselor during the crisis event, which can hurl both client and counselor into the unknown. Perhaps more so than in any other kind of counseling, the crisis intervention counselor has to develop the capacity to accept and to "live with" high levels of emotional intensity and stress. So much is focused upon the "moment at hand."

In a unique way, crisis intervention counseling taps the emotional resources of the counselor and the material resources of the organization and/or the local community material resources, and the crisis intervention counselor must become a skillful orchestrator in utilizing both. Doing crisis intervention is "no place for the timid." The method admits to "mistake making" and this must be factored in to the supervision of this uniquely intensive arena of professional helping. The telescoping of the counseling process, while heightening actual "helping capacity," will also increase the possibility of human error. Crisis intervention counselors must be helped to be skillful and competent in their crisis intervention practice, but they must also be helped to accept their own humanness which is never relinquished in any of the counseling modalities—certainly not in this one.

"Mistake making" is part and parcel of crisis intervention counseling, so the supervisor must nurture the atmosphere of self-critique and ongoing awareness throughout his or her work with one's supervisee. It might be helpful to add here that pointing out "mistakes" should not be done while the counselor is still in the intensity of the "crisis moment." I think that once the counselor has "re-grouped" from the immediacy of the moment, the supervisor can review the "growing edges" which were discovered through the experience of helping. Questions like "Why did you do this?" and "Why did you do that?" are not helpful. The supervisor has to relate to the humanity of the counselor and be willing to "walk with" him or her in understanding the multitudinous dimensions and layers of the helping processes.

There is need for a delicate balance. Certain kinds of mistakes must be avoided for the sake of the client. In situations where the client may be a danger to self or others, the supervisee must know that he or she can and must seek out consultation and supervisory intervention if needed, even if the client must be referred to another helping system, such as the mandated psychiatric treatment systems within the local community. Every effort must be made to utilize consultation and supervision in life-threatening cases. When serious mistakes occur, the supervisor must insure that they were, at least, shared decisions—carefully made.

B. *The Phase of "Crisis" and the Goals of Crisis Intervention Counseling*

We trace its origins back to Erikson and others who recognized "crisis" as a normal part of human development. The notion of "crisis" began to be conceptualized as an experience which prompts and pushes the person on to meet or confront predictable developmental phases of psychosocial maturation (Erikson, 1950). "Crisis" has been further conceptualized to have a growth promoting potential (Rapoport, 1962). "Crisis intervention theory" as a distinct counseling modality was largely developed by Lindemann and Caplan, and concentrates on the state of the reacting person confronted by a "hazardous event" which hurls him or her into the unknown. The perceived "hazard" demands a solution which is not yet part of the person's repertoire of skills, and the resultant experience of this situation is a heightened sense of personal threat and loss. "Habitual problem solving activities" are not enough to restore a sense of balance in the person's experience (Rapoport, 1962).

I think it is important to emphasize that crisis intervention counseling is not concerned about chronic, ongoing problem condition, nor is it aimed at personality restructuring. It is concerned about those situations where a person has been managing in some "satisfactory" kind of way, and is confronted by some event which may be internal, e.g. the threat or loss of self-esteem or self-worth, or external, e.g. the threat or loss of a significant other through death or divorce. In either situation, the person experiences the event as overwhelming and does not have the emotional wherewithal to cope in a constructive fashion. There is the feeling of being a snowball, rolling out of control down an ever steepening slope, gathering volume at ever increasing speed—absolutely terrifying. One need not be a skier to appreciate the analogy, but it helps.

The experience of "crisis" begins when a specific, identifiable event, if not readily conscious, is often preconscious, and literally throws the person off balance. The individual undergoing the crisis experience frequently complains about feelings of "going crazy, losing it, going over the edge," etc. The "crisis" proceeds to a middle phase of "recoil" when the individual's attempts to resolve the problem fail which will usually exacerbate an already upsetting experience. At this point special "emergency problem-solving mechanisms" are called upon (Caplan, 1959), and at this juncture point three things may happen: the problem may be solved, it may be redefined into more manageable terms, or the problem may be avoided—all encompassing "end phase" issues in the "crisis" process (Rapoport, 1962).

The goal of the actual crisis intervention mode of counseling, apropos of any form of brief counseling, is the reduction of the symptoms which impede the client's capacity to handle life stressors. In simplest terms, the object is the reduction of danger to self and the restoration of a modicum of "safety," within which the client is enabled to resolve his or her problematic situation. The method of reaching this goal is through directive and "aggressive" counseling, whereby the counselor does whatever is in his or her capability to help maximize gains and strengths and minimize regression and vulnerabilities, thereby unlocking the growth-potential of the experience and avoiding further deterioration. There is a strong focus on interpretation, partialization, confidence-building, and provision of material resources.

This kind of counseling makes a number of unique demands on the counselor. First of all, it is not for the "faint of heart." A prerequisite here is the personal capacity of the counselor to accept the client's crisis state for "what it is"—along with its irrational, upsetting, and negative "trappings," so as not to become engulfed in the crisis oneself. Secondly, the counselor must be able to help the client clarify and identify exactly "what is going on" in his or her life at this moment, so as to help the client recognize what factors are keeping him or her off balance. Often, these factors are preconscious, so the counselor will have to have skill in bringing this dimension of the client's experience and problematic situation into working consciousness, and thus enable the client to have mastery over them. This in itself is a powerful ego-building experience. "Knowledge is power," and the emotional pay-off for this intervention is invaluable. Here, the counselor must be skilled in facilitating some level of "cognitive restructuring and integration" (Rapoport, 1962), whereby the crisis situation is recast into manageable proportions. Rather than allowing the snowball to thunderously roll "out of control," the counselor acts to "stop the snowball" from rolling out of control in the first place. Once the client experiences "power" over what he had previously experienced as feeling "power-less," the work of crisis intervention is well underway. This intervention of recasting, renaming the "whirlwind" as it were, in itself may resolve the crisis experience.

The third and "hallmark" dimension of crisis intervention counseling is the active and orchestrated use of interpersonal resources and energy and the use of institutional community resources to mobilize the client's energy and strength whereby he or she may discover a new sense of strength and power about himself or herself, to whatever degree this may be. The crisis intervention counselor must appreciate and respect the need for and have access to material resources, e.g. if someone is being severely abused, whether the client is a child or an adult, no amount of counseling alone is going to create the kind of atmosphere of safety and well-being necessary for "maximizing the growth-potential" of the situation which may, in fact, present a danger to the client's life and limb! That is to say that no amount of counseling will be helpful if the "endangered" client does not have a "safe place" during the course of the crisis—the client is too preoccupied with survival.

This brief overview of "crisis intervention theory and practice" is just that, and the reader who is unfamiliar with the literature should read the work developed by Lindemann, Golan, Rapoport, Caplan, Parad, and others in the field of crisis intervention. For our purposes here, we can see that the provision of crisis intervention counseling demands immediate and decisive decision-making on the part of the counselor, and is full of both perceived and actual "risk" to the clients' well-being. For the supervisor of crisis intervention counseling, helping the counselor manage the stress which is inherent in his or her work is the critical issue in the supervision of crisis intervention counseling, in my opinion.

C. The Human Context of Crisis Intervention Supervision

1. *The Effects of Stress: Witnessing Another's Pain* First of all, the counselor who does crisis intervention on a regular basis practices within a uniquely intensive arena of human services. Not only does he or she "sit with" and "minister to" people who are confronting problems in their lives in some kind of reflective or even deliberative manner, a process which might allow the counselor analogously to assume an "armchair position" with his or her client; but also more critically here, the counselor "sits with" people who are being confronted by life problems which are totally overwhelming them. Following the analogy, the counselor who is doing crisis intervention is "sitting with" a client (or a client system, e.g. a marital couple or a family), who is literally and symbolically "sinking into the mire" or "going out of control" which can drive the counselor, appropriately, to the edge of his or her seat with adrenalin pumping at high throttle.

What is it like to counsel clients whose life and well-being may very much depend upon the decision you, the counselor, make? (Remember, we are not doing "client-centered therapy." In crisis intervention, the counselor assumes more control in the counseling situation and is more directive with the client.) If your answer to the question was "I don't know" or anything other than "stressful" you are probably caught up in some form of what I will discuss later in detail as the phenomenon of "institutionalized denial syndrome" of professional stress. In any event, and more important for the topic of this chapter, one must ask, "What is it like to 'sit with' counselors who 'sit with' clients whose life and well-being depend upon what decisions they make and actions they take, which ultimately reflect upon the supervisory experience they have had?" Laying aside any hint of the denial syndrome, the situation of the supervisor is extremely and hazardously stressful to say the least. If there are any doubts about the stressful situation, one need only recall the mounting concern about malpractice suits against professional counselors—a hazard to which supervisors are not immune.

There is shocking, analogical data to suggest that the net effect of the kind of stress which is likely to affect supervisors may be more harmful than one might imagine—if one has ever even thought about it in the first place. Robert Kahn cites a dramatic laboratory experiment which studied the effect of stress comparable to the supervisory situation (Kahn, 1978).

In this experiment, one participant had the responsibility for performance which would either reward or punish both participants involved in the experimental situation. The study has become known as the "executive monkey experiment," not because anyone necessarily wanted to make fun of monkeys nor ridicule executives. The title reflects the executive function of the one monkey which was placed in a separate cage, positioned so as to face another monkey which did not have an "executive" function. The so-called executive monkey had access to a lever which, when pressed, would prevent an electric shock from affecting *both* monkeys. The experiment was conducted during six hour work periods, and the electric shock was administered at regular intervals.

Kahn's conclusion to this clever, almost humorously entitled experiment was anything but humorous! He notes that all of the executive monkeys were reported to have died of gastrointestinal lesions in periods ranging from nine to forty-eight days. Significant also, and in striking contrast to the mortal effects of the experiment on the executive monkeys, was the report that none of the equally shocked non-executive monkeys died, nor did any show the presence of gastrointestinal lesions (Kahn, 1978, p. 61).

What does the "executive monkey experiment" have to do with the supervision of crisis intervention counselors? Certainly we do not suggest that supervisors are like executive monkeys, even though at times mid-level managers may well feel like "the monkey in the middle." (Recall the childhood game where two players throw a ball at the player in the middle with the aim of striking him out.) Supervisors may be involved in other games in the supervisory relationship, and I think it is helpful if the supervisor is aware of their dynamics. Alfred Kadushin wrote a fascinating article on this topic, "Games People Play in Supervision," and I think it is foundational reading for any professional supervisor (Kadushin, 1968).

I think the "executive monkey experiment" vividly highlights the devastating potential of uncontrolled stress on a living organism. There are obvious parallels with the crisis intervention supervisor who sees another's pain once and even twice removed, and, not unlike the "executive" in the experiment, is in a position to minimize the damage caused by the traumatic event and assist in maximizing growth in the resolution of the traumatic event(s) at a "distance."

Anyone supervising crisis intervention counseling (just as much as anyone doing crisis intervention counseling) must be aware of his or her own context of professional stress. But "Isn't this apparent?" you might say. Or better yet, "Shouldn't anyone who is supervising crisis intervention counseling already be aware of his or her stress—and just deal with it?" "Aren't these issues too elementary for experienced practitioners?" "There's a job to be done, and if you're too burned out to do it, quit!" "Maybe you don't belong in the human services field; you know, if you can't take the heat, get out of the kitchen." All of these obviously non-supportive remarks which may be heard in day to day agency interaction only underscore the need in all of us: supervisors, counselors, and administrators, to develop an awareness of our own contexts of stress. We all do not need to follow the fate of the executive monkeys!

2. *A Personal Experience as a Crisis Intervention Supervisor* There is growing evidence to suggest that professional burnout or "burnout stress syndrome" (Paine, 1982) is not only the result of internal psychological factors which may predispose the counselor to experiencing a debilitating reaction to stress (which, in turn, interferes with his or her ability to cope with and to withstand the day-to-day pressures of counseling people in trouble). There are significant external factors as well. The emerging data suggests that there are critical factors at play in the counselor's experience which arise externally in the workplace (Maslach, 1978, 1982; Edelwich and Brodsky, 1980; Bramhall and Ezell, 1981; Munson, 1983). I feel that it is critical for the supervisor to develop an awareness of the effects of both types of stressors upon the counselor and upon himself or herself, the su-

pervisor, if he or she is to be effective in the service and "ministry" of crisis intervention supervision.

From my own supervisory experience, I have observed a phenomenon which I will describe as "institutionalized denial syndrome" of professional stress. What I have perceived, and have consequently conceptualized as a group phenomenon, can and does effect all levels of helping professionals, from line staff to supervisor to program administrator. The phenomenon, which I see as a real syndrome, is perpetuated and promulgated by a dynamic which can be either unconsciously encouraged or officially sanctioned by the system within which these professionals function, and may reflect either inept systems or overly controlled, highly centralized systems, all contributing to the same results—increased distress and chronic burnout!

Exactly what do I mean by "institutionalized denial syndrome" of professional stress? I think the best way to define it is to describe it as I have experienced the phenomenon myself. A phenomenologist at heart, I will utilize a phenomenological methodology of "bracketing out" an experience and describing it, drawing out meaning as it "unfolds" from the description (Merleau-Ponty, 1969), i.e. theorizing from experience, as opposed to the other way around.

Not too long ago (I would like to say "Once upon a time . . ." but I am too aware that what I have to say is no fairy tale) in the frothing wake of the budget cuts precipitated by the tumultuous "Proposition 13 Movement" in the early 1980's, initiating the "citizens' mandate" for massive cutbacks in federal and local social programs which affected both public and private agency settings, I began to sense growing levels of distress both within myself and within staff. At that time, I was supervising four counselors, providing direct crisis intervention services as well as ongoing, longer term counseling. I found myself more and more on edge. While I was not fully conscious of the parallel processes which were at play at the time, I vividly recall the counselors complaining about "feelings of powerlessness," "feelings of being overwhelmed," feeling frustrated by paperwork; there was an undercurrent of suppressed anger and hopelessness. Sometimes these feelings were projected onto me in our regular individual supervisory conferences. Sometimes I found the projection directed toward clients. In addition to feelings of suppressed anger, the projection evoked feelings of guilt—"How could I be angry at my client who just lost his welfare grant?" This example of stress occurred day-in and day-out with little relief. To make matters worse, psychiatrically handicapped clients were being terminated from assistance programs and hurled out of a system which was, for all practical purposes, more disordered than any healthy and stable person could handle, let alone someone with a serious impairment. The net result of such unbridled stress was what I now recognize to be distress, the root cause of "burnout stress syndrome" (Selye, 1974).

There was a growing sense of futility in serving clients, especially those who were experiencing crisis situations—the precipitating events extending from varied, catastrophic personal and social events such as unemployment from the increasing lay-offs at a local steel plant, increasing evictions due to loss of income, to the abrupt and widespread decrease of material resources with which to help clients. These "crises" occurred within the "normal" kinds of crises which were more customary at a family counseling agency, such as the usual life crises experiences of divorce, bereavement, and family relationship problems, and added increased demands on the "helping system." While there was increased demand for services, material resources which had previously been available began to "dry up." Money was gone, and counselors were put in the position of having to say, "No, we are out of rent money . . . Yes, I know you lost your welfare grant . . . I can see the pink eviction notice you received . . . I want to help you . . . (finally) Let me call neighborhood community services to see if they have any rent money . . . Maybe somehow we can find something . . ."

After a few days or weeks of this sort of experience, counselors become almost as desperate as their clients. People do not enter the helping professions to tell people, "I am sorry, I cannot help you . . ." The limited material resources only exacerbated the counselors' experience of their own limited personal resources, and had, I believe, a significant negative effect upon the counselors' feelings about themselves, their clients, and their own work performance.

Whenever anger surfaced, generally against clients, counselors tended to express it passively and it was suppressed—an experience, I think, which confirms Wicks' observation about the provision of helping services within religious settings (Wicks, 1984), and also discussed by Gill in the observation of withdrawing, cynical, irritable, and impatient behavior of the helping person in ministerial settings when anger is suppressed and stress denied (Gill, 1980). Religious zeal has an insidious way of feeding into the denial stress syndrome.

From my supervisory experience I noticed that counselors tended to deny their "negative" feelings about themselves and their clients, and seemed to become passively identified with the helplessness of their clients. This denial seemed to sustain the counselor's own unrealistic expectations of their helping capacities and added to their own feelings of personal powerlessness, and gradually became self-defeating. The denial syndrome takes on a distinct "institutionalized" quality when the organization becomes equally delusional in its expectations of its services and its employees, and becomes just as overwhelmed on a grander scale, as the counselor may become himself or herself.

Since I supervised all the line staff on an individual basis, I was acutely aware of their individual concerns, frustrations, and growing sense of hopelessness. Staff meetings which were largely administrative and superficial in nature became more tense as the counselors inquired about the dwindling resources. Due to the continuing cutbacks at the time, the meager material resources which "appeared from out of the blue" periodically from various private grant sources were distributed by a complex bureaucratic process which took approximately one to two weeks to complete through delving into minute detail of the client's personal and financial affairs, with no guarantees that any assistance would be forthcoming after this process. Paperwork was doubled, resources were cut in half, and frequently the counselor was still in the same boat with the client, this time with "hopes raised" no matter how slightly: "Your application was not approved."

I can vividly pinpoint the experience by which I learned about the phenomenon of "institutionalized denial syndrome" of professional stress, as I have come to identify it. Tension had reached such a pitch during our routine monthly staff meetings, and the suppression of affect so self-defeating among staff, that I decided to "take a risk" and to identify what I had perceived to be happening not only to myself, but to the staff as well. I was heartened by my support-network of a few supervisor colleagues who recognized similar levels of counselor stress in their agencies. I had hoped that my sharing of experiences and observations of stress (as part and parcel) in our provision of crisis intervention counseling might "open up" and invite a discussion of how "we" as a staff could deal with the intense stress (which was perhaps more the distress) we were under. The effect of this initiative was not what I had expected! I very much felt like the "monkey in the middle."

Rather than "opening up" discussion about stress and its effect on ourselves and the counseling process—all topics which I had been able to identify with supervisor-colleagues and individual staff members on a one-to-one basis—I found that staff underplayed and actually denied experiencing stress, in the group setting, under the approving eye of the administrator who chaired the meeting. There seemed to be a tendency to deny personal vulnerability; after all, "Competent professional counselors don't have trouble dealing with stress!" There was virtually no discussion: "Yes, things are a little stressful, but 'it's okay.'" There was some small talk, and following an uncomfortable silence, I sat back in my seat and attempted to make sense of the "madness" I had just witnessed. In the end I realized that there were constraints on open and honest communication. What was shared individually could not be shared in our particular group. Our administrator did not want to hear about staff stress. Maybe he was under administrative stress beyond my wildest imagination. (A recent study done by Sze and Ivker [1986] notes that administrators of private agencies scored higher stress levels than administrators in other social service settings, which I feel is a significant finding within the context of our present discussion.) But in any event, "permission" for open and honest staff sharing was not granted, and staff clearly read between the lines, and the distress continued. It is this "massive group denial" that I have come to conceptualize as "institutionalized denial syndrome of professional stress."

While staff resistance to admitting the effects of stress on themselves and their practice was dealt with in individual supervisory conferences, the group phenomenon proved revelatory for me, providing a personal dimension to the topic at hand, and is an example of living through distress and burnout, and in the end gaining mastery over it. It will not happen to me again. It unlocked growth-potential in me, as I hope it may do for the reader engaged in supervising crisis intervention counseling.

3. *The Dynamics of "Lookin' Good!" or Lessons from the "Tale of the Emperor's New Clothes"* My experience in confronting staff denial of stress they were experiencing in an especially intensive way during the early 1980's put me in touch with my own vulnerability as a supervisor. I felt very much like the child in the tale of "The Emperor's New Clothes," a countertransferential situation of feeling myself observing a charade where everyone really knew about his or her distress, but could not deal with it in the group format. I, like the child in the tale, observed that the emperor (who, in many ways represented all of us in the "helping alliance) ". . . has nothing on." The child's father repeated what the child had observed, and the whole crowd echoed the child's remark. Recall the emperor's response: "The emperor heard them, but he only held his head higher and walked more stiffly than ever, and behind him the two chamberlains carried the invisible train" (Gibson, 1950).

In their article, "How Agencies Can Prevent Burnout," Bramhall and Ezell affirm my observation of the denial phenomenon among professionals. They observe, "Every agency has its own 'emperor's new clothes' phenomenon, its own form of institutionalized insanity" (1981, p. 35). The phenomenon is observed in a whole range of activities, from the trivial, e.g. the way a particular form is to be filled out, to the serious, e.g. to the type and quality of interpersonal feedback given to staff. A good example is the tendency to focus on negative feedback, "when something goes wrong." Bramhall and Ezell point out the tendency for organizations to create their own priorities which may or may not serve their stated function and purposes. They recommend that counselors take part in a support group experience which can act as a "reality check" against the routinely acceptable agency or organizational "idiosyncrasies that are often officially ignored by management . . ." (1981, p. 35).

Ironically, one of the first casualties of our agency's reaction to the wave of fiscal cutbacks, was the closing of the "Training Department," the negative effects of which were sustained by the agency's failure to replace the training function with job-related training programs. A volunteer committee was formed, but few helpful training programs were actually done, and none of them was practice-oriented. Likewise, where supervisory staff from the various agency departments and programs had, previous to the budget cutbacks, opportunities to meet quarterly in a type of "peer support" group meetings, these meetings were suspended, and eventually terminated by administration who felt that "they were just gripe sessions," "time could be better spent in direct service," and "supervisory concerns should be dealt with individually with your administrator." Overall, it was clear that administration did not fully appreciate the need for mutual peer support by supervisory staff. The message came across loud and clear: "We expect you to handle it on your own." Such an attitude expresses an individualistic notion of helping which is ineffective at best and pathogenic at an organizational level at worst.

Fortunately for me, I had developed a supportive network among various supervisors from other human service agencies in the local professional community. "Necessity is the mother of invention!" The net result of an extremely difficult situation was increased networking, not only among supervisors, but among various community agencies as well—we were all forced to share our meager resources and discovered a type of helping power in coordinating the helping efforts. There seemed to be fewer and fewer "turf" battles. Confronted by a new, hazardous situation, we in the professional helping community faced our own "crisis situation," and while it is not over, we have been able to tap new strengths, maybe not in resources, but in cooperatively utilizing and maximizing our combined resources. A serendipitous effect of this shared crisis among the various agencies was the organization, planning, and implementation of two community-based training programs in 1983 which dealt with professional stress. The first workshop presented a panel composed of key public officials from various community assistance programs—the external or objective resources in the community. The second workshop focused on stress management issues which dealt with the internal or subjective resources in the community—the helping person! Both programs received enthusiastic community support, thus confirming the need for the professional helping community to "minister" to its own distress, in particularly distressing times.

I feel there is a tremendous need for the supervisor to be aware of the various forces which come to bear in the provision of any kind of crisis intervention counseling program. The supervisor, whether new to the field or a veteran of supervision, needs to appreciate the complexity involved in his or her professional responsibilities. Proverbial, but true, the supervisor is a key figure in the counseling organization, the linch-pin between management and the actual delivery of services—a point of inevitable tension and stress. He or she is constantly dealing with and intervening in highly charged situations whether in the therapeutic interviewing room, supervisory conference, staff meeting, administrative conference or community activities. Supervisors of crisis intervention counseling services must be willing and capable of confronting two distinct levels of resistance—the counselor's resistance as he or she grapples with and explores his or her far-reaching and sometimes unknown but nonetheless limited parameters of helping via the counseling process, and management's resistance to the parameters of the organization's resources, both materially and humanly which are being tested and stretched, especially in the context of diminishing funding sources.

Supervising crisis intervention services through the twenty-first century, in the present and projected political "climate," is no place for the squeamish. In light of continuing trends in cut-backs in human and social services, I feel that, more and more, the supervisor must become a reliable support and reality-check, and supportive-networker for the counselor, and be willing to "go to bat" for the counselor when needed, especially when the organization's needs and expectations far exceed the human capacity of the staff.

D. *The "Ins and Outs" of Supervision: Assessing the Subjective and Objective Resources of the Helping Process in Crisis Intervention Supervision*

Earlier I described crisis intervention counseling as "the active and orchestrated use of interpersonal resources and energy and the use of institutional community resources to mobilize the client's energy and strength . . ." This understanding of crisis intervention emerged from lengthy collegial discussions with Kurt Walser, Director of Professional Services at Family Services of Chester County. In many ways we both struggled with similar professional supervisory issues, and from this struggle came a workable concept of what we and our respective staffs were experiencing. Aside from his charming Swiss accent, Kurt brought a distinctly European way of thinking about what we were confronting, simply put: "There are objective resources available for helping people and subjective resources available, and we must use both of these things in helping people; otherwise we all just become frustrated individuals" (Walser, 1983). There was more truth to Walser's simple insight than I was able to comprehend at that time. Here, I would like to consider each as I have come to understand them in the practice of supervision. So, the following represents the "ins and outs," the subjective dynamics of the helper and the objective dynamics of the community and organizational structure, and what the supervisor needs to know.

1. *The Subjective Dynamics of the Counselor* As much of my discussion above affirms, I am convinced that one of the most critical issues in supervising crisis intervention counseling is for the supervisor to overcome his or her own resistance to the notion that "helping people can be hazardous to your health," and, along with this, to help one's supervisees muster the same courage to face the pain and discouragement which clients will bring to the counseling session. Everyone involved in the helping process needs to be sensitive to the effects of meeting crisis situations day-in and day-out where the counselor is confronted with the responsibility of making critical decisions which may affect the life and well-being of clients. The supervisor needs to be the first to recognize and accept the reality of stress in this situation. If he or she does not, the stage is set for disaster.

The denial syndrome discussed above can only be sustained if everyone accepts his or her "designated" role in the charade. The supervisor, as a middle-level manager in the human service organization or agency, is in a unique position to recognize and intervene in constructive ways to improve the level and quality of staff performance, on the one hand, and agency responsiveness and program planning, on the other. The supervisor is the critical link which can and must help the counselor and the agency recognize that no matter how skilled and experienced he or she is, the counselor is a human being, and can only do what is human. Even in religious settings, or especially in religiously affiliated organizations, there may be pseudo-spiritual reasons to sustain burnout patterns, where depression and hostility, as "negative" feelings, are suppressed "for a higher good" (Gill, 1980).

After the supervisor has dealt with his or her own vulnerability factor, the likelihood of interferences by parallel processes discussed in depth in Chapter 8 is greatly reduced, or at least brought into consciousness so as to be more "accessible" to the helping capacity of the supervisory relationship. With this accomplished, the supervisor's effectiveness in and capacity to initiate the dynamic supervisory alliance and overall ability to deal with supervisory issues is significantly improved. Critical to building and enhancing the working supervisory alliance, the supervisor must be familiar with the internal effects of stress on his or her supervisee, which is a normal and predictable human reaction for anyone engaged in day-to-day people contact (Maslach, 1978, 1982; Bramhall and Ezell, 1981; Streepy, 1981). Such admission on the supervisor's part will treat job-related stress as "normal" and not a sign of personal defect, which the competent, caring, and dedicated counselor might otherwise assume to be the case as he or she struggles to integrate the personal self with the professional self. With this knowledge in the forefront, the supervisory alliance will become even more humanized which will, in turn, enhance the counselor's capacity to humanize the counseling relationship. Both supervisee and supervisor will be "permitted" to talk about "stress" and more critically become aware when the "stress" may begin to shift to "distress."

(a) *Distinguishing "Stress" from "Distress"* Before a supervisor can distinguish "stress" from "distress" he or she should first of all be knowledgeable about "burnout." What is it? What does it have to do with stress? Who is susceptible to it? Some professionals may look at "burnout" as something that happens to "other people," while others may dismiss it as an excuse for poor performance or a new catch word in professional jargon, another word with which to play mind-games.

It is striking, however, that the phenomenon of "burnout" is observed so often, especially in work settings with high levels of stress in day-to-day activities. The word is heard among virtually all the helping professions; few people have not heard someone or other exclaim: "I'm not so effective as I used to be—maybe I'm burned out . . ." What is professional burnout? First of all, there is no one definition; in fact there are at least two broad approaches theorists take in thinking about the "burnout" phenomenon. Some writers view burnout as a continuum, developing through a series of steps or stages, in a kind of progression (Daley, 1979; Edelwich and Brodsky, 1980). Other theorists view burnout as a cyclical pattern, a response reaction to specific stimulation or, actually, overstimulation produced by certain conditions (Bramhall and Ezell, 1981; Munson, 1983). Suffice it to say, burnout may be viewed in both ways, and it is important for the supervisor to be attuned to the nuances of both as individual supervisees may exhibit symptoms of either: through distinct stages with recognizable progressions or patterned, cyclical responses to specific situations.

The word "burnout" was first used in 1974 in an article by Herbert J. Freudenberger concerning his observation of volunteer workers in "free clinics"; the term soon began to be applied to mainstream professionals including police officers, lawyers, teachers, nurses, mental health workers, clergy, and child care workers, to describe a shared experience: ". . . a wearing out, exhaustion, or failure resulting from excessive demands made on energy, strength or resources" (Freudenberger, 1977); ". . . a syndrome of inappropriate attitudes towards clients and towards self, often associated with uncomfortable physical and emotional systems ranging from exhaustion and insomnia to migraine and ulcer" (Kahn, 1978); ". . . the progressive loss of idealism, energy, and purpose experienced by people in the helping profession as a result of the condition of their work" (Edelwich and Brodsky, 1980).

Hans Selye was one of the first theoreticians to study the physical effects of stress. His early work is still considered foundational in any understanding of "burnout" where he identified the human process of reacting to stress as "general adaptation syndrome" (1974, p. 27). Selye identified three distinct stages which comprise the stress reaction: alarm, resistance, and exhaustion. The alarm stage identifies the person's (bodily) awareness that "something is wrong." This is followed by a resistance stage if there is continued exposure to the stressor wherein the person attempts to resist the stressor. Unsuccessful in resisting the stressor, the person experiences an exhaustion reaction. It is during this final stage where the burnout reaction is likely to arise, for if the stressor continues unabated during the exhaustion stage, there occurs the experience of unmitigated stress. This debilitating experience becomes "distress." The supervisor must be able to enhance the supervisee's management of stress, which may be perceived as "energy," and minimize the supervisee's experience of "distress," which is a destructive force and will become debilitating.

Selye's conceptualization points out the moment when supervisory intervention is most critical—at the exhaustion stage. Here the supervisor must be attuned to the counselor's need to regroup, rebound, and be renewed. This can be accomplished by reducing work load, suggesting alternative and complementary professional activities, e.g. provide opportunities for less stressful client contact, offer time for workshops and continuing education, etc. Whatever it takes, the supervisor must help the counselor regroup once he or she has reached the exhaustion stage. Even here, the supervisor must be prepared to deal with resistance as discussed above in the denial syndrome phenomenon.

Stress is an inherent part in any modality of counseling; it is heightened in crisis intervention counseling. Since much of what happens in crisis intervention counseling is telescoped in time and energy, the accurate and prompt recognition of the stages of "general adaptation syndrome" is even more critical in crisis intervention supervision if the supervisor is to provide the kind and quality of supervision which will maximize the counselor's own potential and growth. The supervisor must be able and willing to assess the counselor's stress reaction stage, and be ready to intervene in a direct way—modeling, in a sense, in supervision, what the counselor provides in his or her counseling intervention with the client in crisis. Here the concept of the "supervisory alliance" is very much tied to the "helping alliance" which is comprised of counselor-client-supervisor-agency—all intimately linked in significant ways!

The supervisor of crisis intervention counseling must instinctively know when stress is turning into distress. In many ways, the recognition occurs preconsciously, in the supervisor's sense that a particular worker seems edgy, withdrawn, defensive or avoidant of client contact. This instinctive awareness must be made conscious, and clear intervention must reduce the stressors in a meaningful way to allow the counselor to return from his or her stage of exhaustion to well-being again. The dictionary definition cuts through the intellectualization which appears in the literature, and while it certainly does not replace a thorough reading of the various theories of stages and progressions of burnout, it is revelatory nonetheless. Consider these definitions:

"stress: 1. Special weight, importance, or significance."
"distress: 1. To inflict suffering upon, cause agony or worry to; afflict; harass."

Supervision has the capacity to intervene in both situations. Unfortunately, supervisors do not always intervene in ways which are perceived by supervisees as helpful or supportive of them (Munson, 1983). It is incumbent upon the supervisor to handle this responsibility with the utmost of care, sensitivity, and sound knowledge about the issues involved in supervising this unique area of counseling practice.

In my practice of supervising crisis intervention counseling, I have found that the use of a standardized "agenda" which includes ample room for "feelings" reflection is extremely helpful in monitoring, recognizing, and sometimes uncovering denied counselor stress and distress. The push to deny personal vulnerability can be so strong in the counselor, and the phenomenon of institutionalized denial so inherent in helping systems, that very deliberate and planned measures need to be taken by the supervisor to assist in the recognition of these issues, and to activate the process of transforming them into positive professional development. In the long run, such a procedure would have a positive effect on improved service provision, staff morale, and affirm commitment to the working alliance which I think is absolutely necessary in the supervision of crisis intervention counseling.

The format that I use for the supervisory agenda is an adaptation of the form developed by the Pastoral Counseling Department at Loyola College. Questions include: (1) What were your feelings about this supervisory session? In anticipation? During? During the subsequent week? (2) Identify supervisory issues addressed. (3) Describe the quality of response from the supervisor. (4) What did you learn from this supervisory session? About yourself? About your client? About the counseling process? About the supervisory process? I have found that while supervisees are likely to resist using such a structured format for supervision, it makes evasion of the critical issues of supervision discussed above difficult, if not impossible. I use the form with flexibility and, together with the supervisee, review each item to learn how best it can apply to *this* counselor. Anything that does not fit is adapted to meet the particular counselor's need. Areas of resistance to using the form are carefully examined. Sometimes counselors may fear that the form will be "used against him/her" in an evaluative way, and will be reluctant to share openly with it. Here the supervisee must be assured that the form is not an evaluation form, but a discussion tool to help focus on underlying supervisory issues that have bearing on the case discussion which will take place. Usually this kind of assurance is enough to clear up the remaining difficulties with the form. While supervisees may periodically complain about not having enough time to fill out their agenda, they usually find it helpful, nonetheless; and even this "press for time" to complete a simple and short form, which the agenda is, focuses supervisory discussion on use of time, limit-setting, and need to take time for self—in this case, taking time for supervisory preparation. The supervisory agenda forces both the supervisor and supervisee to take their time together seriously, not that the time together "has to be grim," but serious, in the sense that supervisory time becomes more planned and focused. The use of a structured agenda, which includes opportunity to "process" feelings, I think, enhances, streamlines, and cuts through to where the supervisor and supervisee need to be with each other. It gives the counselor the clear signal: "I expect all kinds of feelings to surface in supervision—and it is okay to talk about them in an open and honest way."

I think that if the supervisor can accept the "stress" and the possibility and danger of "distress" in the counselor's experience as "normal," even predictable reactions in the supervisees' practice experience on an ongoing basis, a more meaningful and genuinely supportive kind of supervisory alliance can actually take place and be realized in a mutually enriching manner. Conversely, if the supervisor is not willing to risk himself or herself, or cannot accept these day-to-day reactions as normal or acceptable in the supervisee, supervision deteriorates into a routine, administrative exercise in reporting numbers of clients seen, forms completed, and other assorted bureaucratic issues. Such behavior may deal with "administrative supervision," but misses the mark in attending to the issues of "supportive supervision." I have found that an overemphasis on "administrative supervision" fails to attend to the supportive needs of the counselor. This failure has a way of setting the supervisory conference up for "gameplaying" (Kadushin, 1968), and exacerbates the risk of professional burnout by missing the affective issues that the supervisee may need to withhold from sharing, not only with you, the supervisor, but with himself or herself as well. The use of a structured agenda in a flexible and open way helps to side-step gameplaying in supervision. If gameplaying is already in process, confront it directly, for as Kadushin states:

> Confrontation implies a refusal to accept the game being proposed by seeking to expose and make explicit what the supervisee is doing. The supervisory situation, like the therapeutic situation, deliberately and consciously rejects the usual rules of social interaction in attempting to help the supervisee (Kadushin, 1968, p. 32).

Games occur in supervision, in many ways to sustain the "denial syndrome" discussed above, for as Kadushin notes, "The supervisory tutorial is a threat to the student's independence and autonomy" (p. 24). Games, which Kadushin discusses whimsically but very seriously in his article, play out the supervisee's resistance to the full participation in the supervisory alliance. An especially critical issue in crisis intervention, gameplaying cannot continue unchecked where clear, honest, and trusting communication must be the rule of thumb.

Unfortunately, supervisors play games with supervisees, and vice versa, and the risk of burnout is increased by the functioning of the "petty bureaucrat" whom Maslach sees as the prototype of the burned-out professional who does not have to get involved with real people or take responsibility for unpopular or painful or uncomfortable decisions because all you have to do is "fall back on the rules" (Maslach, 1978). I am sure most experienced supervisors have had some exposure to this professional phenomenon (assuming he or she is not a "petty bureaucrat" himself or herself): "I'm following procedures" whether or not those procedures have a needlessly hurtful effect on the delivery of service—that is not the bureaucrat's concern. "If you don't like the rules, you can always leave . . ." Dialogue is impossible in this kind of atmosphere. There needs to be a "give and take" in the supervisory relationship *if* it is to develop into and function as an "alliance."

(b) *The "Fine Art" of Mistake-Making* The "fine art" of mistake-making may be trickier than may first appear. First of all, in order to excel in this important crisis intervention counseling skill, the counselor must be "self aware"; the counselor must be acutely aware of his or her effect upon the client. If the supervisee is not aware of himself or herself, he or she will flounder when it comes to this critical crisis intervention skill, look at the supervisor when confronted by a "mistake," and not know "what you're talking about." From this we may detect the high level of skill needed for successful and professional mistake-making. The skilled crisis intervention counselor is acutely aware of his or her capacity to make mistakes in the counseling process. This recognition gives him or her power to control mistake-making, regroup from difficult mistakes, and possibly provide backup interventions when mistakes are detected. People who do not take to the "fine art" of mistake-making, or, worse yet, professionals who "do not make mistakes" (and there are some of these types around), do not make very good crisis intervention counselors.

As I discussed in an earlier section, crisis intervention counseling is a telescoped counseling modality which takes place in stressful, sometimes extremely stressful human situations. Active and directive intervention is needed if the crisis intervention is to be successful: assessing the crisis situation, precipitating event, and client's capacity to respond to the crisis intervention counseling process. All of these elements, combined with the counselor's humanness, set the context for mistake-making. The issue here is not to be frivolous about the seriousness of counseling. The issue is to be serious in recognizing that "mistakes will be made." Better that they be recognized for what they are than have the counselor fall victim to the denial syndrome in yet another context, e.g. "If you are a competent professional, you won't make mistakes." This should be: "If you are a competent professional, you will be aware of your mistakes, and will have the capacity and wherewithal to learn from them and find ways not to repeat them." I have become acutely aware of my own capacity for mistake-making, and believe it is a key issue for anyone supervising crisis intervention counselors. Always sensitive to the possibility of parallel processes, the supervisor must attend to his or her own skills of mistake-making before he or she can be helpful to the counselor in developing his or her skills in this crucial area. Just as the supervisor must "give permission" for the supervisee to admit his or her stress reaction, so too the supervisor must give clear "signals" verbally as well as non-verbally, that mistake-making is also a part of the counselor's experience, not as an end in itself, but as a tool for improved service and continuing professional growth.

How "should" the supervisor of crisis intervention counseling "deal" with counseling mistakes? The first answer is already implied by the question itself. The supervisor must, first of all, be willing to "deal" with them, meaning he or she must be skillful in confronting the mistake as a "mistake," nothing more and nothing less.

Assuming that the counselor has been screened for sound professional judgment, training, and ability and knows what is expected of him or her in providing crisis intervention counseling, there is an underlying foundation of trust between counselor and supervisor. The supervisor, who oftentimes views the work of the supervisee second-hand, at best via audio-visual tape, and perhaps occasionally by directly "sitting" in on interviews, must make his or her performance expectations known to the supervisee as clearly as possible. The job description is critical here, and should be a "working document" in the supervisory alliance. The limits of the kind of crisis intervention counseling that an agency does should be as explicit as possible. Whether or not twenty-four hour emergency coverage is expected of the counselor, and how this is to be done, etc., are all important for both supervisor, counselor, and administrator to understand.

If a counselor lacks training in a specific counseling area, e.g. intervening in the crisis inevitably provoked when criminal charges are brought against a suspected child molester or when a protection order is served on an abusing spouse, the supervisor should see to it that training opportunities are made available to the counselor—and if this is not possible, be ready to refer the case to another practitioner. Big mistakes by counselors can be prevented by responsible case assignments by the supervisor who needs to know the strengths and weaknesses, growing edges and limitations of the counselors whom he or she is responsible for supervising. This, too, is an important part of the art of mistake-making: avoiding mistakes which arise from inaccurate assessment. This goes back to the initial intake phase of the case and the process of case assignment. I do not believe case assignments should be "self-assigned" as they say. I believe such a practice is, in effect, a relinquishment of supervisory responsibility. There are other views on this, but I am convinced through practical experience with this practice that it is seriously faulty. The responsibility of case assignment falls squarely upon the shoulders of the supervisor! Otherwise, the supervisory alliance is threatened, and counselors can easily become a group of "frustrated individuals."

As I pointed out earlier, crisis intervention calls for directive intervention on the counselor's part. The manner in which mistakes are handled in supervision can greatly influence how the counselor will perceive himself or herself as a crisis intervention counselor. An accurate sense of competence and confidence is essential if a counselor is to do crisis intervention. Otherwise the counselor goes adrift with his "sinking client." When a mistake is observed by the supervisor, it is important to wait until the counselor is in a position to integrate it into his or her learning. For example, a counselor inappropriately advises an abused spouse "to go home, and just stand up to him, and if he tries to punch you, call the police." The woman goes home, confronts her husband with her "new found" courage, and he brutally batters her.

Two things, I think, must happen in the above example situation. One, the counselor must experience the supervisor's *affirmation* and not judgment. Two, the counselor must be able to explore the reasons for the particular advice given, to understand why it was not appropriate in this situation. If the supervisor approaches the counselor in a judgmental way, pointing out the "inappropriateness of the counseling intervention," or, worse yet, if the counselor is "called in" to discuss this "bad advice" by an administrator, the rug will be effectively pulled from under the counselor's feet, and damage will result. Trust will be broken, and the next time the counselor may be hesitant being "directive" with his or her client, when he or she needs to be purposefully directive. Other damaging "fallout" from this kind of situation may be the supervisee's feeling reluctant to discuss another similar situation with the supervisor, and be left guessing "Why was *that* inappropriate?" The tour de force response from the supervisor who is inept in the genuine and skillful art of mistake-making and mistake-mending will likely be something like: "What do *you* think was inappropriate in what you did?"—answering the proverbial "question with a question," sending the counselor, in my opinion, on a senseless "guilt trip."

I feel that professional supervisors should have the courage to be open, honest, and direct with their supervisees, especially in helping them, first of all, to recognize their mistakes, and, secondly, to help them learn and explore new ways to intervene in crisis situations in an empathic and direct fashion. One supervisory response to the above example could well develop as follows:

Supervisor: Since your client had a long history of severe physical abuse, was hospitalized three times in the last two years from beatings by her husband, I think it was a mistake to expect her to all of a sudden be able to "stand up to him." I understand your frustration. It is not simple working with these kinds of situations. You

	handled a very difficult situation and miscalculated. When situations like this arise, you need to think about safety issues. Whenever there is active abuse, safety comes first.
Counselor:	You know, I can really see where I went off . . . I get so angry at these guys who think nothing of hitting their wives. I really wanted to see her take care of herself. I gave her the emergency number and the police number . . . I didn't take the threat of her husband as serious as it was . . . I can see that now. It's good to talk about it.
Supervisor:	Your client is very much connected to you . . . she can draw strength from you, but on her terms . . . maybe what you can do is help lead her to safety the next time. Why don't you visit the women's shelter with her, so she can see what it's like with someone she trusts?

Interactions such as this accomplish two important things: recognition of a miscalculation, a mistake, and affirmation of the counselor's humanity while inviting the counselor to expand his or her repertoire of crisis intervention helping skills, in this case by facilitating the client's accessibility to the shelter, if and when a "safe place" is needed.

I share these critical issues in this section of my chapter not from some lofty point of knowledge, but from a humble vantage point of having struggled through my own supervisory mistakes. I struggled through numerous parallel processes, not knowing what they were, but, once learning about them, I felt deeply insightful into the dynamics of supervision. When I advise against holding a judgmental attitude against one's supervisees, I do so, having practical experience of feeling judged and judging others—the vicious cycle of the "do unto others" model of supervision. I have learned from my mistake-making. I hope this reflection is helpful to the reader in sharpening his or her skills in the art of "mistake-making" and "mistake-mending."

2. *Objective Resources of the Helping Process.* As I discussed earlier, crisis intervention counseling is unique and distinct from other counseling modalities because of its active use and "orchestration" of material and/or other community and institutional resources. The "outs" of crisis intervention counseling fall within two major components: the geo-political, socio-economic community milieu within which context the counselor practices, and the ideological and structural dynamics of the organization

within which the practitioner is employed. We will now consider some of the key issues relating to the "objective" resources.

(a) *Community and Institutional Resources* The crisis intervention counselor must be skillful both inside his or her office and outside the office in developing a working knowledge of the community in which one provides crisis intervention counseling. The counselor needs to be familiar with the workings of the local Department of Public Welfare, Employment Office (sometimes inadvertently referred to as the Unemployment Office), Drug and Alcohol Detox Programs, Child Welfare or the Children and Youth Services Department, and Legal Aid Services, to name a few basic community resources which the crisis intervention counselor may turn to through the crisis intervention counseling process.

In addition to the many publicly funded resources which many of the above generally are, the counselor needs to be aware of the availability of various "private" community resources which are sponsored by the private sector, oftentimes through church organizations such as the Salvation Army, Catholic Social Services, Jewish Family Services, YM/YWCA Programs, Big Brothers, etc. Usually with supervisees who are new to the position of crisis intervention counseling, as an integral part of their orientation, I will review "key" community agencies and programs which they should know. Time is scheduled for the counselor to visit select agencies and to meet a designated contact person who can orient the counselor to the services available through the different agencies. The time is usually very well spent, as this provides an update to me and the rest of staff when the new counselor shares his or her experience after the field visit. The time invested at this point in counselor orientation avoids the frantic scurrying at the time when a client presents a crisis and the counselor "starts from scratch" as it were: "Now, where is the Department of Public Welfare again?" The personal contact also reduces the risk of situations where "clients fall through the cracks" in the systems.

Failure to do this homework assignment may not necessarily spell disaster to the new counselor, but any uneasiness which the crisis intervention counselor may feel about making a referral to a community resource will be readily perceived by the client who is already overwhelmed, and any insecurity on the counselor's part will only exacerbate a difficult situation and, in fact, undermine the goal of crisis intervention, i.e. the reduction of symptoms, by adding the counselor's "crisis": "Whom should I talk to? My client is 'losing it' with her kid." Community systems are not quite so mysterious as they need to be for the counselor engaged in crisis intervention. If you do not feel satisfied through one level of contact when you call the Welfare Office (and most likely you are speaking to a hurried receptionist), request to speak to a supervisor, and ask each person you speak with what his or her name is, and tell him or her yours. While many of the public systems do represent inhumanly complex bureaucracies, the crisis intervention counselor must make the effort to make the various systems respond to meet the needs of his or her client. Only if the counselor has gained a "working knowledge" of the community resources and agencies can he or she possibly be in a position to then "orchestrate" the "objective" resources with the "subjective" resources which the counselor himself brings to the relationship.

Even for clinicians who may already be familiar with the community resources, it is important periodically to update one's "resource file" (which should be organized in a cardex in ready reach) on one's desk, as community resources are, for better or worse, in a constant state of flux. It is also advisable to have a particularly smooth working relationship with the community mental health service program and child and youth agency whose procedures may change depending upon changing legislation and regulations, sometimes very rapidly.

Neither the "ins" nor the "outs" of crisis intervention counseling are simple. This section simply serves as a reminder of the complexity one is up against when providing crisis intervention counseling. The "helping alliance" transcends individuals and particular agencies and programs, and takes on a very real socio-political dimension of which the practitioners must be aware. What is or is not available in this broader community resource will have a very real impact upon the quality and effectiveness of the counseling done in your office. Community networking, i.e. developing working alliances with other helping organizations for mutual support and sharing resources, is a reality of the 1980's and most likely into the twenty-first century.

(b) *Organizational Structures which Enhance or Impede the Helping Process* The administrative directive was clear: "I expect each worker to schedule twenty interviews per week." There was no invitation for discussion, nor was there any sense from this administrator that different counselors had different interviewing needs. A crisis intervention counselor might very well have to spend, literally, hours on the telephone tracking down resources and firming up plans to assist a client. A family counselor may spend an entire afternoon in a conjoint family session, while another counselor may have individual counseling sessions and on this basis will be able to schedule individual counseling sessions on the basis of the so-called "clinical hour." I was struck by the fact that qualitative human services were being put into quantitative figures. There was a sense that staff was perceived as a commodity to be used to accomplish the agency goal, not unlike the "dixie-cup" attitude cited by Bramhill and Ezell—"use them up and throw them away" (p. 34). "There's always more from where they came . . ." Sadly, organizational goals and attitudes may very well run contrary to the goals and attitudes required by the "supervisory alliance." This section will consider some of the issues pertaining to crisis intervention counseling which arise from the organizational structures of the human service agency.

First of all, the "dixie-cup" mentality runs counter to good, humanistic, and professionally acceptable standards of practice. It is ironic how our natural resources are so readily abused whether they are situated in the magnificent mountains or whether they are situated in the less sublime office next door to you. There seems to be a propensity to take our natural resources for granted. The supervisory alliance requires that the supervisor respect the innate dignity and uniqueness of the counselor. While productivity and statistics play an important role in any agency, especially in the tightening fiscal restraints, the unique needs and abilities of each counselor must be taken into consideration in an open, honest, and dignified way. The supervisory alliance which is recognized as key to the process of supervision does not allow for any "disposable" people. Each person in the helping alliance has a unique perspective and role in the overall delivery of services. Mutual respect, recognition of dignity, and various competencies, based upon knowledge and trust, form the underlying supports for professional growth, and where these supports have been undermined, professional growth is impeded.

Zischka and Fox (1983) point out the "pivotal position" of the supervisor within a social agency to "cushion the impact of bureaucracy on staff and thereby to prevent or to reduce burnout" (ibid.). They continue, and I think accurately observe, "At no other level of the hierarchical structure does any one individual possess a comprehensive view of the impact of policy on clients, as this policy is implemented by staff" (p. 47). So it would stand to reason that the supervisor is a key figure in setting the organizational tone and attitude among the staff. Sadly, this is not always the case. The supervisor can play an integral role in buffering the negative effects of bureaucracy on the counselor, which Zischka and Fox describe as the "catalytic role," provided certain basic requisites are met.

According to Zischka and Fox, the supervisor must first look to himself or herself, in the light of four basic "characteristics":

1. high level of morale;
2. ability to cope with stress;
3. ability to differentiate between situations which lend themselves to change, and those which do not;
4. belief that their work is understood and appreciated.

In many ways these observations affirm much of our discussion regarding supervisor self-awareness. Where Zischka and Fox are especially helpful, I think, is in their development of guidelines for assuming the "catalytic role" (p. 49). While supervisors may have developed high levels of self-awareness and expertise in their field of practice, unless they are just as aware of the structural and organizational climate within which they practice, their self-awareness will have a "one dimensional" quality to it.

Supervisors must also be able to accurately assess the organization in which they may or may not be able to function in a "pivotal" capacity. Turning once again to my dictionary, which I like to do to let "language work" for me, I found that "pivotal" is an adjective of the noun "pivot" which is defined as "1. *Mech.* Something upon which a related part turns, oscillates, or rotates . . . 2. A person or thing upon which an important matter hinges or turns." How does the supervisor gauge whether or not he is pivotal? The "guidelines" outlined by the above authors give specific areas to consider in order to derive an answer. I will quote them at length, as they give concrete tools to assess a critical element in the helping system, the organizational climate. The supervisor needs to know:

1. Are the lines of responsibility and authority in the agency's hierarchical structure clearly delineated?
2. Does the agency have a structure for obtaining feedback from all levels of staff re indications for policy changes to improve client services?
3. Do supervisors participate in the agency's decision-making process?
4. In spite of the complex bureaucratic structure . . . does the agency give meaningful recognition to staff dedication, commitment and skills?
5. Does the agency provide realistic opportunities for professional advancement?
6. Does the agency have an effective in-service training program, related to job requirements of all the staff, and can this learning be implemented within the requirements of the position?
7. Does the agency provide the necessary supports for staff to carry out the requirements of the work?
8. Does the agency have some provision for flexible working hours to help staff at all levels meet both professional and personal obligations?
9. Is the agency hierarchy male dominated, causing women supervisors to compete on an unequal basis?

10. Do the agency's policies regarding both professional practice and personnel policies in any way reflect ageism, racism or sexism? (pp. 49–50).

'organizational climate" thus identified by answering these key questions, the supervisor is in a better position to determine whether or not his or her agency's structure and atmosphere is amenable to developing and sustaining the "supervisory alliance" which is being set forth in this book on supervision. How one responds to the above questions suggests whether, and to what degree, there is an organizational foundation for this model of supervision. While an overriding negative response to most of these key questions would not necessarily rule it out, I think it would serve to impede a real working alliance from adequately functioning. The supervisor is, in no stretch of the imagination, an entity unto himself or herself. The supervisor is a part of a much larger "helping system" which like any system has limitations and boundaries—some wider some narrower than others that he or she needs to take into full consideration in one's overall practice of professional supervision.

Conclusion

I hope that I have not "lost" the more clinically-oriented practitioner over the course of this complex discussion. It is very appropriate to ask, "What does all this have to do with crisis intervention counseling?" Let me bring together the seemingly "loose threads" of this piece of professional tapestry by an analogy.

Over the course of my experience in both doing and supervising crisis intervention counseling services, I have come to perceive the actual "doing" of the crisis intervention as comparable to seeing and recognizing a client who is "situationally" being "swept away" by powerful currents in a churning and overpowering journey down an unknown and uncharted river with the possibility of being washed over the falls after the next bend. The actual crisis intervention, then, entails jumping into the churning water and assisting the client who is being overwhelmed and hopelessly swept away. In doing this sort of "hazardous work" neither the counselor nor the supervisor, who is "standing at the shore," can take anything for granted. The counselor who "jumps in" must have the basic knowledge and skills to negotiate the pressures of the currents he or she will be facing. The counselor cannot do this alone. He or she must be able to rely on his or her supervisor who likewise must be well equipped for this responsibility. The supervisor will need to help muster the needed equipment to "pull the client out of the river," and should be prepared to have a life-line in hand. Knowing that there are "back up" rescue workers is extremely important for the crisis intervention counselor, for the statistics on professional burnout attest that the helping professional can also be swept away too!

My conclusion to this discussion of supervising crisis intervention counseling is that supervisors must be acutely aware of their responsibility to provide support to their supervisors which takes precedence, I believe, over the other supervisory functions of administrative and evaluative supervision and educational supervision—although they are intimately linked. The supervisee engaged in crisis intervention counseling must know that the supervisor is "there for him," ready with life-line, life-saver, maybe even a few blankets for warmth when he or she comes out of the river.

Unfortunately some organizations which provide crisis intervention counseling may not always provide this kind of "safety." There may be organizational dynamics which effectively impede and interfere in the provision of supervisory support. Budget constraints and the push for expanded services in the face of decreasing resources can place an agency at odds with itself. It is here, in the middle of complex stressors, that the work of crisis intervention supervision is done or undone. I hope this article will be helpful to supervisors in getting "undone" and more focused on what they need to be doing.

References

Martha Bramhall and Susan Ezell, "How Burned Out Are You?" Part One, *Public Welfare*, Winter 1981, pp. 23–26.

———, "Working Your Way Out of Burnout," Part Two, *Public Welfare*, Spring 1981, pp. 32–39.

———, "How Agencies Can Prevent Burnout," Part Three, *Public Welfare*, Summer 1981, pp. 33–37.

Rachel Callahan, "The Ministry of Crisis Intervention," in *Pastoral Counseling*, ed., Barry K. Estadt, et al. Englewood Cliffs, N.J.: Prentice-Hall, Inc., 1983.

Stephen J. Catalano, "Crisis Intervention with Clinical Interns: Some Considerations for Supervision," *The Clinical Supervisor*, Vol. 3 (1), Spring 1985.

Jerry Edelwich with Archie Brodsky, *Burnout: Stages of Disillusionment in the Helping Professions*. New York: Human Sciences Press, 1980.

Michael R. Daley, " 'Burnout': Smoldering Problem in Protective Services," *Social Work*, September 1979.

Erik H. Erikson, *Childhood and Society*, Second Edition. New York: W. W. Norton & Co., Inc., 1963. First printing 1950.

H. J. Freudenberger, "Burn-Out: The Organizational Menace," *Training and Development Journal*, July 1977, pp. 27–29.

Katherine Gibson, "The Emperor's New Clothes," in *Fairy Tales*. Racine, Wisconsin: Whitman Publishing Co., 1950, pp. 121–137.

James J. Gill, "Burnout: A Growing Threat in Ministry," *Human Development*, Vol. 1 (2), Summer 1980.

Alfred Kadushin, "Games People Play in Supervision," *Social Work*, July 1968.

———, *Supervision in Social Work*. New York: Columbia University Press, 1976.

Eva M. Kahn, "The Parallel Process in Social Work Treatment and Supervision," *Social Casework: The Journal of Contemporary Social Work*, 60: 520–528, November 1979.

Christina Maslach, *Burnout: The Cost of Caring*, with a prologue by Philip G. Zimbardo. Englewood Cliffs, N.J.: Prentice-Hall, Inc., 1982.

———, "Job Burnout: How People Cope," *Public Welfare*, Spring 1978.

Maurice Merleau-Ponty, "What Is Phenomenology?" in *Phenomenology of Religion*, Joseph Dabney Bettis, ed. New York: Harper & Row, 1969.

Carlton E. Munson, "Combating Burnout," *An Introduction to Clinical Social Work Supervision*. New York: The Haworth Press, 1983.

Whiton Stewart Paine, ed., *Job Stress and Burnout: Research, Theory, and Intervention Perspectives*. London: Sage Publications, 1982.

Lydia Rapoport, "The State of Crisis: Some Theoretical Considerations," *Social Service Review* 6, June 1962, pp. 211–17. Reprinted in Parad, *Crisis Intervention*, pp. 23–31.

Hans Selye, *Stress Without Distress*. New York: Signet Book, 1974.

Peter E. Sifneos, "Brief Psychotherapy and Crisis Intervention," in *Comprehensive Textbook of Psychiatry III*, ed. Harold I. Kaplan, et al. Volume 2, Third Edition. Baltimore: Williams and Williams, 1980.

Joan Streepy, "Direct-Service Providers and Burnout," *Social Casework: The Journal of Contemporary Social Work*, June 1981.

David K. Switzer, "Crisis Intervention and Problem Solving," in *Clinical Handbook of Pastoral Counseling*, ed. Robert J. Wicks, et al., 1985.

William C. Sze and Barry Ivker, "Stress in Social Workers: The Impact of Setting and Role," *Social Casework*, 67, March 1986, p. 147.

Kurt Walser, Taken from a conversation during a planning meeting at

Family Service of Chester County, "A Forum on the Poor and Unemployed in Chester County," April 25, 1983.

Robert J. Wicks, "A Threat to Christian Communities: Angry People Acting Passive-Aggressively," *Human Development*, Vol. 5 (4), Winter
1984.

Pauline C. Zischka and Raymond Fox, "Burnout and the Catalytic Role of
the Supervisor," *The Clinical Supervisor*, Vol. 1 (2), Summer 1983.

Recommended Readings

Lucille N. Austin, "Basic Principles of Supervision," *Social Casework: The
Journal of Contemporary Social Work* 33, December 1952.

Gerald Caplan, *Principles of Preventive Psychiatry*. New York: Basic
Books, 1964.

Samuel L. Dixon and Roberta G. Sands, "Identity and the Experience of
Crisis," *Social Casework: The Journal of Contemporary Social Work*,
Vol. 64: 223–30, April 1983.

Barry A. Farber, ed., *Stress and Burnout in the Human Service Professions*. New York: Pergamon Press, 1983.

Lillian Hawthorne, "Games Supervisors Play," *Social Work*, May 1975.

Stephen G. Kaplan and Eugenie G. Wheeler, "Survival Skills for Working
with Potentially Violent Clients," *Social Casework: The Journal of
Contemporary Social Work*, Vol. 64: 339–46, June 1983.

Naomi Golan, "When Is a Client In Crisis?" *Social Casework: The Journal
of Contemporary Social Work*, July 1969.

Charles S. Levy, "The Ethics of Supervision," *Social Work*, March 1973.

Kenneth W. Watson, "Differential Supervision," *Social Work*, November
1973.

Nancy Boyd Webb, "Developing Competent Clinical Practitioners: A
Model with Guidelines for Supervisors, *The Clinical Supervisor*, Vol.
1 (4), Winter 1983.

Richard W. Voss, A.C.S.W., M.T.S.

13

Family Counseling

I. Why Is Family Counseling
a "Special Issue" in Supervision?

First of all, the very fact that much of this book focuses upon supervisory issues related to individually-oriented psychotherapy and pastoral counseling makes it all the more critical to include a chapter on the supervisory issues which are unique to the supervision of family-oriented counseling services. Primarily because family-oriented counseling is a fundamentally different type of counseling intervention (Carroll, 1964, pp. 180–182; Minuchin, 1974, pp. 2–4), it stands to reason that family counseling will entail a different approach to supervision.

Unfortunately this difference is not universally recognized. Professionals who are committed to a "generic" foundation to supervision, i.e., that there are common elements of practice applicable in diverse situations, basically a "generalist" approach, will likely assume that the supervision of family counseling "is not much different" from the supervision of individually oriented counseling (Munson, 1980). There are basic limitations to this assumption which I hope to address in this chapter, and thereby help the reader avoid some of the pitfalls which may arise from applying or, perhaps, "misapplying" generic principles (which do function on a basic level, but do not reflect practical realities) in family-oriented modes of treatment, which is a unique field of supervisory practice, separate and distinct from individually-oriented modes of counseling supervision.

This chapter is aimed at providing a practical discussion of the supervisory issues pertaining to supervising family-oriented counseling. By way of disclaimer, this chapter is not intended to provide an authoritative or theoretical discussion of family counseling, its merits or demerits, advantages or disadvantages. While the field of family-oriented counseling and supervision is not without controversy and professional debate (see discussions by Berger and Dammann, 1982;

Constantine, et al., 1986, and Johnson, 1986), the reader is referred to the many experts in the field in order to familiarize himself or herself with these specific issues.

Additionally, for the reader who is unfamiliar with family-oriented counseling, *Handbook of Family Therapy*, edited by Alan S. Gurman and David P. Kniskern, 1981, is a helpful and comprehensive summary and overview of the field of family counseling. This work provides a good purview of the diversity of the field as well the common elements in the theory and practice of family counseling. The reader who is new to the field of family therapy (I use the terms "therapy" and "counseling" interchangeably) is encouraged to review the Handbook for an orientation to this exciting, challenging, and expanding field of professional counseling.

I think it is important to state that this chapter will be geared to the practicing supervisor in a general counseling center, social service agency or community mental health clinic where one encounters the day-to-day press of supervisees' needs for support, direction, and ongoing training, along with the press for the actual delivery of service. This chapter is not geared to the specialized training issues one may encounter in a family therapy training center. The reader is referred to an excellent article by Susan H. McDaniel, et al., entitled "Multiple Theoretical Approaches to Supervision: Choices in Family Therapy Training," which gives a thorough summary and clear comparison of the distinct supervisory approaches utilized by each of the major "schools" of family therapy, which for our purposes here are too specific.

I have selected some of the practice issues one is likely to encounter in supervising family counseling services in a general counseling setting, appreciative that these issues can never be reduced or contained in any single checklist. This chapter is my attempt to share experiences and insights which I have drawn from approximately eight years of supervising not only family counseling services, but individual and marital counseling as well. Having supervised the broad spectrum of counseling services within a social service family counseling agency, I do not intend to suggest that any one modality of counseling is "better" or "more effective" than another.

Family counseling is by no means a panacea or a "cure-all." It is a valuable treatment modality which, when used in a competent and selective manner, can enhance an agency's ability to intervene effectively and make a difference in a client's struggles. I believe it is a timely reminder that, while in the process of writing this chapter, I noticed Harriette C. Johnson's article entitled "Emerging Concerns in Family Therapy" in a recent copy of *Social Work*, and feel that this article provides a realistic sense of context and caution about our topic, so as to better approach this practice area with an accurate sense of balance and perspective. With these introductory comments completed we now turn to some of the "issues" of supervision in family-oriented counseling.

II. The Supervisor of Family Counseling Must Nurture a Profound Awareness of the Complexity of the Family-Client-System

Just as one approaches individual counseling with a profound awareness and sensitivity to the "mystery of the human person in all its complexity" (Estadt, 1983, p. 7), the counselor engaged in family-oriented counseling must nurture that profound sensitivity to the magnificent complexity of the client-system of the family, which has been described as one of the "most complex" of social groups (Simmel, 1964). Inasmuch as the supervisor of individual counseling is an ongoing and "objective" reference point of client dignity, I think that so too in family counseling must the supervisor be that "reference point of client-dignity" in the tremendously complex and often conflicted milieu of the family.

I am a firm believer in stating the obvious, and as such feel that anyone supervising family counseling services must appreciate and recognize that family counseling, as a distinct mode of counseling, is a complex form of treatment (Munson, 1980, p. 132). Not only does the process of family counseling involve the interaction of counselor with an individual client, but frequently family counseling involves the interaction of the counselor with a whole group of people, an entire family, comprising the "client system" meeting at the same time and within the same space.

Whether through actual physical presence of nuclear and extended family members, utilizing the method of conjoint interview, a practice employed by the Structural, Strategic and Experiential Schools of Family Therapy (Minuchin, Haley, Satir, and Whitaker) or through a thoughtful "re-membering" process, as I like to conceptualize it, where an individual client is approached from a family-context perspective, meeting with select and even individual family members, employed by Family-of-Origin and Contexual Schools of Family Therapy (Bowen, Nagy, and Framo), the focus of all these approaches is on the person-in-family-relationship and upon the "orchestrating" of this system to effect change. What is common to all of these approaches is that problems and people are viewed, not in social isolation, but in the inter-personal connectedness or dis-connectedness of the family system or family heritage.

While the movement and thrust of family counseling need not be antagonistic to the more individualized forms of psycho-social treatment approaches to counseling, it is, nonetheless, fundamentally different. Family counseling functions on a level of complexity which is incomparable with individual modes of counseling, and this heightened level of complexity will make special demands upon the counselor about which the supervisor must be acutely aware. While the family counselor takes a more active and directive role in the counseling process, the very complexity of the counseling setting places limitations on what the counselor may or may not do. There is a relinquishment of power in this form of therapy (Luthman, 1974, pp. 225–230), which increases levels of stress within the counselor. Anyone will recognize the difference in working with a client individually who "talks about" one's frustrations in dealing with "Johnny's temper tantrums," from working with a client-system, where Johnny is present and actively having a temper-tantrum with all the emotional reactions from other family members and counselor alike.

I feel that, perhaps more so than in any other type of supervision, the supervisor of family counseling services is involved in one of the most exciting, dynamic, and challenging activities a supervisor is likely to encounter, because the mode of treatment is so dynamic and complex. Both supervisor and counselor become active partners in a therapeutic alliance within a system which is constantly changing and interacting. Assessment and diagnosis becomes an ongoing process not only from session to session, but often from intervention to intervention—moment to moment. The supervisor finds himself or herself sustaining and supporting the counselor's interaction not only with one client, but also with two, three, four, five, six, and sometimes more clients in an oftentimes intensely conflicted family-client system.

Murray Bowen has conceptualized the interactional complexity in a fascinating illustration which I will cite, in part, in the accompanying chart. The chart (Bowen, 1971) reflects some of the objective and quantitative complexity of the family counseling interview which, I think, sets forth, by sheer statistics, the fundamental difference between family-oriented counseling and individually-oriented modes of therapy. Notice the escalating numbers of possible interactions which appear in the right-hand columns as additional client-members are added to the family-system. The interactions are viewed in relation to "Two-Way Interactions" between one family member and counselor and "Three-Way Interactions" between two family members and the counselor at any interaction. I think this illustration provides solid statistical evidence of the complexity with which the counselor must cope in providing family counseling.

Number of Clients	One Counselor	
	Two-Way Interaction	Three-Way Interaction
1	2	—
2	6	6
3	12	24
4	20	60
5	30	120
6	42	210
7	56	336

In addition to the statistical complexity of family counseling there are subjective elements which the above table does not show. The subjective elements intensify the complexity of the family-client-system, and include such variables as age differences, role expectations, sibling positions, and maturational crises which occur among individual family members.

So, the first critical issue in supervising family counseling is clearly the actual complexity with which the counselor is engaged, and which makes the supervision of family counseling vastly more complex than individually-oriented counseling supervision. To ignore or fail to appreciate the impact of the complex nature and unique demands which family counseling will make upon the counselor-supervisee sets the supervisory experience up for disaster, and as I have already discussed in my earlier chapter on supervising crisis intervention counseling, line staff who are engaged in highly stressful areas of practice report that supervision is likely to intensify their feeling of distress rather than help resolve it (Edelwich and Brodsky, 1980).

III. Burnout Prevention and Family Counseling

If, as a responsible supervisor, one is cognizant of the impact of distress generated in many "crisis" counseling situations on a one-to-one basis, how much more intense is the experience of distress when the counseling modality itself places the counselor within multiple and simultaneous "interacting" crises? Since, frequently, family counseling is initiated when one or more family members are in active and acute conflict with each other, the family counselor must be aware of his or her levels and reactions to the stress which will likely be an inherent part of providing family counseling. I think that the potential for burnout is all the more intensified for the counselor engaged in family counseling, and the supervisor must be attentive to this reality from the onset of the supervisory process.

Just as the crisis intervention counselor is required to make difficult "on the spot" decisions with his or her clients in a directive fashion, so too is the family counselor in the position of making difficult "on the spot" decisions which will affect all the members of the family-client-system. Not infrequently these decisions will be met with increased stress, as the family is faced with the possibility of change, which even if needed will be resisted in view of the family's push for *homeostasis* (Carroll). The family session is a key arena for crisis, and this places the counselor within the interplay and drama of multiple interacting crises within which the counselor plays an interacting role himself or herself. The hazard of burnout is ever-present.

Robert Friedman points out this danger in his article, "Making Family Therapy Easier for the Therapist: Burnout Prevention" (1985). In this article Friedman lists a number of practical "tools" which the family counselor can use to minimize the risk of burnout; I feel they are worth reviewing here with a little elaboration.

First of all, with the exceptions of such "extreme situations" as suicide, homicide, and child or spousal abuse, Friedman notes that ". . . the major responsibility for positive change rests with the family, not the therapist, and that the problem belongs to the family, not to the therapist" (p. 550). The counselor must accept the limitations of family counseling. Inasmuch as family counseling is not a panacea, neither is it a "cure-all" and the family counselor and supervisor must always keep their awareness clear that the counselor can accomplish only what the family system will allow him or her to accomplish in light of the family's need for *homeostasis*, a key principle in family dynamics (Carroll). While the family counselor can invite and even "provoke" change in a family-client, he or she cannot make the change happen. I think it is helpful for the family counselor to identify this reality with the family, placing the locus of responsibility for change with the family itself: "I don't know your family as well as you do. What do you think about Johnny's behavior?" Here the counselor defers assuming the role of outside "expert" and places the responsibility on the family members themselves.

The above example also illustrates another tool for the counselor, and that is defining one's role with one's family-client. While the family counselor is someone who is an "expert" in family counseling, this does not mean that he or she is an "expert" about *this* family. On the contrary, as an expert family counselor, he or she knows that the family-client members are their own family-experts, and will only share with the counselor what they choose to share. The counselor will never know more about them than they do of themselves, and this is a relief for anyone who struggles with the complexity inherent in family counseling. I usually point out to counselor-supervisees that any family has had a long history and experience together—"even longer" when one considers "inter-generational" perspectives, and the counselor will only be involved with the family for a relatively "brief" time. He or she will only know what the family-client shares in the counseling session—nothing more, nothing less. Such role clarification helps set realistic limits upon the counselor's expectations and helps to keep the "rescue operation" (Luthman, p. 226) in awareness.

Another important tool useful not only to prevent burnout, but also integral to family counseling intervention itself, is the counselor's open and honest sharing of one's feelings in a purposeful but still spontaneous manner (Luthman, 1974; Carroll, 1964). The counselor's use of self-disclosure accomplishes two functions; it is a reality check for the counselor's self-awareness, enabling him or her to be aware of one's stressful experience, and it can also be therapeutic in identifying and even "mirroring" feelings which may be shared by family members. For example, when the counselor shares: "I'm sitting here becoming more and more distracted and upset as Johnny continues his temper-tantrum (Johnny is screaming loudly and kicking an office chair against the desk), and I'm wondering if it's getting to you as much as it's getting to me," here the counselor is expressing his or her feelings in an open, honest, and even exploring way with the family and accomplishes two things: he or she identifies the real distress of the "live situation" which is occurring, and he or she invites a discussion of specific therapeutic issues at the same time: "I'll bet it's easy, at times, just to 'give in' to Johnny's demands when he does this behavior (?)." Other tools which Friedman suggests to prevent burnout include the use of humor, flexibility, and confrontation regarding counseling impasses. The only tool with which I would disagree is that of leaving the session to allow the family to work on their issues without the counselor. I feel that if a family has come to counseling, the least the counselor can do is "work with" them, and leave "homework assignments" for home, which I think is more responsible, considering that most clients are paying a fee for the counselor's presence.

So far I have discussed general issues of family counseling supervision which address basic assumptions about complexity and burnout. I would now like to address some of the more specific issues of supervising family counseling. I am sure my list is not exhaustive, but I have chosen those which seemed important from my experience in supervising family counseling.

IV. "Let's see how you're doing . . .":
Making a Case for Direct Observation
in Family Counseling Supervision

Even though, in most counseling agencies and centers, there is a press for appointment or clinic time, I believe there is a need to utilize some method of direct observation of family counseling sessions by the family counselor supervisor, whether this be through the use of video tape recording of select sessions, by live supervision "through the looking glass" of the one-way mirror, or by supervisor co-therapy. The very complexity of the family counseling modality makes it difficult for any one human being to attend to more than one client at a time, and taking into consideration the tremendously complex interactional schema discussed above, the value of "self-report" which is acceptable in individually oriented counseling is highly unreliable and inadequate when it comes to family counseling supervision.

I believe that counseling agencies need to make time for such a supervisory tool if they are to provide meaningful family counseling supervision. This does not need to be on a case-by-case basis, but should be done with select rotating family cases on a feasible supervisory schedule. For example, if one supervises a "mixed" group of counselors, including individual, marital, and family counselors, I would recommend bi-weekly group conferences with those counselors who are engaged in family counseling, whereby counselors take turns presenting a family tape for peer and supervisory critique. Ideally, one interviewing room can be set-up for family sessions minimizing the time spent on setting up technical equipment, etc. Such technical accommodations help everyone involved to recognize and appreciate the special nature of family-oriented treatment, the special demands made upon the counselor, and the overall therapeutic needs of the client-system, entrusted to the treatment system. There is nothing more destructive than a highly conflicted family meeting with a highly distressed and burned-out family counselor.

Agencies and counseling centers which provide family counseling must attend to the professional requirements of family counseling as well as the technical requirements of family counseling supervision, or else they need to consider whether or not they are willing to make a commitment to the provision of this specialized service area. While family counseling has been perceived as a highly "cost-effective" counseling alternative, in that a group of clients can be seen at the same time, it is not a "cheap" or inexpensive alternative. Any cost-cutting measures taken by counseling agencies should not cut adequate supervision, which I feel, necessitates providing the means for direct observation, on some basis, by supervisory personnel. Without such provision I think there is the temptation to perceive the supervision of family counseling as "no different from any other counseling supervision," a matter that was addressed at length above.

Aside from helping the counselor-supervisee cope with and manage the stress inherent in family interaction, another central reason for the need for direct observation of the counseling interview is that one aim of the family counselor is to "join" the family-client-system, becoming an interacting participant in the family counseling process (Minuchin and Fishman, 1971). The "joining" process enables the counselor to intervene with the family system effectively, and it also makes the counselor more vulnerable to getting "caught up" in the family dynamics himself or herself. Thus, the work of "joining" is an invaluable and essential task to be accomplished by the family counselor, but it also can entangle him or her in the process or web of complex interactions. Thus, the need for direct observation of what the counselor may need to know, but may not be in a position to perceive. This complex attending to multiple interactions makes video taping or other direct means of supervisory observation an essential element of supervision, and not a mere training "luxury" as some observers may view it. I would even go so far as to say that without such supervisory tools, it is impossible to supervise family counseling effectively. I would like to illustrate this point by a vivid and yet "ordinary" example from my own supervisory experience.

One of my supervisees who was engaged in "family-oriented" counseling with a middle-aged couple had expressed her frustration about the lack of progress in the case. The couple had come to counseling because of an intense and long-term family conflict regarding the wife's feelings of rejection by and alienation from her in-laws, exacerbated by her desire and need to be accepted emotionally as a "daughter" by them. The counselor had been voicing her increasing frustration about the impasse in the counseling, and was at the point of wondering whether or not she ought to terminate counseling. It was in response to this specific question and situation that I suggested to the apprehensive, but highly skilled counselor, that she video-tape a series of conjoint family (couple) sessions, as all previous supervisory material was reviewed indirectly through the counselor's self-report. Even though the thought of video-taping provoked a high level of anxiety in this counselor for the first time, both she and the clients agreed to the experience.

Even though we did not do "live" supervision which would require counselor and supervisor to be available at the same time and place, a considerable amount of coordination and planning was needed even in utilizing "delayed" or replay methods of taped material, requiring administrative support, patience, and coordination and cooperation with other staff, representing a significant commitment from a typically busy family counseling agency. After overcoming the innumerable and expected "technical problems" such as setting up and coordinating time, space, equipment, and personnel, the counselor taped a series of four counseling sessions which were then viewed at length in subsequent supervisory conferences which followed a few days after the actual counseling session.

As I reviewed the first tape, it became obvious that the counselor had "joined" this family system of the couple. Both spouses interacted spontaneously with the counselor, and she with them. What came into clear focus was that in the "joining" process, the counselor had, in fact, become "aligned" with the husband, in an oppositional stance against the wife. The counselor was not aware of this "alignment," and to the extent that she was unaware, she did not attend to the wife's alienation and loneliness which seemed to make up the threads of most of her interactions with him (and the counselor alike). As this interactional pattern persisted through the interview I became aware of how the wife's manner seemed to draw the same response from the counselor as she elicited from her spouse (and probably from his family as well). The counselor was responding experientially to the same dynamics which were keeping the client in the predicament she so desperately wanted to change. Rather than engage her husband in a positive "affectionate" interchange, the wife evoked a "lecturing" attitude from her husband. The more the husband assumed this lecturing posture, the less his wife seemed to listen to him, continuing the pleas for acceptance and understanding, focusing upon the in-laws. The two were locked in seemingly endless arguing. So maddening was the arguing that the counselor gradually began to side with the husband's reasonableness, in an effort to move the couple off center. However, in doing so, the counselor, in experiencing the same frustration as the husband, failed to perceive the wife's unsuccessful attempts and growing hopelessness to gain an affectionate response from her husband. It was no wonder that counseling had reached an impasse. The counselor's self-reporting on the counseling process did not include nor did it focus upon the wife's issues. The counselor was caught up in the "madness" of this family (sub)system.

What the counselor failed to perceive about her alignment with the husband's pleas for reason to his wife was clearly recorded in black and white on the video tape. A progressively derisive tone was noticed in the husband's voice, and while he began on a "reasonable" train of thought, the "reasoning" gradually took on a condescending and ridiculing quality. The content of what the husband said continued with the original benign rationale, but the feeling level had changed dramatically. While this went unnoticed by the counselor, the wife had picked up on this ever so quickly and sensitively. More and more this mismatched feeling-interaction became the primary issue, but, tied in with the husband in his growing frustration, the counselor missed it.

It was not until the tape was replayed three or four times, focusing upon the counselor's body language, eye contact with the husband, and "lecturing" style which she had herself assumed toward the wife, that the counselor was able to "see" what I was perceiving as a more neutral observer. The counselor had, in fact, gotten caught up in the alignment she shared with the husband and family system on the whole (as she experienced the negativity the wife spontaneously evoked in others), and lost sight of the wife's perceptions and needs. It was only through a careful examination of the video tape that the interactional pattern was observed and confirmed by the counselor's own experience of it herself. As an experiential participant in this family system comprised not only of the husband and wife in the interviewing room but also the in-laws (who lived out-of-state, but nonetheless were very close to the dynamics of this family) the counselor needed the objectivity which was available through supervision by the direct observation of her video tape. This supervisory tool enabled the counselor to "step back" from her experience of the interactional family pattern and "see" the larger interactional picture.

Transcending verbal content, and replaying select portions of the tape, frame by frame, we were, together, able to "see the forest" and "the trees." The family counselor has to do both as he or she attends to the entire system and to each interacting part of the system. This example illustrated some of the complexity of working with just two family members, the spousal subsystem, in relationship to both itself and to the extended family, the in-laws. The complexity intensifies as numbers and subsystems are increased. If the method of direct observation was critical in this limited subsystem, how much more important (and essential) it is in working with larger family groups! Direct observation is the supervisor's most reliable and valuable tool whether through video-taping, live supervision, or co-therapy sessions with the supervisee, and the supervisor ought not underestimate the need for, at least, periodic and selective use of this tool in his or her supervision of family counseling. I say this with a deep awareness of the pressures which discourage the practice of direct observation, because of time and fiscal constraints which push for increasing direct service as well as the added pressure of coordinating and planning around the practical and technical obstacles one is likely to encounter. There is also the understandable resistance of the counselor-supervisee who must "risk" self in the process of self-learning.

I believe that there is pressure to "short-change" supervision, and that this is not likely to disappear as fiscal restraints become even more stringent. Quantity versus quality is an unacceptable standard in determining supervisory method, especially when one considers the need for direct observation in the supervision of family counseling. While family counseling has been described as an "economical" and cost-effective method of treatment (Carroll), it is not a "cheap" alternative to see more clients faster, quicker, sooner.

I would like to include a word of encouragement to any supervisor considering the use of direct observation in his or her practice, and also a word of caution. In order for it to be a productive and growth-enhancing experience for both supervisor and counselor alike, the supervisor needs to set the stage for a non-threatening, albeit exciting and challenging learning experience. To this end I would not recommend that the taping be used as an "evaluative" instrument as such, but utilized within the trusting and supportive supervisory relationship. My experience of this supervisory tool has been that if the counselor-supervisee is accepting and trusting ("comfortable" is not completely accurate), then the clients are apt to be more accepting of it too. The very use of any of the tools of direct observation gives immediate credence and communicates a genuine recognition that family therapy is complex work, and helps the supervisor assure the highest quality of service possible.

Rather than feel overly threatened by the experience, most clients feel that they are receiving "specialized" treatment when involved in direct observation family treatment. Often I have found that "actions speak louder than words," and clients seem to take it to heart that not only is the counselor involved in the helping process, but the supervisor as well. I think clients are assured that "even if my counselor misses something, it can be picked up by the supervisor." Usually it is only the highly paranoid client or a client who may be in litigation that will refuse to be taped, in which case the client's wishes are to be respected. Of course, authorization to video-tape the family counseling session should be obtained in writing by the client's parents or legal guardians before beginning the taping of sessions. This authorization should be in writing and clearly explain that the tape will be used for "professional purposes" and that confidentiality will be maintained and the tape erased within a mutually agreed-upon period of time. Specific questions can be addressed with the family at the time of the first interview, unless there is reason to defer to a later time.

V. The Art of Giving and Receiving Criticism

So far we have examined the complexity and the need for carefully and caringly observing the complexity of family counseling and the work of the family counselor. While I feel that the supervisor must exercise caution and care, and not emphasize the evaluative function in direct observation supervision, the level of human activity and spontaneous interaction which are part and parcel of family counseling open the path for ongoing critique.

The supervisor must help the counselor learn how to deal with criticism in a constructive, non-defensive and non-destructive way. The best way to do this, I feel, is to let the counselor know that criticism will be an ongoing part of the supervisory process, not as an indication of defect or inadequacy on the part of the counselor, but because of the complex nature of the family counseling process itself. Since I believe that the supervisor of family counseling can utilize all the tools he or she may have at one's disposal, I found Carlton E. Munson's "Guidelines for Dealing with Criticism" in his article "Supervising the Family Therapist" (1980) potentially helpful to review with one's supervisees. These Guidelines may be helpful, not as rigid rules to follow, but as thoughts to consider by supervisor and supervisee alike in entering more fully into the supervisory process. These Guidelines should be used as a tool to stimulate and enhance open and honest supervisory discussion, "giving permission" to open up topics rather than "close them down." I quote Munson at length:

1. Listen to the criticism in detail. Do not rush to defend yourself or your position.
2. Evaluate the validity of the criticism in your own mind. If the criticism is fair, formulate ways in your own mind that you could change your performance.
3. Try to gain more understanding through asking for more detailed information about the criticism. If the criticism is very general, as it often is, ask the supervisor to be more specific. Ask how the activity could have been done differently or better.
4. Do not imply that the supervisor has some personal motive. Keep the criticism on a professional level and always relate it to professional performance.
5. Do not get angry with the supervisor and lose self-control. This accomplishes nothing.
6. Do not shift the responsibility to someone else.
7. Do not attribute the criticism to personal weakness and do not present yourself as a total failure in all areas.
8. Do not shift off the criticism by expressing that you cannot deal with negative comments.

9. Do not change the subject to avoid any direct discussion of the criticism.

10. Do not repeatedly admit that you were wrong, and do not continually question the supervisor as to what you can do to make up for the criticism.

11. Do not focus the conversation on a discussion of justifications and excuses for what you did.

12. Do not shift responsibility onto the supervisor by saying that the supervisor is over-reacting or is just looking for something to criticize.

13. Do not turn the criticism into a joke or verbal one-up-manship.

14. Clarify for yourself, or ask the supervisor, how your behavior was inadequate. If the supervisor cannot offer an explanation, then you must assess whether the criticism is valid.

15. Regardless of whether you accept or question the criticism, let the supervisor know you heard and understood the criticism.

16. If you accept the criticism, acknowledge it, and offer an alternative for the future or ask your supervisor for possible alternative behavior.

17. Remember that criticism is not a threat to you personally or professionally. It is a way of gaining new information about different and perhaps better ways of performing (p. 134).

Both the supervisor and counselor-supervisee must understand from the onset of supervision that they are part of a unique helping alliance, which especially in the case of family counseling supervision is extremely complex. Both must understand that neither the counselor nor the supervisor "can go it alone" and that they will need to rely on each other's openness to the learning and therapeutic process with their client(s). They will examine the treatment process carefully and thoroughly, deeply aware and profoundly respectful of client needs within the family system—which will never be fully comprehended.

VI. Conclusion: A Baptismal Context for Family Counseling Supervision

The pastoral counselor who provides family-oriented counseling may frequently experience himself or herself "plunging" into the unknown waters of the living family with an "immediacy" unequaled in many modes of individual counseling. If a particular conflict between mother and daughter, for example, is the focus of the counseling session, it will, most likely, play itself out "right before the counselor's very eyes." He or she can easily be immersed in the unique human/family situation in the "here and now." The intensity of this experience can be extremely unsettling and "nerve racking" for the counselor, who frequently must let go of pre-conceived notions and ideas in order to experience "what it is like to be in this family, at this time." This experience can be very frightening. The counselor cannot assume a detached stance; no, here he or she "plunges into" the family experience and, while he or she is part of the changing process, is himself or herself transformed in the experience of becoming an interacting participant. I believe that it is this unique process inherent in family counseling which carries with it profound "baptismal" implications, for it is only in the action and activity of "joining" the family system, with all its hurts, pains, and distortions, which is a real dying to pre-conceived notions of what family life "should be" or "should not be," that the family counselor can then invite the family to discover new modes of living.

In the therapeutic activities of joining, detaching, aligning, stepping back, listening, challenging, confronting and consolidating, family counseling may be viewed as a deeply baptismal ministry. It involves a certain faith commitment to enter into a new and frightening experience, often fraught with destructive conflicts and twisted distortions, to allow oneself to be immersed into a family experience and then be open to be drawn back through the supervisory process to explore avenues of change and new patterns of living, profoundly aware that while the counselor can invite or prompt change, the power for change resides in the family system itself.

In many ways the pastoral counselor who provides family-oriented counseling has a unique perspective from which to meditate upon a disturbing yet fascinating Gospel paradox from Luke 12:49–53:

> Do you think that I have come to give peace on earth? No, I tell you, but rather division; for henceforth in one house there will be five divided, three against two and two against three; they will be divided, father against son and son against father, mother against daughter and daughter against her mother, mother-in-law against her daughter-in-law and daughter-in-law against her mother-in-law.

Here, Jesus validates the place of conflict in the baptismal ministry; conflict is not something that one necessarily seeks to avoid "at all cost" (Stuhlmueller, 1968, p. 146). Conflict can be a transforming reality which leads to a new mode of life, to a new way of seeing oneself—even in relationship to one's family members.

Conflict is an inescapable part of baptismal reality, not the exception. At times the family counselor will be the one not "to bring peace" but to prompt divisions and conflict by which change and family transformations may occur. It is from this point of reference that we can perceive the family counselor and supervisor as charged with the tasks of stimulating, inviting, challenging and encouraging clients to face their own baptismal dying experience.

As supervisors we provide the support for the counselor and the family to penetrate their family problems, suffering, and upsetness with a sense of hope that through this dying to self, to dysfunctional patterns of living, new forms of life and family living may be discovered.

References

Michael Berger and Carrell Dammann, "Live Supervision as Context, Treatment, and Training," in *Family Process*, Vol. 21, Sept. 1982, pp. 337–344.

Murray Bowen, "The Use of Family Theory in Clinical Practice," in *Changing Families: A Family Therapy Reader*, ed. Jay Haley (New York: Grune and Stratton, 1971), pp. 163–71.

John A. Constantine, Fred P. Piercy, and Douglas H. Sprenkle, "Live Supervision-of-Supervision in Family Therapy," in *Journal of Marital and Family Therapy*, Vol. 10 (1), 1983.

Edward Carroll, "Family Therapy—Some Observations," in *Family Process*, March 1964, pp. 180–182.

Barry K. Estadt, ed., "Profile of a Pastoral Counselor," in *Pastoral Counseling* (Englewood Cliffs: Prentice-Hall, 1983).

David L. Fenell, Alan J. Hovestadt, and Samuel J. Harvey, "A Comparison of Delayed Feedback and Live Supervision Models of Marriage and Family Therapist Clinical Training," in *Journal of Marital and Family Therapy*, Vol. 12 (2), 1986.

Robert Friedman, "Making Family Therapy Easier for the Therapist: Burnout Prevention," *Family Process*, Vol. 24, 1985.

Alan S. Gurman and David P. Kniskern, eds., *Handbook of Family Therapy* (New York: Brunner/Mazel, 1981).

Harriette C. Johnson, "Emerging Concerns in Family Counseling," in *Social Work*, Vol. 31 (4), July-August 1986, pp. 299–306.

Shirley G. Luthman and Martin Kirschenbaum, *The Dynamic Family* (Palo Alto, Cal.: Science and Behavior Books, Inc.) 1978.

Susan H. McDaniel, Timothy Weber, and James McKeever, "Multiple Theoretical Approaches to Supervision: Choices in Family Therapy Training," in *Family Process*, Vol. 22, 1983.

Salvador Minuchin, *Families and Family Therapy* (Cambridge: Harvard University Press, 1974).

Salvador Minuchin and Charles Fishman, *Family Therapy Techniques* (Cambridge: Harvard University Press, 1971).

Carlton E. Munson, "Supervising the Family Therapist," *Social Casework*, Vol. 61 (3), March 1980.

Vernon C. Rickert and John E. Turner, "Through the Looking Glass: Supervision in Family Therapy," in *Social Casework*, Vol. 59, March 1978.

G. Simmel, *Conflict and the Web of Group-Affiliation* (London: Macmillan, 1964).

Joseph W. Ciarrocchi, Ph.D.

14

Addiction Counseling

Pastoral counselors frequently work with clients experiencing addiction problems. To give a single illustration, studies suggest that at least one patient in three on medical-surgical units in general hospitals are there due to an alcohol-related medical problem. A hospital chaplain, by implication, sees addicted persons continuously whether he or she is either interested or skilled in dealing with this particular client population. Supervisors of pastoral counselors cannot expect to be experts in all phases of addiction without specialized training, and indeed few clinicians anywhere have expertise in treating all addictions. Nevertheless the field of addiction treatment has reached a point where general principles and effective strategies are available. This chapter will focus on those disorders which are generally labeled as substance abuse disorders, namely problems associated with inappropriate alcohol and/or drug use. Disorders such as eating disorders, compulsive gambling, and tobacco dependence are excluded. The focus of this chapter is directed toward the generalist supervisor rather than the specialist in addictions, although the specialist may find the points addressed here to be useful. The chapter will also be limited to a discussion of the more common situations likely to be encountered in supervision. Numerous resources exist for those interested in further specialization (e.g. Royce, 1981). Accordingly, this chapter will be divided into three sections. The first section briefly discusses some shifts in the counseling model which are necessary to accommodate the needs of the specialized population. The second section deals with counselor issues such as required competency, technical knowledge, and emotional maturity essential in the process of counseling substance abusers. Finally, the remaining section elaborates upon the various practical issues which ordinarily occur when counseling addicted clients and will suggest strategies for the supervisor.

I. Expanding the Counseling Model

Standard counseling models (e.g. Egan, 1975), without a doubt, are prerequisites for helping clients with addictions. One of the more common fallacies involved in the field of addictions is the notion that treating addicted persons demands harsh, confrontative methods, and that unless one engages in therapy by insult the addicted person will not recover. Well-meaning but unskilled counselors often drive clients away from accepting treatment because of too early confrontation, and then justify the outcome on the basis of the client's "denial." While it is true that some small percentage of addicts may respond to strong confrontation, addicted persons do not fall into any one personality category and, therefore, no single approach works for everyone. Relationship building is as important with an alcoholic as it is with a depressed person, and the basic building blocks of counseling such as communicating primary empathy and positive regard are also essential (cf. Chapter 2).

Nevertheless, there are also important differences in counseling addicted persons which necessitate adapting the standard model to fit the client's needs. Many of these differences revolve around the disease model of addictions. Most addiction specialists view chemical dependency as chronic, progressive illness which, though treatable, is never cured. The treatment consists of maintaining abstinence from the addicting substance. Unless abstinence is achieved, deterioration is expected. While a disease model is not inherently antithetical to a humanistic counseling model (for example, counseling terminally ill patients), some strain is notable. Humanistic counseling models avoid labeling and diagnosis whenever possible in the view that categorizing the illness results in losing the person's individuality and uniqueness. In treating the addicted person it is paradoxical how frequently the disease model is experienced as liberating. From the wellsprings of confusion, intense self-recrimination, destroyed relationships, and shattered health, the client gradually discovers hope once the demon inside is named. Despite the utility of such a model the pastoral counselor is hesitant to try a therapeutic style with which he or she has had little experience.

A second conflict with traditional models revolves around the futility of insight-oriented therapies in treating most addictive disorders. These therapies have been utilized for more than a half century in the attempt to treat addictions, and by and large have resulted in failure, as recorded in the one empirical laboratory available to us, namely human experience. Many clients have attempted insight-oriented treatment, and although they develop much self-knowledge they also continue to drink or use drugs. In short, insight alone appears to have little value in influencing long term recovery.

This latter observation leads to the final and probably most salient conflict, namely the necessity of an active and directive role for the counselor. Standard client-centered counseling models acknowledge the importance of problem solving during counseling. Taking such an active role is often also the case in addiction counseling with one important difference—proper timing. In addiction counseling the counselor takes an active and directive role much earlier in the relationship. In this respect addiction counseling is similar to crisis intervention (cf. Chapter 14), also requiring a more directive counseling style.

My own supervisory experience suggests that it is beneficial to explore these model issues early in the supervisory process. Counselors come to us from such disparate theoretical backgrounds that it is unwise to assume a counselor's theoretical stance toward treating addictions. The learning process for a counselor to become proficient with a wider range of clients involves considerable risk-taking while under supervision. This may be conceptualized as the counselor becoming desensitized to attempting counseling styles different from his or her customary one. The supervisor can facilitate the process by discussing these issues at the level of theoretical models, rather than simply making technical comments on the unfolding counseling process. Counselors are more open at this level since it provides them a framework to conceptualize the application of new skills.

II. Counselor Issues

A. *Countertransference*

While countertransference issues are present in all counseling and supervisory relationships, it may be that dealing with addictions ranks among the most emotionally charged. It is a truism that negative cultural attitudes toward problems such as alcoholism have impeded its proper diagnosis and treatment. Although it is beyond the scope of this chapter to explore the many historical antecedents of these attitudes, it is certainly wise to examine the concrete effects this history may have on the individual counselor at the preconscious level. Several lines of negative attitudes are likely to converge on the counselor which may require the supervisor's help in identifying their impact on the counseling relationship.

First, negative feelings can easily arise out of the counselor's personal history with addictive disorders. Probably the most common source is chemical dependency in the counselor's own family. Failure to have worked through a parent's alcoholism, for example, will reduce the counselor's objectivity and clinical acumen. One common mistake is overidentification with the non-alcoholic spouse which leads the counselor to advise marital separation before therapeutic strategies are even attempted. In this case, the counselor may be acting out his or her aggressive feelings toward the addicted client. A consensus is emerging that persons raised by family members with chemical dependency may be predisposed to demonstrate certain psychological patterns in adulthood. Some specialists who work with adult children of alcoholics, for example, believe that clearly identifiable personality patterns emerge in these adults (Black, 1981). A counselor who has been raised in such a family may need to be informed non-judgmentally that there is increasing study of the developmental effects arising from such circumstances, and could be invited to become familiar with these studies. It would be wise to point out that these studies, to date, are clinical impressions and await research validation. Further, from an ethical point of view, the supervisor may want to alert counselors that exploring these areas may generate personal issues, and the counselor may wish to decide if this is the optimal moment for such exploration, and supportive resources may be pointed out to handle any fallout (for example, personal therapy). Nevertheless, counselors with chemical dependency in their family background along with supervisors need to be alert to the likely countertransference issues generated by such circumstances. A special but not uncommon case occurs when the counselor himself or herself is in recovery from chemical dependency. These individuals face unique countertransference issues. Some may feel propelled evangelistically to convert the ignorant, and this fervor frequently leads to overdiagnosing the addiction, thereby leading the counselor into needless confrontation with clients. At other times the effect is for the counselor to focus on his or her own addiction history and to project inappropriately onto the clients what worked for him or her. One likely attitude may be, "My road to recovery was harsh, and so should be the client's". Such approaches lack objectivity, and while it is true that the counselor in recovery brings a personal, lived experience about addiction, this knowledge alone is no guarantee that it will be applied strategically.

Negative feelings toward clients may also arise out of adherence to a moral model of addictive behavior. This may be particularly problematic for counselors whose religious traditions proscribe even social use of alcohol and drugs. When faced with addicted clients the counselor must be able to shift from a moral model which prohibits these behaviors to a disease model which views the *addicted person* as one suffering from an illness, the source of which has not been willful. While this shift is not a difficult one cognitively, resolving the issue at the emotional level requires careful self-monitoring. Developing a non-judgmental stance is a task for all counselors. Yet the conflict is most real when the counselor's religious tradition sees the person's behavior in moral terms while the behavioral sciences approach it as an illness. The theological model of forgiveness and redemption which pastoral counselors utilize effectively with the repentant is likely to intensify denial in addicted persons since they already view themselves as morally outcast. The supervisors task is to allow the counselor to explore these conflicts and thereby integrate a theological-moral understanding of human nature with the disease model of chemical dependency which, when acknowledged by the client, is the first step in his or her ultimate recovery.

Finally, some counselors bring a bias toward addictions in viewing them simply as the expression of an antisocial personality disorder. Since many professionals view the antisocial personality as not amenable to change via traditional counseling methods, such a view generally renders the counseling process impotent. While it is true that a subgroup of substance abusers are antisocial, the overwhelming majority of persons diagnosed as chemically dependent arc not. The supervisor may be helpful in assisting the counselor to apply the diagnosis in a rigorous fashion in accord with the strict criteria of the *Diagnostic and Statistical Manual of Mental Disorders* (DSM-III 1981), rather than using the label in a generic, imprecise way to describe anyone who has ever had legal involvement. Sometimes it is used imprecisely to describe anyone the counselor deems "manipulative." In applying the criteria strictly the supervisor will also instruct the counselor to distinguish when possible between antisocial acts which are a consequence of the chemical dependency and those which operate independently. Lying, stealing, cheating, using people, and being irresponsible are common to many alcoholics and drug addicts, but for the overwhelming majority who attain recovery these behaviors cease.

On a final note, it is conceivable that many of the issues described in this section as counselor issues may also belong to the supervisor as well. In this case the supervisor needs to be aware of how such issues will influence the supervisory process particularly with regard to attitudes the supervisor conveys about addicted clients. This would be a classic example of parallel process, an issue which is explored in depth elsewhere (cf. Chapter 8).

B. Practical Issues and Strategies

In the preceding pages, I have attempted to deal primarily with counselor issues related to the areas of self-knowledge and countertransference which are most likely to arise when working with addicted patients and the role of the supervisor in facilitating this process. This section focuses on issues directly related to working with the individual addicted client and how the supervisor may guide the counselor in attaining the necessary skills in assessing addictive disorders, developing effective intervention strategies, and mobilizing appropriate environmental supports for the recovery phase.

1. *The Setting*. For some time I have supervised counselors in addictions from a wide variety of professional backgrounds, including pastoral counselors, psychologists, social workers, alcohol and drug counselors, and I have become increasingly impressed with the importance of the counseling setting or environment. I am not referring here to office space or furniture, but to the type of agency, the amount of staff resources available, and the circumstances of client referral. In counseling the chemically dependent these conditions are paramount, perhaps to a greater degree than most other disorders. I have become sensitized to this fact primarily by listening to counselors who relate negative experiences with the chemically dependent. I have heard a number of counselors with excellent skills state that they would "never work with addicts again." In each case I feel that the discouragement these students experience has less to do with their own competency or the intractable nature of the disorder and more with the circumstances of their field placements. In short, given the nature of the disorder many counseling experiences with addicts are set-ups for failure. To hear counselors relate their discouragement is particularly disheartening to one who has derived an immense amount of professional and personal satisfaction from participating therapeutically in many clients' recovery from chemical dependency.

Yet it appears that these students have a point. To counsel addicts in an outpatient setting when there is no "clout," i.e. when there are no real consequences for failure to recover such as legal sanctions, marital dissolutions, or job discipline, is in many instances simply whistling in the dark. Very few chemically dependent persons have such inner controls that they will spontaneously seek and remain committed to treatment. Also, to work with the chemically dependent in the early stages of recovery and not have access to alcohol and/or drug screening often ensures failure. Years of treatment experience with addicted individuals demonstrates the necessity of environmental sanctions for failure to comply with treatment recommendations, along with the availability of objective methods for evaluating such compliance. Failure to provide such a structure does more than simply waste counselors' time, for it reinforces manipulativeness and grandiosity which are hallmarks of the disorder. The counselor who initially approaches his or her task with enthusiasm gradually comes to understand the structure he or she works within and senses the impossibility of meaningful client change. The student translates this experience into the "fact" that such clients cannot be helped or at least not helped by this student.

2. *Pre-Counseling.* A second difficulty arises when either due to the counseling setting as described above or due to the client's denial it becomes evident to all concerned that the client will not or cannot recover. It may be profitable to use a term analogously which was popular a number of years ago in religious education, namely pre-catechesis. This referred to situations in which cultural circumstances were so alien to religious meaning (e.g. extreme deprivation, severe barriers of language/custom) that direct preaching of the Word would be ineffectual, and that ministry involved more generic "doing of good deeds" which might thereby generate receptivity to the spoken Word. Something analogous takes place in addiction counseling. When recovery appears futile there is still the potential for the counselor to experience this as a learning opportunity. For such conditions I have coined the expression "pre-counseling" wherein the counselor is preparing the ground, so to speak, for when and if the seed is planted. If the chemically dependent individual is actively drinking and/ or using drugs the counselor may engage in pre-counseling and still develop skills. For example, refusing to see clients who are obviously under the influence is necessary, for it states to the client, "No work is possible under such circumstances, and I will not be victimized by this disease as you are." Pre-counseling also provides excellent opportunities for counselors to develop appropriate confrontation skills. The counselor has the chance to point out to the client as often as necessary the real life consequences of his or her ongoing addiction. Statements such as "I know I must be sounding like a broken record, but your relationship with your wife cannot possibly improve as long as you're drinking" will in time desensitize counselors to the fear of a beginning therapist that a client will somehow break if faced with the truth directly. Further, if the counselor adapts his or her own expectation to pre-counseling situations, greater growth is possible. One can learn such important lessons as one's own powerlessness over the disease, the influence of larger social networks and bureaucracies upon the therapeutic tasks of individual clients, and the necessity of in-

volving the client's significant others in the counseling endeavor, as well as the adequacy of a disease model of addiction.

The supervisor can greatly facilitate the counselor's growth under such circumstances. Beginning counselors are often trapped by a results-oriented mentality which is antithetical to the counseling relationship, and paradoxically generates poor results. The supervisor, by focusing the counselor's energy on the process variables of attending, exploring and personalizing, will greatly assist the counselor in giving up the desire to control the outcome. Substance abuse perhaps more than any single problem demands from the counselor the emotional stance of letting go. Yet the stance once taken frees the counselor to develop genuine relationship building skills and to assess their effect on the client's problem. Relationship building is generally not difficult with substance abusers. Aside from those who are antisocial, many are intelligent, interesting and insightful. The supervisor can provide valuable guidance for the counselor who will learn that, despite the counselor's technical competence and the client's insight, change may still not occur. This is difficult to assimilate at any level of counseling experience, yet it is best learned when receiving supportive supervision. The concept of pre-counseling permits supervisor and counselor to establish suitable goals for counselor growth even when the circumstances for helping the chemically dependent are less than ideal.

III. Supervisor-Counselor Issues

This final section explores the role of the supervisor in facilitating development of counselor skills in the theory and application of the *structure* of addiction counseling. This refers to developing an understanding of the various stages in the treatment of chemical dependency as well as guidelines for the minimal environmental supports without which healing rarely occurs.

A. *Assessment.* Assessment of a drug or alcohol problem is quite obviously the foundation of addiction counseling. Nevertheless, this statement is not merely a truism. An early task for the supervisor is evaluation of the counselors' assessment skills; if they are faulty the entire counseling endeavor goes awry. In teaching psychopathology to graduate students I like to say that every client, even those presenting complaints about an ingrown toenail, should be assessed in the two areas of substance abuse and suicidal ideation. Beginning counselors tend to ignore both subjects and supervisors often need to guide counselors into assessing those topics. Substance abuse problems are often ignored in the context of many pastoral counseling settings. One such setting noted at the beginning of this chapter is the general hospital. If the chaplain fails to inquire about alcohol abuse when his or her patients have liver disease, the chaplain may be missing an opportunity to give hope to the person who has just "bottomed out" due to alcoholism. The only way to uncover such problems is to have a high suspicion index regarding substance abuse and the frequency of its occurrence. Similarly, marital counselors who fail to assess substance abuse travel at their own risk since much energy can be wasted on treating the symptoms of marital discord instead of its underlying cause.

A common mistake is to believe that assessment takes place in the first few interviews while in reality assessment is a continuous process through-out therapy. Denial may cloud the substance abuse picture during early sessions, so the supervisor keeps alert to behavior patterns which signal high risk situations for substance abuse problems. These include such cir-cumstances as chronic physical problems, severe marital and/or family dis-cord, those presenting with a history of physical or sexual abuse, legal problems in general with assault and drunk driving charges in particular, employment difficulties and school problems. The presence of any of these problems increases the probability that substance abuse exists and often their true scope is perceived only gradually during counseling. This re-quires ongoing assessment as new clinical data become available.

The assessment process itself assumes some knowledge of the criteria for chemical dependency and familiarity with basic concepts such as tol-erance, dependence, addiction and general diagnostic criteria for the sub-stance abuse disorders classified in the *Diagnostic and Statistical Manual* (1987, Third Edition, Revised) of the American Psychiatric Association. Spelling out these criteria are beyond the limits of this chapter, but sources are readily available (Ciarrocchi, 1984; Cohen, 1981; Milam 1981). From the supervisor's standpoint the most difficult aspect is feeling com-fortable with the counselor's assessment. As a supervisor I am often uneasy about the adequacy of the counselors' evaluation and in such cases suggest areas for further inquiry. Listening to session tapes can validate one's impressions, since counselors, particularly in the early phases of training, are often hesitant to question clients directly. The supervisor may have to model assessment approaches which gather the necessary information yet remain respectful of the client's disclosure level.

Another issue relevant to the assessment of chemical dependency is the question of dual diagnosis. Since a significant number of chemically dependent individuals have accompanying mental disorders (Mirin, 1984), supervisors need to be alert to ongoing assessment of psychopathology. This is a difficult task in any event since active substance abuse mimics a wide variety of symptoms such as anxiety, depression and characterolog-ical disorders. Only when the substance abuse ceases can one be more confident about an additional diagnosis. Nevertheless, intense symptoms such as suicidal ideation, psychotic thought processes, and violent behavior certainly warrant full professional evaluation whatever the current substance abuse status.

B. *Intervention*. Intervention is a term used technically in the substance abuse field to refer to a formal process wherein a consulting professional and/or significant others confront the chemically dependent person in such a manner as to maximize his or her acceptance of the need for treatment. This process has been formalized and guidelines have been established (Johnson, 1980). Briefly, data regarding the effects of the client's substance abuse are gathered systematically and presented, often in a group setting, along with a recommendation for treatment. Intervention in this formal sense is too complex in most cases to trust to a beginning counselor, so it would be best for the supervisor to steer the counselor away from attempting this unless the field placement is in a substance abuse treatment program with resource personnel who can assist in planning the intervention. In most cases intervention will refer mainly to the process of the counselor conveying his or her assessement as to the extent of the client's substance abuse problem along with treatment recommendations.

Perhaps few behavior problems lend themselves more to mobilizing large social networks to best achieve success. Significant others frequently need to be involved for the counselor to (a) assess the scope of the problem accurately and without the prejudice of the client's denial and (b) insure some hope of compliance with the treatment recommendations. Family members with first-hand knowledge of the frequency of substance abuse and its effects must often be present in the early phases of assessment and intervention. So too, employers may be needed to spell out both the effects of the substance abuse on job performance and to confront the client with the reality of job loss with continued deterioration. In most programs counselors spend the majority of training developing skills in one-to-one or group counseling methods. Little time is spent focusing on organizing broader social networks to achieve therapeutic goals for clients, yet this is a crucial skill for addiction counseling. In my experience the supervisor becomes especially helpful in this stage from both the practical and the theoretical standpoint. Counselors have difficulty negotiating the demands of maintaining the client's confidence while at the same time enlisting the support of persons interested in the client's welfare. Counselors often feel bewildered by the potential conflicts here and find it much easier to simply ignore these social networks. The supervisor's task will be to suggest practical strategies for obtaining help from significant others and to help the counselor understand the theoretical importance of such strategies. Ignoring social networks simply plays into the client's denial system and sabotages the counselor's attempt to assess accurately or achieve effective intervention.

Supervisors may be helpful in alerting this counselor to the philosophy of substance abuse intervention which is based on the premise that few chemically dependent persons initiate treatment for substance abuse and that some type of pressure is often necessary. This philosophy often conflicts with existential-humanistic models which many counselors adhere to. Alerted in this fashion, counselors will not feel as tentative and awkward about stepping out of their customary role in assuming more directive ones. Furthermore, good intervention like good interpretation is often unaccepted by clients. Supervisors will support counselors with their sense of failure, frustration and at times intense anger at their own lack of success. The lesson taught in Al-Anon is also useful for any of us engaged professionally with substance abusers, namely we are as powerless over the disease just as surely as the alcoholic or drug addict himself or herself.

C. *Relapse.* Addiction counselors face several types of relapse, and counselors would do well to acknowledge the distinctions and not react similarly in each case. The first pattern represents relapse after only brief abstinence. In this instance it is doubtful whether one can even speak of recovery having taken place, but rather the brief abstinence from substance abuse is more a prelude to recovery rather than its commencement. The supervisor's concern here is to help counselors maintain perspective on such events, seeing the necessity of maintaining the tight social networks in intervention systems that were employed originally to obtain the client's commitment to treatment. Some therapists will develop contractual arrangements with clients which permit severe negative consequences for repeated use or drinking. For example, clients may agree to permit counselors to contact employers or legal authorities such as parole or probation officers should drinking or drug use resume. For many pastoral counselors such measures may appear extreme and the harshness of such effects need to be balanced by a considerate judgment of the ravages of the continued addiction. In any event, dealing with relapse in the early stages of treatment involves more of a fine-tuning of procedures. Each relapse pattern portends its own demoralizing impact on the counselor, and this pattern often traps counselors into thinking that sustained recovery is not possible or that addiction treatment is "hopeless." This confirms the importance of seeing relapse patterns psychologically as a prelude rather than fulfillment.

The second pattern of relapse occurs after many weeks or months of abstinence followed by substance use whether starting out as "controlled" use which swiftly deteriorates characteristically into loss of control or substance use followed by an immediate plunge into binges. In this pattern the addicted person eventually "comes to his or her senses" and stops using. The self-help groups conceptualize this pattern according to the disease model of chemical dependency. In this model chemical dependency is viewed as a chronic, progressive illness which, though treatable, is never cured. Relapse is both confirmation and symptom of the disease. This model is also useful to counselors who tend to feel discouraged when their clients relapse. Relapse can be so demoralizing for a counselor because it is often so baffling. One is often hard pressed to find the "cause" of the relapse, and clients and counselors engage in seemingly endless analysis. At such times the most sensible statement that can be made is that the person drank because he or she is an alcoholic. Self-help groups, moreover, often provide useful observations about pre-relapse behavior and use such terms as "dry drunk" or "white-knuckle sobriety" in an attempt to elucidate the behavior patterns or mental attitudes which precede relapse. One such example is the mnemonic HALT which stands for hungry, angry, lonely and tired, the antecedent conditions for many relapses. The wisdom taught here is avoidance of prolonged relapses.

Behavioral counseling approaches emphasize looking at relapse as a learning experience by discovering what led up to it, what coping strategies the addicted person failed to use, what lifestyle imbalance issues may have led to a state of deprivation and hence resentment toward sobriety, and finally what one would do in the future to cope with similar circumstances. In addition this approach attempts to prepare the client for understanding what is termed the "abstinence violation effect," that rush of self-loathing and failure likely to accompany any slip. This approach minimizes the harmful effects of the slip and offers practical advice on regaining self-confidence (Marlatt, 1985). Despite differences in nuance and language there are many similarities in the strategies espoused by both self-help groups and behavioral science. The supervisor interested in such approaches has a wealth of professional material to draw from to support counselors.

A third pattern of relapse is less common but frequent enough to deserve comment. This pattern is reflected in the client who has lengthy abstinence of many years and yet unfortunately relapses. Both the disease model and the behavioral science methods outlined above are also useful here, yet it is alarming that despite lengthy abstinence the relapse is often more prolonged and devastating. In this pattern, expectations of sobriety from family, friends, employers and self-help groups may be so high that the client has difficulty rebounding because of the shame connected with having fallen from his previous level. Depression with this pattern may be more intense than with others and the risk of suicide should be carefully evaluated.

D. *From Addiction Counseling to Integrative Therapy.* As recovery strengthens in the dependent person the focus of counseling becomes less and less on maintaining abstinence and gradually resembles the process and structure of integrative therapy. While it is not necessary for counselors ritualistically to mark this transition, they need to be aware that such a shift has occurred and to incorporate their more general counseling approaches. Two features about this stage are noteworthy. First, the counselor should not forget that the addiction is a chronic condition, and clients often deny this fact. Second, counselors assist clients by comparing and contrasting current client behavior and defenses to those employed when actively drinking/using. This both reminds the client of the illness' chronicity and at the same time reinforces him or her for developing more adaptive coping skills. Elsewhere (Ciarrocchi, 1983) I have outlined a developmental model for counseling the recovering addict. Such a model takes into consideration the transitions which occur throughout the various phases of addiction counseling, and supervisors may find such a model helpful. My major point now is that addiction counseling even well into recovery remains somewhat specialized, yet as recovery progresses the flow of counseling more closely resembles the standard counseling procedures.

Supervisors need to remember that recovering addicts have special needs not just because ignoring the fact may provoke a relapse. Addiction counseling, rather, is a positive force for the total growth of the client—who happens to be chemically dependent. The supervisor who facilitates the counselor's growth will be adhering to a model which is both cautious and growth-centered at the same time.

15

Spiritual Direction:
A Model for Group Supervision

In his *Living Flame of Love*, John of the Cross uses some very harsh words to describe spiritual directors who impose their own insecurities on their directees, specifically during the period when they are being led by the Lord from more discursive prayer to contemplative prayer. He calls them to task in this way:

> These directors do not know what spirit is. They do a great injury to God and show disrespect toward Him by intruding with a rough hand where He is working. It cost God a great deal to bring these souls to this stage, and He highly values His work of having introduced them to this solitude and emptiness . . . so that He might speak to their hearts. . . .[1]

Who among us who has ever done spiritual direction does not pause before such a judgment and wonder whether he or she has ever been a source of harm to a directee.[2] Hopefully all of us will allow ourselves a moment of healthy self-doubt. Who has not wished in certain ambiguous situations for the opportunity of having talked with someone more experienced or simply with other directors, and thus had the reassurance that comes from doing spiritual direction in dialogue rather than in isolation?

For those of us who have had the experience of doing spiritual direction in some form of colleagueship, it seems profoundly right. Facilitating

---

1. John of the Cross, *The Collected Works of John of the Cross*, translated by Kieran Kavanaugh and Otilio Rodriguez (Washington, D.C.: ICS Publications, 1973), p. 631.

2. For those for whom the language and reality of spiritual direction is unfamiliar, I would recommend reading Kevin Culligan's chapter in the Loyola Pastoral Counseling Faculty's earlier book. Also since there is some resemblance between transpersonal counseling and spiritual direction, Bruce Scotton's article would be a helpful complement to what I am presenting in this chapter. Both of these references are listed below.

other people's relationship with God is an awesome task and some kind of community setting makes sense experientially.

There are several settings in which many people in this country are discovering the graciousness of this type of spiritual direction community. Probably the oldest is the daily team meeting during directed retreats.[3] These gatherings are normally centered either around topics agreed upon by the group of directors or on issues which arise during their experience of working with the retreatants. These meetings are generally very enriching and have paved the way for another increasingly common form of colleagueship: the regular peer group meeting of spiritual directors outside a retreat setting.

As during the retreat experience, these ongoing peer groups normally address both topical considerations as well as the continuing ministry of the members. Unlike the retreat setting however, these groups form themselves more spontaneously from among people in a given geographic area who experience a felt need for support in their work of spiritual direction.

Another form that this search for colleagueship in the ministry of spiritual direction has taken is the quite recent phenomenon of supervision. It exists for the most part in training centers and takes a variety of formats. This article will draw upon our six years of experience with supervision in spiritual direction in the Loyola Pastoral Counseling Department (LPCD).[4]

While this search for colleagueship is born, as I have suggested, in a felt existential need among spiritual directors, it is also founded in a basic theological reality. All ministry in the Church is communal, and spiritual direction is no exception. This is true of ministry because religious experience is by its very nature primarily that of the community; for we are called by God *as a people.* The individual is invited and challenged to participate in this call with all that is particular to him or to her but most fundamentally by becoming one with the history and experience of the larger faith community.

---

3. A directed retreat is an extended and intensive private prayer experience. The person on retreat meets daily with an experienced director as a means of becoming more aware of how God is leading him or her and how he or she might best cooperate with the promptings of the Holy Spirit. Traditionally these retreat experiences last either eight or thirty days. When there are enough retreatants at any one time to require several directors, then the team of directors often meet daily for prayerful support and mutual guidance.

4. Historically, supervision of spiritual direction trainees was introduced into the LPCD several years after the pastoral counseling program had begun. An obvious strength of the LPCD has always been the fine and extensive supervision of its degree candidates. This supervisory environment directly influenced the approach and style adopted in 1981 for both the individual and group supervision of spiritual direction.

Therefore, even though the classic setting for spiritual direction is the one-to-one encounter, it does not make sense theologically or existentially for this ministry to operate completely in isolation. That it has done just that for some time is easily explainable, given the more individualistic approach to spirituality which has characterized the recent past. Also the tendency in the Catholic tradition to link spiritual direction with confession, until recently devoid of any clearly communal setting, has reinforced this privitization. However, as our vision of Church, sacraments and spirituality becomes more communal, then our approach to this *ars artium* is invited to change in the same way.

Spiritual direction supervision takes place in both individual and communal settings. This chapter will deal with the group setting as it has evolved over the last six years in our training of spiritual directors in the LPCD. This has been our primary way of doing supervision in our program. We have also offered individual supervision four times a semester to our trainees, and they have certainly valued this more personalized and sustained look at their ministry. However, since something has been written on individual supervision and nothing substantial on group work, I have chosen to share our rich experience of the latter in this chapter.[5]

I. The Foundations of Group Supervision

In the group supervisory process, the students present their work to a group composed of their peers together with one or two experienced facilitators for the purpose of growing in the practice of this art. The fundamental focus of supervision is the same as the focus of spiritual direction itself. Thus just as the goal of spiritual direction is to facilitate the relationship between the directee and God, then one of the main purposes of supervision is to facilitate the director's relationship with God specifically as a director. Therefore the issues of faith, hope and love are always at the center of this process. Ideally an atmosphere of prayer and openness to the Spirit of God characterizes these sessions.

There are two foundations to supervision. The first is explicitly expressed in any helping relationship: *the working alliance*. Obviously in a group this is experienced somewhat differently than in the individual setting. Nevertheless, it remains equally essential that a good trusting relationship develop not only between the supervisees and the facilitator(s)'

---

5. The literature on supervision in spiritual direction is limited to the two references at the end of this chapter. Both come from the fine work of the Center for Religious Development in Cambridge, Massachusetts. They deal with individual supervision primarily but *The Practice of Spiritual Direction* mentions group supervision, pp. 188–91.

but with the whole group. This allows the members to present their spiritual direction ministry in a non-defensive manner and to experience both support and challenge in a helpful way. This is the only way that group supervision can be meaningful. It will take time for a deep alliance to build, but my experience has been that people come to this with enough basic good will to allow even the early case presentations to be helpful.

The second foundation which enables and enriches the working alliance is the *contemplative attitude*. There are many ways of understanding contemplation. What I mean here is a type of presence to one another which affirms the group's openness to the working of the Holy Spirit in the spiritual direction enterprise. It is obviously a faith stance which not only listens to and cherishes what is expressed and lived as a sacred human reality, but also intuits the power and grace of God in and beyond the actual case being considered.

Barry and Connolly (1982) devote two helpful practical chapters (pp. 46–79) to cultivating this essential attitude in the directee. For further treatment on how the contemplative posture is foundational in spiritual direction and thus *a fortiori* in group supervision, I would suggest reading that material.

Thus we should remember that this working alliance is always multifaceted. Not only is there an alliance building in the group, but also the group and its members as individuals are developing a working alliance with the Holy Spirit, who has always been considered traditionally as the principal spiritual director. Therefore the term "working alliance," as it applies both to spiritual direction and to its supervision, indicates first and foremost the gracious and active relationship with God and only secondarily the relationship between the various human agents. This relationship is nourished by the belief that before we appeared on the scene as director or supervisor, God has been at work in the life of the directee or supervisee and that God is with us as we carry on our ministry. Therefore a life of prayer is essential to the group and its members in order to nourish this faith-posture. Only if we remember this can we keep from losing the focus which distinguishes this ministry and its supervision from other forms of counseling.

II. Group Supervision

A. *Background and Theory for Our Practice*

In the past six years, the LPCD has offered weekly small group supervision to our directors in training. These groups have met for two semesters of about fifteen weeks each. As you will soon note, we have adopted a clinical model for these sessions which has worked quite well. Before looking at this procedure it is important to understand something further about the nature of the group supervision itself.

By mutual understanding these small groups are task groups gathered to assist one another in the ongoing ministry of spiritual direction. This is a given and the basis for the weekly meetings. Because of the nature of the ministry itself, the chances are good that it will become also a community of faith. Obviously this can not be programmed, but it can be invited and nurtured by beginning with prayer, which sets us directly before God as a gathered group intent on responding to God's initiative in the lives of our directees and in us as directors. My experience is that these sessions are more effective and helpful if the group sees itself as a community of faith as well as people gathered for a task.

The group provides three basic services to its members: personal support, insight and challenge. The personal support is very important, since most of the people in our program have had only limited previous experience as spiritual directors. They often feel insecure before the task and feel the need for ongoing support as they risk undertaking this beautiful and awesome ministry.

Insight happens in several ways. First of all, the weekly reflection on the cases presented generally offers some perspective, information and understanding to everyone in the seminar. More particularly, the person presenting receives something of the accumulated wisdom of the group, most of which is by intention directed to the particular case in question.

The insights generally focus both on process and content. Thus along with the reflections on what is happening in the session, in the directee and the director, there is also some furnishing of more cognitive insights through references to theological, psychological or spiritual frameworks which people judge to be relevant. At times a book or article is suggested and is often made available to the members of the seminar. Generally once or twice a semester, either part or all of a session will be set aside to discuss some issue or idea which the group thinks will be helpful to their growth as directors. One of the valuable services which our program provides is an ongoing concern for the interrelatedness of the spiritual and the emotional which is characteristic of a pastoral counseling program.

As the level of trust grows in the group, then it is more possible to challenge one another to look at and deal with needs for growth as a director. In this same process, the participants will feel increasingly more comfortable in presenting situations in which they are particularly vulnerable and sense that they may be in need of further growth in their ministry as directors. Generally it takes eight to ten sessions before the group is comfortable dealing with their "growing edges." This depends on how quickly and how well the group "working alliance" develops. In my experience this can vary considerably from group to group and depends to some extent on relational variables which escape the conscious control of the group or the facilitator(s).

There are three possible foci for the work of group supervision: the situation and journey of the directee being presented, the relationship between the directee and director, and the director's way of being with the directee. Generally, the group is comfortable plunging into the first. As trust grows they also tentatively approach the second and the third. The group facilitator is in a good position to model work on the last two aspects because of his or her role, and this strategy will normally invite the others to risk in these areas as well. However, this generally takes time.

It is certainly crucial in the first session to deal explicitly with the issue of confidentiality. This agreement is important enough not to be presupposed. The group should make a verbal contract that nothing of the presentations of the directee and the subsequent discussion will ever leave the room. The written case presentations should be destroyed at the termination of the group and the tapes should be erased.

Our group sessions last for one hour and fifty minutes. Some groups have chosen to schedule two presentations of fifty minutes each with a ten minute break in between; others have only one. There are advantages to both. The double session allows people to present more often and thus get more feedback. It also provides a more varied experience for everyone. On the other hand, the single session allows more easily for the type of in-depth consideration that brings forth elaborated insights and clear specific challenges to growth for the director and the seminar alike.

B. Structure

With these general considerations in mind, I will share with you the structure we have adopted for our weekly group meetings. The session format includes an opening prayer, a written case presentation, questions for clarification, listening to a tape, discussion and conclusion.

1. *Opening Prayer:* The facilitator(s) can open the first session with prayer and then ask for volunteers to lead prayer in the following weeks. In general, the participants have preferred not to lead prayer and to present a case in the same session. It is important to limit the time for this formal prayer or it can increase in length little by little, leaving less time for the group task. Five minutes seems an appropriate length.

2. *Reading the Case Presentation:* With few exceptions the groups have preferred to make a brief write-up available as background to the case

under consideration. It seems like a more efficient use of this moment with more information being conveyed in a shorter length of time than could be done orally. This is the outline that we use:

Identification of the Directee: Basic facts such as first name (real or fictional), age, sex, marital status, employment, etc.

Origin of the Relationship: It can be important to know this to understand the context of the spiritual direction work. For example, if the directee is a parishioner of the director, we understand that there are several levels to the relationship which may help and/or hinder the development of the necessary spiritual freedom for growth in faith. (Often in our program we find directees for our participants, since many of the latter are from outside our geographic area.)

General Impressions: The presenter should attempt to describe briefly the directee in enough ways so that whole group can have an image in their mind of the person: for example, appearance, behavior, manner of self-presentation, faith commitment, maturity, etc.

Situation for Consideration: What session is this? What immediate background can help the group best understand the specific part of this session that we will hear and/or see?

Relevant Background: This would include biographical data; family history; medical history; psychological history; faith history, including the experience of previous spiritual direction, significant retreats, conversion experiences, important spiritual images and patterns.

Most Important Issues: What is the person dealing with at this point in his or her journey? Four types of issues are addressed here: physical, psychological, theological and spiritual.

Process: What are the director's goals in working with this directee? What are the directee's own stated goals? How would the director describe his or her relationship with the directee? What role is the director trying to fulfill? Does the director bring habitual agenda to the sessions? If so what?

Prospect: Does this look like a long term direction situation? Does the directee understand spiritual direction? Is he or she committed to it?

Assessment of Ministry: Does the director believe that he or she is listening well and understanding what is being said? Does he or she feel competent to work with this person? What has the director found helpful and what would he or she change and why? What are the director's growing edges?

Normally it takes about *five minutes* to read this type of write-up which is in the average two to three pages in length. Then another *five minutes* is taken for any questions people might have about the written case presentation. This is not the moment to enter into the discussion of the case but rather to clarify anything in the write-up which is ambiguous or to seek further information that people might judge appropriate.

3. *Reviewing the Tape:* Both audio and video tapes have been used for this part of the presentation. In general the audio tape is more practical and less intrusive, so it has been preferred. We use tapes rather than verbatims simply because we feel they are more helpful. Verbatims "lie!" Tapes capture the actual moment with pauses, tone of voice, inflections and an actual feel for the interchange between director and directee. At the beginning of each new group, we spend a few minutes talking about how to tape a session. People are urged to experiment with their recorders so as to obtain a good tape. There is nothing more annoying and deflating to a session of this type than an inaudible recording. A good moderately priced external microphone is essential. The built-in condenser microphones are not adequate.

Only rarely have participants in the seminar raised the question of the appropriateness of taping spiritual direction sessions. As long as the confidentiality is assured, there seems no reason not to, and the advantages for the group work are clear. The reason for taping and the assurance that the tapes will only be used for supervision are conveyed to the directees in a matter-of-fact way. They are told that if they ever wish to stop the tape during a session they may do so. To my knowledge, in the past six years, directees have refused to be taped only twice, and only on very rare occasions has a directee actually requested that the recorder be shut off. Often a directee will comment that he or she is happy to be able to help the director-in-training in this way. It makes the experience mutually rewarding and helps create an atmosphere of companionship in faith which is characteristic of spiritual direction sessions.

We listen to about *fifteen to twenty minutes* of the tape. The director chooses one or more sections to give the group an idea of what is happening in his or her work with the directee. Normally he or she will take *one or two minutes* to put in context the part of the tape the group is about to hear.

4. *Discussion:* After the tape review, the group members begin sharing thoughts and feelings about what they have read and heard. As I said above, the focus moves easily to the directee's situation and only more slowly to the directee/director relationship and the assessment of the director's way of being with the person.

It seems from experience that it is better for the facilitator(s) to exercise some restraint about entering the discussion, since that can inhibit the others, especially early in the group's life. It is important that the leader value the contributions of the members of the group when appropriate as a way of reinforcing participation and facilitating the working alliance.

5. *Conclusion:* It is important to check with the presenter to see if his or her needs were met in the discussion. If the presenter was confronted, it would be good to see how he or she is feeling and, if necessary, process that with him or her. The facilitator should begin this concluding moment when there is still enough time to achieve whatever he or she senses needs to be accomplished with the presenter. This *may* also be a time for a "teachable moment" where the leader may wish to offer some relevant content to the seminar which would advance the focus of the day's session. In my experience, such teaching moments should be short and to the point. If there is need for something more substantial, the facilitator can suggest either a reference or the scheduling of a longer discussion sometime in the future.

C. A Fictionalized Example

(This was the group's ninth meeting.)

Jill is presenting Sam, a forty-two year old married man who responded to a notice in his parish bulletin about the possibility for spiritual direction. He would like to develop more of a prayer life. Up until now, he has concentrated mostly on work and family. He says that he has been a "faithful but not overly devout Catholic." Jill and Sam have been meeting every two weeks and she is presenting their sixth session to the group. They seem to have a good rapport. He is trying to share something of his heart, but has been so accustomed to living in his head that he finds himself unable to talk of his feelings and intuitions. Frustrated with Sam and the process, Jill is asking for the group's help.

1. Case Summary

Sam was an only child. His mother has been a recovering alcoholic for the last six years. His father divorced her when Sam was fifteen. After his father left home, he was raised by his maternal grandparents. Sam had the normal struggles with masturbation during puberty and experienced severe scruples for about six months when he was sixteen. This painful period came to an end when he attended a high school retreat. He was deeply touched by the retreat director's eloquent message of God's infinite love for sinners. In the months that followed, he thought of becoming a priest but decided to study engineering instead. After college he married a woman whom he met in his first drafting class. They have two boys, ages nineteen and fourteen and one girl who is seventeen. Sam and his wife have grown apart in the last five years. He says they do not seem to have much in common anymore and he is somewhat bored with the relationship. Nevertheless he does not want to leave her and the children. He feels rooted in his family. "It's not all that bad, it just isn't all that good either." He has remained faithful to her, choosing not to have an affair with a divorcee last year.

For Sam God is a just judge, who expects our best, but understands our weaknesses. He is sure that he believes in God's love for us but has not been able to reexperience the feeling of this love since the retreat experience of eighteen years ago. Sam has a cordial but somewhat distant relationship with his mother. His father died of a heart attack when Sam was thirty-seven.

2. Discussion

The group wanted to hear more about Sam's prayer life. Jill said that he often turned to God when he was in pain and occasionally offered thanks for certain blessings, like the health of his children and a recent promotion in the engineering firm where he works. He finds Sunday Mass less prayerful now than when it was in Latin, but he is occasionally moved by something in the Scripture readings or a good homily. Other than that he does not take much time for prayer, but wants to develop this dimension of his Christian life.

The group session focused first on Sam's image of God, which struck several as fairly abstract. They wondered what impact his father's "abandonment" of the family and his mother's inability to raise him had on his inability to experience God's love more deeply. (This prompted a short discussion on the relationship between the emotional and the spiritual and how to facilitate such an exploration and remain faithful to the spiritual direction context.) Jill said she had hoped to work on that with Sam sometime in the future but wondered now if doing that in the next session might not help bring Sam closer to his feelings.

Someone in the group suggested that Jill might want to ask Sam to close his eyes and sit with the image of the just but understanding judge, using some active imagination as a way of moving beyond the rational. Jill appreciated that suggestion, but admitted her own lack of skill and comfort with doing that. Several other people said the same. The leader said he would be willing to make a presentation on the use of imagery in spiritual direction in a future session. The group seemed interested. Several people commented on how well they sensed Jill was attending to Sam. They sensed that the rapport was good. They found her interventions and questions to be right on target.

Another person recalled her own thirty-day retreat and how she had spent it meditating on various relevant images of God in Scripture, e.g. God as judge in Matthew 25, the tender God of Hosea 11, the forgiving God in Luke 7 (adulterous woman). She wondered whether Jill could suggest a few texts to Sam and offer him a method for prayer with Scripture. Jill said she had tried assigning Sam some "homework" (spending time between their sessions reflecting and praying with selected Scripture texts) after the second session. He did not have much success with it but seemed interested. Maybe she would try it again.

Jill said she felt uneasy exploring Sam's relationship with his wife. The group spent some time looking at this with Jill. She came to realize that her fifteen years as a religious woman had offered her many good friendships but not much really intimate sharing. Except for "going steady" with a boy at age seventeen, she had never had any close relationships with men. In fact she admitted that she is somewhat afraid of getting close to others. She felt she wanted to bring this to her own spiritual director in their next session. She also told the group that she was thinking of entering therapy during this year. They supported her in both those intentions. The group leader further suggested that understanding Sam's approach to intimacy in his marriage might reveal something in a "mirrored" way of the inner processes which seem to be blocking the development of intimacy with God.[6]

One member of the group said she had been struck by Sam's decision not to get involved with another woman. She felt it was significant that he would choose to remain faithful given his own background of abandonment and neglect, and she suggested that Jill point this out to Sam and invite him to contemplate this as an effect of God's grace in his life. The leader seconded this idea and recommended that Jill ask him to share his own understanding of why he made this choice. Has he always seen himself as faithful or is it a more recent development? What events or people have brought him to this attitude and behavior? Someone else added that even

---

6. The image of "mirror" here refers to 1 Corinthians 13:12: "For now we see in a mirror dimly, but then face to face. Now I know in part; then I shall understand fully, even as I have been fully understood." It is a given in spiritual direction ministry that the work of God in people's lives is most often shrouded in mystery. While a person's experience of prayer can offer some indication of what God is about, the ordinary experiences of life may be of equal or at times greater help in discovering how God is touching the directee. For example, Sam's struggles with intimacy in his marriage could very possibly "mirror" a concomitant call of the Holy Spirit to deeper intimacy with God. In this situation it is possible that similar inner obstacles may be impeding both the development of Sam's prayer life and intimacy with his wife. Learning more about his marriage relationship may give Sam and Jill some clues about how he might further his stated desire to deepen his life of prayer.

if Sam is not used to finding God in the midst of his own inner life, beginning to be in touch with grace in this way could help him greatly in his desire to develop a solid prayer life.

Since there were only about six or seven minutes left, the leader "checked in" with the presenter. Has she found this helpful? Jill said that she was quite pleased and grateful for the feedback and felt it would help her and Sam to continue moving forward. He also asked her whether there was anything else she wanted to say. Jill added that she appreciated the affirmation and welcomed the challenge to deal with her own issues in direction and probably now in therapy as well. She intended to call her doctor that week and set up an appointment.

There was still a minute or two left, and another member of the group wanted to up-date the others on some progress he had made in working with the directee he had presented to the group three weeks earlier. Everyone rejoiced with him. The session then came to an end.

Although this example is fictionalized, it offers a true picture of how our particular approach to group supervision has actually worked in practice. As you can see, it provides many opportunities for cognitive, affective and spiritual growth. Since this group spiritual direction supervision is situated in the pastoral counseling program with its strong clinical emphasis, the group matures in its ability to understand the relationship between the spiritual and the emotional. In the process they acquire a more nuanced sense of how God speaks to us through the realities of everyday life.

The members of the group not only support each other as they develop a good working alliance but they also help develop the contemplative attitude without which spiritual direction makes no sense. Certainly a group by its very nature represents more manifestations and incarnations of how God works in the hearts and souls of people than is true in individual supervision. One of the tasks of the group is to become more attuned to contemplating that richness as it illumines their ministry of spiritual direction.

It is my hope that in reading about the experience in this chapter, more people will be moved to seek some form of group supervision for their spiritual direction ministry. As I said in the beginning, those of us who have had this experience believe that it is profoundly right. The format we are using in the LPCD could be adopted for use by various groupings of spiritual directors whether in an academic setting or not. Hopefully some day the isolated spiritual director, fulfilling his or her call to this wondrous ministry without the benefit of such colleagueship, will be the exception rather than the rule.

References

William A. Barry and William J. Connolly, *The Practice of Spiritual Direction.* New York: Seabury Press, 1982.

William A. Barry and Mary C. Guy, "The Practice of Supervision in Spiritual Direction." *Review for Religious* 37 (November 1978): 834–42.

Kevin G. Culligan, "The Counseling Ministry and Spiritual Direction." In *Pastoral Counseling*, pp. 37–49. Edited by Barry K. Estadt. Englewood Cliffs, New Jersey: Prentice-Hall, 1983.

Bruce W. Scrotton, "Observations on the Teaching and Supervision of Transpersonal Psychotherapy." *Journal of Transpersonal Psychology* 17 (1985): 57–75.

Part 4

Special Issues in Supervision

Rachel Callahan, Ph.D.

16

Religious Issues

I. A Case Study

A counselor brings in a taped work sample of her latest session with her middle-aged female client. Client and counselor have been working together for six months and have moved into mid-phase therapy. The counselor is a mature, seasoned, and quite gifted therapist and for several previous supervisory sessions has had concerns about this particular client.

The client entered therapy after sustaining a number of personal losses. It was not her first therapeutic experience. From the beginning of their work together the counselor had concerns about this client's depersonalization and her tendency to withdraw to "another world" where she could communicate with God with ease. At the same time she consistently reported problems with human communication. The client is an overtly religious person who talks freely about her religious experiences and prayer. The counselor is sensitive and respectful to religious issues.

The following verbatim exchange is taken from the session following the client's birthday. Should the counselor be concerned?

Client:	My birthday was Sunday.
Counselor:	Happy birthday.
Client:	Thanks. I woke up and previous to that I had taken on a different relationship with God. It was best friend type. So we spent the day. And it was His day. He made the choices. It was interesting, a beautiful day. I didn't do anything that He didn't give direction. It was His day and He only wanted to hear Mozart. It was interesting because He's very proud of His better creations—Mozart being one of them. That's all we listened to.
Counselor:	How does that relate to you, Claire?

241

Client: It feels very good. (Client is tearing up.)

Counselor: What are your tears about, Claire?

Client: It was just . . . they're tears of joy and awe and also a
               little anxiety that you'll think I'm silly.

Counselor: Anxiety that I would think it's silly that you and God
               would have a day together?

Client: Well—now why would I think that you'd think that's
               silly? No confidence. Anyhow, I had a great day. I
               think He did too. He chose to go to the (art) gallery. It
               was interesting. Parking spaces surface and all kinds of
               things when God is there.

Counselor: How did you know what God wanted you to do,
               Claire?

Client: He told me. Well, I asked first. It was a dialogue,

Counselor: Did you get a feeling of what would be right, or . . .

Client: Oh, He talked to me. I'd say, "Now what are we going
               to do today? It's my birthday and I'm one of Your
               creations, good, bad, or indifferent." So He was very
               pleased and thankful that I chose to spend the day
               with Him. So I said; "Well, this is kind of what I'd like
               to do. What would You like to do?" And some of the
               things I wanted to do, He didn't. "Do you really think
               we should do this? Would it be as enjoyable as that?"

Counselor: How did He communicate that to you, Claire?

Client: Well, it's kind of a feeling, but it's also an awareness of
               speech, and when I'm communicating I can't separate
               out whether it's my voice or somebody else's or what
               it sounds like. I can't discern but it's speech. It's very
               clear. He touches me. In fact there was one occasion
               when He took hold of my arm and I could feel it. We
               went to the gallery. And I know the ones He likes
               very much. He likes them all, but some He's more
               proud of. Rembrandt He's proud of but He thinks he's
               a cheek.

Counselor: Thinks he's a . . .

Client: A cheek. Very cheeky.

Counselor: You know, I can't imagine what it was like for you to
               have that day. I've never had that kind of
               communication with God. It's an experience I haven't
               had.

Client: It's nice—the nicest day I ever spent. I spaced out
               quite a bit—forgot your appointment. I had to

organize the day (today). But if there's time, let's go to the gallery.

The counselor, having tactfully dealt with the therapeutic boundary issue, continued to draw Claire out about her birthday, and as the session unfolded it became clear that nobody had remembered her birthday and that she was struggling with some profound issues of loneliness. As a supervisor, how would you respond to this work sample? What feelings does it stir up in you? What assessments about Claire? Should my supervisee have heightened concerns about her client's welfare and how she is coping or should she affirm Claire's self-report of such a satisfying birthday celebration?

Your own responses will probably raise some of the complexities of dealing with religious issues in supervision. Most immediate, for both supervisor and supervisee, are the self-awareness issues. What is my own history and current status regarding religious belief and experience? What are my own feelings about religious matters being brought into therapy? As we move through the 1980's there is more tolerance for the acceptability of religious experience as something more than a regressive phenomenon. But the *Zeitgeist* of scientific positivism which has certainly informed the study of the behavioral sciences in the United States does not leave much room for faith which is basically neither a provable nor a disprovable phenomenon of human experience.

When working with religious issues in supervision, as with any issue, the first consideration needs to be client welfare. What might be some of the considerations in dealing with the client presented above? The first consideration needs to be an awareness of Claire's own religious beliefs and experiences and a respect for these. In this instance Claire is a Roman Catholic who reports a prayer life of familiar conversation with God. As the transcript above illustrates, it is difficult to assess what she means by "conversation," whether she is using the term in an analogous way to report a sense of felt intimacy or whether she is using it in a delusional way— i.e. reporting hearing voices. She regularly uses the defense of splitting and views the material "real" world as someplace hurtful and scary whereas the "spiritual" world is a sanctuary, a haven. On another occasion she had shared with her therapist the following experience that occurred during a Mass while she was on retreat.

I had a beautiful experience, I'd just like to be there all the time—a very sweet song. The priest just waited. He didn't break it (the host) or anything, which made me feel he was all part of it; in fact, I *know* he was. It was a state of being. The only way I can describe it is to try to visualize it. We were all in the room. There was a cloud above all the people. And coming up to this cloud were beams of rays and those beams were all collective adoration and we all gathered in this cloud in a kind of collective. It was an enormously wonderful place to be and I didn't want to leave. It took two or three minutes but it seemed like an awfully long time. The priest broke it, but he broke it with terrible sadness that he had to break it. Now I'm more and more having that experience.

Statements like this flagged a great deal of concern for me because they suggested loose ego boundaries which sounded almost delusional. This concern was heightened by the client's preference for that world instead of the one where she lives.

What frightens me here is the material world. I have to logistically live in the material world. I have to get a job. That's immobilizing to know I have to do that. It's infinitely more pleasant to be there.

The client reported her father as an aggressive, dominant, unpleasant workaholic, a distant father except for an incident of trying to fondle her breasts when she was a young adolescent. He was definitely not the kind of person one would enjoy spending a day at the art gallery with. Nor was her marriage to an alcoholic husband which ended with his death in 1979 a model of intimacy. In this particular situation Claire's religion was a part of her defense system and not too helpful to her in a growthful, integrative way, and yet the fragility of her ego led her counselor to be respectful of her defenses without colluding in them (cf. counselor's last response).

II. Assessing the Role Religion Plays

The case study presented above illustrates only a few of the delicate assessment questions in trying to evaluate how religion "serves" a client. Robert Lovinger (1984) points out that religion gives order and meaning to the physical, social, and interpersonal world of a believer. He cites the study of Argyle, & Beit-Hallahmi (1975) which presents a taxonomy of how religion functions organized around three basic concepts: *origins* of religion's function—i.e. how it gets started; *maintenance*—i.e. why and how it keeps going; *outcome*—i.e. consequences.

Some of the theoretical hypotheses presented under each of these concepts include:

Origin

   a. *Cognitive needs*—religion helps a person to deal with meaning questions. What is life all about? How can death and evil be explained? What should my life goals be?
   b. *Father (mother) projection*—Freud suggested that the idea of God represented a father projection. Later theorists would expand the notion to include mother and/or family projection. Yalom (1982) talks about the universal need for an Ultimate Rescuer.
   c. *Superego projection*—as a child internalizes parental dos and don'ts, these gradually get projected onto God, the clergy, the Church.

Maintenance

   a. *Social learning*—religion gets transmitted via formal instruction and family learning. But while this accounts for the passage of knowledge, it hardly accounts for the motivational power that religion holds for many people.
   b. *Compensation for deprivation*—over the centuries religious beliefs in a better life after death have served a compensatory function. Hope is a central element of religion as a sociological phenomenon.
   c. *Relief of guilt*—the relationship between guilt and religion is a complex one. Religion not only serves an expiatory function but there is also ample evidence of how it functions abusively in producing guilt as well as relieving it.
   d. *Dealing with death*—the ultimate human limit situation is death, and religion is one of the ways that a person copes with the anxiety of this reality.
   e. *Sexual motivation*—there is the intriguing question of how religious behavior competes with sexual behavior. Lovinger suggests that religion and sex are alternate forms of commitment.

Outcome

   a. Personal integration—religion can and does produce growth.
   b. Social integration—religion has long functioned as a means of socialization.

These theories, like most theories, tend to be somewhat reductionistic and obviously do not address theological issues. They are useful in trying to order and conceptualize from a psychological point of view how religion functions for the individual and for the group.

The very reductionism of the theories, however, calls us to a larger issue which needs to be addressed in a chapter like this. We need to look at the difference between "religious experience," which can be examined according to the principles of behavioral science, and the human "experience of God" which although less positivistic is no less real. "Religious experience" and the human "experience of God" are not interchangeable phenomena. Deni Edwards (1984) has a splendidly readable treatment of the larger topic—i.e. the human experience of God. This is harder to examine in terms of a "pure" behavioral science model. Mystery does not allow that kind of scrutiny. Faith is a far broader concept than cognitive or intellectual assent to a set of beliefs. It is an affective, relational phenomenon and somewhat beyond the grasp of human "proof."

Edwards uses the word "grace"—a word that has distinct meaning in different theological traditions as the way to describe how the mystery of God is mediated in human experience. He cites experiences of "grace" in some of the rich life experiences—love, creativity, forgiveness, beauty—where there is some sense of transcendence, a "more than" what is. And likewise he points to "grace" in limit situations—the human experiences of vulnerability where we let ourselves become aware of how fragile is our grasp on human existence with all of its contingency. The Challenger explodes and we share this as a nation. Death, failure, loneliness, alienation often are the experiences which lead a person to therapy. The pain and anxiety which are connected with these "limit situations" often motivate a person to seek help. Religious issues may not be overt but they are often covert as individuals struggle with issues of life and meaning.

III. Practical Applications for Supervision

With the preceding pages as background, what are some of the practical issues that a supervisor needs to be alert to in working with supervisees during each of the major phases of therapy? As practitioners we realize that therapeutic process looks much "neater" and more orderly in the books than in the uniqueness of human experience. Thus any of the issues surfaced under each of the phases might appear at any time.

In the beginning stage when the client is searching for help the foundational question, often not articulated, is: "Can you understand and help me?" And out of this question a client may ask straightforward questions about the religious affiliation of the therapist. An honest response is best. Being with a client in an empathic way in initial interviews builds the ground for trusting and tolerating differences, but if the differences look as if they will be an obstacle to therapy it is better to recognize that limit from the start.

Early on in working with a client it is useful to listen for covert religious issues. Paul Pruyser (1976) identifies some useful variables to attend to. What is the person's *awareness of the Holy?* What (if anything) is *sacred* to him or her? Has the person *experienced awe or bliss?* When? Where? How? How does the person *embrace creatureliness?* Do the ordinary limit situations of human existence outrage or paralyze the person? What is the way to cope with those fantasizing about a blissful hereafter in order to avoid dealing with life? Does the person have any *sense of Providence?* Does the person look to God to do magic, to be an Ultimate Rescuer from life's limits? Does the person have faith (as distinct from Faith as an identification with a denomination)? Does the person embrace life, have a commitment to his or her life experiences? Where is the person with regard to *grace?* No matter what the specific denominational differences in the theologies of grace, there is the commonality of the notion of unearned gift and its connection to forgiveness and guilt. Does the person perceive self as "unforgivable"?

Mid-phase issues become clearer as transference, countertransference and resistance emerge. How might a person's image of God appear as a transference issue? In the case sample presented earlier it was clear that Claire used reaction formation and splitting in her image of God. How a person views good/evil, God/Devil, is significant and might suggest some early disturbance in object relations. In listening for this it is important to be aware of how a person's specific denomination might inform this perception.

On the continuum of defiance/submission which usually gets right "into the room" as mid-phase work unfolds, where is the client? How does he or she turn the therapist into "god"?

Countertransference issues related to this topic include, first of all, unresolved religious issues that the therapist might be carrying. In the supervisory setting the supervisor can deal with this directly by inquiry or listen attentively to where the supervisee tends to get "hooked." Sometimes a religious person can present a "holier than thou" attitude. The narcissism of "I thank God that I am not like the rest of humankind" can stir up feelings of anger or boredom in the therapist. A critical issue for intervention in this situation is timing. An assault on a client's narcissism that comes too early could be wounding and could precipitate premature termination. Many religious persons are at least covertly narcissistic. The sense of being specially chosen and of being the world's worst sinner can both be rooted in a sense of more than human specialness.

Another countertransference issue could be mobilized by counselor feelings about dependency and/or idolatry. If a client transfers onto the therapist his or her desire for an Ultimate Rescuer, it is bound to stir up all sorts of feelings which become grist for the mill in supervision. Probably the most "dangerous" to client welfare is for the therapist to get seduced by being treated like god and waste therapeutic time in a collusion which feeds the therapist's own sense of omnipotence and grandiosity.

The resistance issues that emerge include variations of the following two. A client can use "god talk" or other ways of spiritualizing matters as a way to refuse to deal with critical issues. Another resistance phenomenon which can wear several masks is triangulation. If a person is a religious person and God is never mentioned, I get curious about the absence of conversation about what appears to be a significant relationship. If a client is simultaneously engaged in spiritual direction and therapy, it is important that the two processes are complementary and they do not get played off against each other in triangulated resistance.

Other religious issues may also emerge. What if a client asks the counselor to pray with him or her? How might religious imagery be useful? Answers to these questions have to be decided individually with the guiding question being: "How would this enhance (or detract from) the therapeutic journey of this particular client?"

The goals of therapy and religious conversion have many similarities. Both include journeying toward a sense of personal freedom and autonomy; a realistic embrace of one's gifts and limits and of one's "one and only life"; responsibility; forgiveness and reconciliation; personal integration. Religious experience can be part of the change of heart and behavior that marks both conversion and a healthy psychotherapeutic journey.

When both client and counselor have journeyed to "well enough" in this process, termination occurs. While the person is never finished in the life process of change and integration, he or she has arrived at a place to stop therapy. This "letting go" and "getting on" can be a religious issue for both client and counselor and might be ritualized in some way, if that seems appropriate.

Epilogue

The preceding pages represent some of the religious issues that might surface in working with supervisees. A chapter on religious issues needs also to include a word about the idolatrous potential of supervision. Most of us supervisors are also practitioners and know the press of feeling stuck with clients and the yearning that our more "expert" consultants will have answers and strategies that we do not have. If there is potential for a client to look to the therapist to be the Ultimate Rescuer, there is the powerful parallel process that goes on between supervisee and supervisor. It is easy to get hooked by this affirmation of expertise. Perhaps one of the greatest services we can render to our supervisees is to let them see our own ragged edges and limitations, to share our questions as well as our answers, and to help them celebrate that the power of the therapeutic process is precisely in the humanness of "good enough" and not in impossible quests for trying to do "perfect therapy."

17

Ethical Issues in Supervision

I. Some Theoretical Considerations

At the risk of oversimplification, but in the service of some theoretical background, I suggest that there are traditionally three ways in which we have articulated ethics. Each of these has a long history and can be identified with ancient sources, and each is given emphasis in various contemporary theorizing. In the complexity of life, such a typology is intended to give us some organizing touchstones. However, typologies by their nature are always oversimplifications. Indeed, as our later discussion will show, these categories are not mutually exclusive.

H. Richard Niebuhr, who taught me to think about ethics, said that these three approaches could be simply stated in a series of questions. First, there is the *deontological* approach (having nothing to do with ontology, the study of "being"), so named after the Greek word *deon* which we translate, "it is necessary." Deontological ethics is the ethics of absolutes, laws, timeless imperatives. The questions which frame a deontological ethics are: "What is necessary?" "What is required?" "What ought or must I do or refrain from doing?"

The second approach to ethics is also Greek in its origins. This is the *teleological* approach, from the Greek word *telos,* meaning end or goal or accepted good. The questions which frame a teleological approach are: "What is our goal?" "What are our ends?" "What actions will best serve our goals or ends?"

The third approach will seem on the surface to be a more modern way, with the relativity implied which informs so much modern thought. However, it can be argued that its roots lie in the farthest reaches of the Judeo-Christian tradition. It is variously called *situational* or *contextual* ethics. The questions one asks when ethics are considered contextually or situationally are: "What is happening?" and "What is an appropriate or fitting response to what is happening?" In this approach, responsibility does not imply obligation as it does in the deontological approach, or subservience to agreed upon ends as in teleological ethics. Rather, responsibility here means "the ability to respond." That is, behavior is decided after a judgment is made about the situation at hand and that behavior is chosen as consistent with the needs of the situation at hand. Thus, behavior which "fits" one situation might be out of order in a second situation and one's judgment is called for to choose the appropriate action. The words "situation" and "context" here also imply that ethics is a function of relationship. That is, the relation which exists between two or more parties or a person and a group will greatly influence what behavior is appropriate.

Clearly, each of these approaches has its place in our discussion. There are imperatives which apply to the ethics of supervision, and the goal of leading novice counselors to become seasoned therapists seminally informs the way we do supervision.

However, it is that relational dimension of contextual ethics which makes it particularly germane to our discussion of ethics in supervision. For supervision takes place in relation, or, in fact, usually in a series of relationships. For example, in addition to the relation to the supervisee, a supervisor is likely to be related to some institution, or in addition, to a professional community. Often a supervisor is responsible to a particular professional organization which has its own standards of practice, criteria for evaluation, and a mandate to offer the public services which meet certain criteria of accepted practice. All of those relationships which the supervisor maintains impinge upon and inform supervisory practice. Thus, the supervisor makes ethical decisions against the background of "responsibility" to one or more academic, theoretical, or institutional relationships in addition to the relationship with the supervisee.

The supervisee typically has, in addition to the relationship with the supervisor, a series of relationships as well. In early stages of preparation, the supervisee is likely, in some academic settings, to be examined on the theory and practice of a therapeutic school or schools of which the supervision is a part. Beyond the academic, typically, a supervisee seeks recognition, or, at later stages of professional enhancement, higher levels of recognition from some organization, school, guild, or government bureau which licenses professionals.

Additionally, the supervisor and supervisee are both in relation to the client or clients whom the supervisee presents for supervision. The professional and legal definitions of "vicarious liability" signal the supervisor's responsibility for a supervisee's client, to whom the supervisor may be unknown. It may also be that both parties to supervision are themselves in therapy, or have been in therapy, and each may even be receiving and

offering supervision to and from others. Specifically, the supervisor may
be in supervision of supervision and the supervisee is certainly offering
counseling or therapy to clients. I review all of this to underscore the complicated series of relationships which inform and influence the relationship
between supervisor and supervisee and to emphasize that however we
speak of ethics in supervision we must take seriously the relational aspect
of multifaceted accountabilities which are part of the interaction.

I further emphasize the relational dimension to signal my own bias.
With the exception of those few conditions which we know to be geneti-
cally derived, it is my conviction that skewed early relationships between
infants-children-adolescents and important adults are the source of the
problems or personality issues which persons bring to therapists, *and* that
the essential healing effect of therapy or counseling is a function of the
quality of the relationship which exists between the help-seeker and the
helper. Such matters as setting, particular therapeutic approach, technique, relative professional expertise, titles, diplomas, etc., are all considerably less important than the quality of relation which a client/patient and
a counselor/therapist are able to establish, make use of, work through to
mutual satisfaction, and surrender or terminate. In fact, apart from the
establishment of such a relationship or therapeutic bond, the exercise of
the skills and techniques of therapy can be experienced as manipulative
and thus can be counter-therapeutic.

Additionally, I believe that the ability of a counselor to offer such a
relation is a function of his or her own important relations. If those relations have nurtured the therapist in such a way as to enable him or her to
become an open, receptive, empathic, non-judgmental, decisive, non-defensive person, then the person has the essential ingredients needed to
provide his or her part of an intimate bond with a help-seeker. Obviously,
by important relations I mean not only the therapist/counselor's early experiences with parents, but those important later experiences of confirmation which reinforce early experiences or which correct or heal them—
relations with teachers, religious leaders, therapists, et al. Not the least
important and difficult tasks of a supervisor of therapists is to judge which
of a supervisee's weaknesses are academic or supervisory and which are
therapeutic, calling for the student to pursue his or her own therapy in
protection of the student's clients, and to exercise supervisory authority
or influence to direct the student into therapy.

I further believe that this relation-making enterprise of counseling or
therapy can only be effectively taught *in relation*, i.e. in supervision with
a recognized journeyman practitioner who offers yet another relationship
as the primary medium of teaching a novice counselor how to offer therapeutic relations to clients. That is, in the course of supervision, a rela-

tional bond is formed which becomes the experiential model (though the content is different) of what a healing relation can be. This is hardly to suggest that supervision and therapy are not different enterprises but only that they share in common *relation* as the medium of change, *and that* a skewed supervisory relation will be counter-productive because it models brokenness, alienation, and frustration which will, in turn, negatively influence the supervisee's relations with clients. This is not to suggest that problems will not inevitably arise in supervision, but only to emphasize that those problems left unaddressed will lead to disintegration of the relation and be poor modeling for the student.

II. Supervision as a Mentor/Protégé Relation

I have exposed another bias. It is my conviction that the supervisory relation, if it is to be effective, is *not* an adversarial relation, marked by constant critique, manipulative distancing, confrontation, and challenge, but rather a mutually respectful mentor/protégé relation marked by the protégé's willingness to expose weaknesses, fears, and failures, in the confidence that the mentor will be receptive, respectful, and gently encouraging and supportively didactic. In an early experience in supervision I was greeted in the first hour by this statement: "The executive committee has decided you need supervision. I am the only member who was willing to work with you. So you better make good use of this, or you will be out of a job." Months into that experience we were so badly stuck that he suggested that we mutually seek consultation about our work. The consultant listened to each of us for some time and then suggested that my supervisor and I were nearly enough peers that the relation was doomed. We terminated shortly. I did need supervision. I did not need threats or abuse. I could have made very good use of a mentor, but was not offered that.

It *is* the supervisor's task to teach, correct, challenge, and evaluate. Those tasks can be accomplished best, I believe, in a relationship of mutual respect. Obviously, it is that same sort of relation the supervisee is attempting to make with a client to form a working therapeutic bond. It is difficult for me to see that an essentially adversarial relationship with a supervisor will model the quality of intimacy needed to do effective therapy. On the contrary, I suspect that arrogance and so-called professional distancing which blocks healing in our work with clients is learned or at least reinforced in supervision which is established on an adversarial base.

Certainly this emphasis on parallel therapeutic and supervisory relations as the media of therapeutic and supervisory effectiveness does not as clearly apply to those counseling modalities which are oriented essentially to technical rather than relational healing. For example, in systemic family therapy where artful manipulation and the well-timed exercise of self-conscious technique is the approach of choice and demonstrable effectiveness, the supervisory medium will be essentially didactic, with the supervisor teaching the use, choice and effective timing of techniques. The same would likely apply to behavioral therapy supervision, where, again, technique rather than the offering of a corrective relation is the operative healing modality. In such modalities, the prevailing ethic would likely be teleological since the goal of behavioral change of persons or systems is mutually understood, accepted and contracted for, and those means of change which serve that goal are the accepted means.

To return to the mentor/protégé relation as my model for effective supervision of relationally oriented therapies, what can we say about that relation which helps us comprehend its ethical dimension? We will look at its potential distortion and its potential usefulness.

First of all, the mentor/protégé relation is subject to the same potential distortions as the therapist/client relationship since each is beset by the confusion attendant to the transference phenomena. The supervisee, anxious to please, eager to grow, fearful of failure, will bring to the relation unrealistic expectations for the potential of supervision, the potency of the supervisor, and the limits of his or her own potential. In addition, all the supervisee's accumulated conscious and unconscious feelings about persons in authority will be in play. Those distortions, mixed with the height of the stakes on success or failure, make the supervisee a very vulnerable person at the outset—an "easy mark" for exploitation or manipulation by the supervisor. Needless to say, depending on the supervisee's psychodynamics, this vulnerability may be transparent and clearly and non-defensively acknowledged, or, more likely, masked behind a variety of covers and possibly only vaguely comprehended by the supervisee. In those cases where supervision is being sought less than willingly or enthusiastically, all of these distortions will be further complicated by a more or less freely acknowledged sense of resentment or hostility in the supervisee.

The mentor, for his or her part, will have countertransference responses in both the senses in which that word is used in the literature. First, like the supervisee, the supervisor has expectations of self, protégé, and the supervisory enterprise which influence receptivity to the student and influence early responses to the student. These are more or less transparent as a function of the supervisor's psychodynamics. Second, in response to the protégé's transference, the mentor will exercise his or her own countertransference. That these countertransference phenomena are often a mix of positive and negative responses to self, others, task, and eventually to the third parties to this enterprise, the protégé's clients, only serves further to distort and confuse the picture. It is out of this morass of ambivalent feelings, needs, and expectations that a useful learning bond must be forged.

When a supervisor has a positive countertransference to a student, and views him or her as a promising therapist-to-be, there lurks in the shadows the potentially envy-creating sense that the mentor may one day be out-distanced by the protégé. When that is a realistic possibility, the parties will have to work through the supervisor's envy and the mix of guilt and triumph which will accrue to the student's experience of success. A good argument can be made for supervision to be done outside of the employment location as a protection against the worst sort of exploitation by either party which could derive from either the mentor's sabotaging or the protégé's manipulating of this circumstance.

When mentor and protégé are mixed gender (or same gender with either or both homosexually oriented) the potential for sexual transference confusion on the part of either or both parties can skew the relation and lead to potential exploitation. Here, all three sorts of ethical questions seem to apply. It is difficult to believe that lovers can also maintain a workable professional teacher/student relation. The teacher's affection for the student will blind him or her to the student's weaknesses, and the student's desire to please the lover will make him or her guarded in presenting weakness. Worse, the desire to be protected and taken care of will lead the student to stay in a needy, subservient position, especially if the maintenance of the supervisory relation is the front-occasion for the two to be together. Worst, the power the protégé may take on in a love relation opens all sorts of potential for exploitation personally, structurally, and professionally, reversing the appropriate symbiosis of mentor and protégé. Such a relation clearly if subtly exploits systems of accountability and clients as well. So, quite apart from the obvious moral concerns, such as the possible violation of other established relations of the two parties, acting out sexual attraction in supervision is deontologically, teleologically and situationally unacceptable. As in therapy, where the same temptations arise commonly, it is the prerogative of the more experienced professional person in the mix to control acting out no matter how tempted or severely provoked.

However, the occurrence of sexual attraction between the parties creates important supervisory opportunities. If we accept that sexual attraction is a transferential phenomenon and thus pre-ethical (feelings are neither right nor wrong, only actions bear moral evaluation), the careful working through of these feelings, acknowledging their limited importance, their potential for the destruction of the supervisory relation, and their respectability as expressions of esteem for one another, will model for the student a way to make use of and thus not be phobic of the same sexual transference and countertransference issues which arise in therapy. Thus, the mature supervisor will make use of an otherwise frightening and potentially destructive circumstance to further the student's understanding and equip him or her to deal with some potentially troublesome therapeutic experiences with clients. Such an experience in supervision will model the transformation of transference (being "in love") to reality-syntonic growth and healing (loving). In the process, the mentor will necessarily risk his or her own vulnerability through self-disclosure and thus model for the protégé the appropriate transparent use of one's self and feelings in a healing relation.

III. Some Specific Ethical Issues

In noting some of the potential problems in the mentor/protégé relation, we have already dealt with specific ethical issues. We will now look at several other ethical issues which arise in supervision.

Among the issues we have to address in our field is that of professional cloning. There is an ethical issue which arises when we become possessive of a student or a former client, or both, and seek to offer supervision to that person. Our propensity to clone ourselves and the propensity of those whom we have influenced therapeutically or academically to become clones presents us with real temptations. I recall a former teacher of mine whom I revered and whose very junior colleague I became as a young college teacher/administrator. It was his ambition for me that I become a college administrator and move to be a college or university president. After years of distinguished teaching and writing he had become a dean. He put his ambition for me in a winsomely seductive but grandiose way: "Bob, between the two of us we could influence nearly a century of higher education." Similarly, when a particular client or student shows promise (surely influenced by counter-transference) we are tempted to hold on to him or her, and he or she may be tempted to cling to us. Who else, we wonder, could mold this very promising young star as effectively as we? (How else will my professional immortality be insured? is likely the more honest question.) The potentiality for the exploitation of mutual grandiosity is rife in such issues as these. As in human development, the youth who wins the Oedipal battle likely loses the developmental war. Appropriately, we let students and clients with professional promise go, to be influenced by others, encourage them without possessiveness and avoid exploitation for our ego's sake. In the process, we make a larger contribution to the enrichment of our field by avoiding incestuous cloning and encouraging random professional cross-fertilization.

Another issue which raises ethical concerns of a more subtle type is that of the male dominance in our field—reflective of our culture to be sure, but in need of reform as the culture is struggling to do, or at least to appear to do. In a field which can be inclined to privatized attitudes, we need to be more sensitive to our social impact and to the potential for social reform in the work we do. We do not serve women who are becoming therapists well when we teach them in male dominated faculties, teach male-biased developmental and psychotherapeutic theory, always refer them to male therapists, always assign them to male supervisors, and then expect them to establish themselves as female professionals, especially in a profession in which the creative use of one's *self*, including sexuality, is of such significance. When we add the irony that we still see a predominantly female clientele in therapy, such a training process not only does an injustice to female therapists-to-be, it makes a would-be healing enterprise into one which perpetuates counter-therapeutic ideas, postures, influences, and relations. Our mandate to heal argues for us to lead in the correcting of old societal griefs and grievances, and one place to start is to increase the number of women teaching in our field and to provide female supervisors for female students. It could be further argued that many males who seek to become therapists would benefit from a female supervisor as a means to be further sensitized to the subtleties of prejudice toward their female clients and as an experience of accountability to a seasoned female professional. The wise use of the transference issues raised by that arrangement would go far to addressing on-going attitudes of entitlement among males. In group supervision, where more than one faculty member or supervisor is involved, a male-female team models for all students the possibility of mutually respectful sharing of equal authority.

The issue of fees charged for supervision is rife with ethical considerations. It would be difficult to account for how fees for therapeutic and supervisory services are established. In fact, it would be hard to find any rationale for fees apart from the "whatever the traffic will bear" rule. Since much of supervision is offered to novice professionals or graduate students and since those persons constitute a captive clientele by virtue of either academic requirements or the criteria established by certifying organizations or governmental rules, and since we supervisors are in the position to influence those criteria or rules in such a way as to restrict competition and perpetuate our hegemony, we would be well-advised to consider a careful review of our fees. "Whatever the traffic will bear" is not an adequate ethical base for establishing fees. Nor is the argument that a therapeutic hour "sells" for so much (often with third-party support), and therefore any fee less than that represents a loss, adequate for establishing supervisory fees. In fact, it is my experience that doing supervision offers professional and personal rewards far beyond its financial returns. Supervisory fees, except where they are built into a larger tuition arrangement, might well be established in terms of a supervisee's ability to pay rather than on a fixed fee. Even in the case of academic requirements, as supervisors we likely have more influence on policy-setting than our tendency to protect ourselves financially inclines us to exercise. Given the captive clientele we create with our rules and criteria, we do well to model for our protégés a generosity of spirit which they can carry into their work. In this, as in so many other aspects of supervision, we are unwittingly providing the primary model our students have of professional integrity. Bearing that in mind, as we establish or negotiate or modify fees, take seriously our larger responsibility for influencing the future of our craft.

In our work with our supervisees we have a legally explicit but a more compelling morally implicit responsibility for the well-being of the third parties to our contract: the students' clients. When a protégé's work with a client is potentially harmful to the client or the student's refusal to engage at a therapeutic level leaves a needy client without adequate support, challenge, or care, we are responsible for leading the student to take responsibility for the work. In my experience, students who are novices in the field or whose own lack of personal awareness blocks intimate engagement with a client are likely to revert to the exercise of technique to substitute for a healing relationship. Technique by its very nature is potentially violent, and in the hands of a green and therefore insecure counselor it is often used against the client rather than for him or her. We likely recognize this at those points where we are tempted to use technique ourselves as a defense against our discomfort with what we are seeing in the student's work. With that, or any other internal "early warning system," we signal the need to engage the supervisee in depth with us in the service of experiential learning. Often a time like this is pregnant with the potential for putting before a student the need for further or on-going therapy if he or she is to be effective in this work which requires self-knowledge, the working through of old personal pain, the forgiveness of our parents, and the acceptance of ourselves *before* we engage the pain of clients. Reversion to the seeming safety and specificity of technique is often a clue that the novice has not done that hard personal work which is the *sine qua non* of effective practice.

A final issue is subtle. In my experience, there is a widespread tendency in therapists to a quality of arrogance, entitlement, pomposity, and professional posturing which is difficult to understand in professionals who offer a naively innocent public only the most vague specificity of "treatment" for the pains endemic to the human condition. Our generation of established therapists came to maturity at the height of the so-called human potential movement. Twenty years later, we are, if we are listening to our clients and attentive to our own foibles, personally, relationally, and professionally, more aware of the compelling impotentiality of our humanity. Yet, we posture on, as though we (or anyone) were, in fact, superior to anyone else, to our clients, our students, or fellow practitioners of other therapeutic modalities. Before and beyond our training, our own therapy, and our receipt of various certificates, diplomas, and titles, we were and are human beings, beset by all of the difficulties which plague our species and immune to none of the ills our clients bring to us. It is precisely that humanity which is our best hope for truly understanding and empathizing with clients so that we may form a healing relation. I recall as a green therapist in an early supervisory experience that I began to hear myself on audio tape aping my supervisor, his style, his vocabulary, even his vocal inflections. The seeds of transference—such is the powerful influence we often have on a protégé. Thus, if we posture our superiority, we invite our students to become arrogant, and a new generation of professionals perpetuates destructive, dehumanizing, and distancing self-presentation at the expense of clients already tempted by the inequality of our stylized setting to make us Gods. In the mentor/protégé relation we have been exploring, our claiming our humanity with all the impotentiality implicit in existence best serves our supervisees' needs to acknowledge their limits, the limits of their clients, and the distinct limits of our craft.

Conclusion

Despite our claims to moral neutrality as therapists, we have inherited the priestly mantle of moralists in a secular society. We are asked to tell a confused and frightened society—one at a time, in groups, in the books we write, in the media—how to raise children, deal with existential loneliness, combat stress, fix broken marriages, heal old griefs, resolve guilt, et al. When we answer, either directly or with the inevitable verbal and non-verbal signs of agreement and reinforcement or disagreement and challenge to a client's words and behavior, we are acting as moralists, judging, approving, or disapproving. So also with our protégés in supervision. Wittingly or not, they seek the illusive "one right way" to "do" an art which has more to do with "being" than with "doing" and we sit in judgment of their work, leading them ever so gradually to accept the non-specificity of our craft and to live with the anxiety of their own essential weakness in the face of the brokenness, terror, rage, apathy, and despair their clients present. In the process, we hear ourselves reaffirming our vocation even as we accept its and our limits, and we see our supervisees gradually surrender the quest for magical specificity to accepting the reality of the power of the healing relationship.

The "shoulds" and "oughts" of deontological ethics with their assumption of a categorical imperative, timeless truth, and some sort of accountability to some higher authority seem, usually, incongruent with the relativity of so much we deal with as therapists and supervisors. It seems to me that morality only begins where we run out of rules, exhaust the lists on various codes of ethics, and face the need to *choose* and to take a stand. It occurred to me about three-quarters of the way through this chapter that I was writing about ethics, held strong opinions, and yet was not saying "we should" or "you ought" or other imperative statements. With the exception of sexual acting out in supervision, very little of what I have said arises out of or is best explicated in the rigid categories of deontological ethics. And even that issue can be clearly explicated teleologically and contextually.

Teleological ethics, on the other hand, with its questions "What is our end or goal?" and "What actions best serve our goal?" have informed much of what I have written. Our goal is to initiate a new generation of therapists into the mysteries of our vocation. That goal provides a focus for how we spend our time in supervision and sets limits on our actions and interactions.

However, in the complexities of everyday contact with our protégés, it seems to me that the questions of a situational or contextual ethics serve us best: "What is happening?" and "What is an appropriate or fitting response to what is happening?" Whether our attention in a given moment is on the establishment, the working through or the surrendering of the mentor/protégé relation itself, or on the supervisee's work with a client, or on the intricacies of parallel processes between and among the parties, attention moment by moment to what is happening and to fitting responses to what is happening takes seriously the relational context in which we and our protégés work. In contextual ethics "responsibility" is rescued from its popular definition of "obligation" and refers to the more difficult and subjective definition: the ability to respond. There, freedom, choice among options, and the need to live with our choices create tensions which seldom accrue to simply meeting obligations. That we raise the contextual questions of ourselves and of our protégés within the limits of our teleologically defined task does not diminish the usefulness of the contextual approach. In the process, we again model a way of being together which will serve our supervisees well as they surrender their hope of finding "the one right way" and take up the harder work of being with their clients, bereft of agenda and at risk of suffering with others. When we have suffered with them, they will find the avenue more credible, for they will have experienced the healing power of careful attention and patient waiting.

Joseph A. Heim, M.S., C.A.S.

18

The Social Justice Issues in Supervision

Supervision and social justice may not seem to have much in common, but there exists, in fact, an organic link between the two. The nature of the counseling and the supervisory tasks, although highly individualized processes, requires an awareness of the broader social issues in order to effectively carry out their purposes. There is a profound interdependence between the individual and the social forces that influence human existence, and those in the helping professions have long been concerned with the relationship between the two. The concern, however, has not remained on the level of mere interest or intellectual curiosity; it has carried over into commitment and action. Alfred Adler, one of Freud's first disciples, was concerned about social issues before becoming a psychiatrist and maintained that concern throughout his life. He felt that the psychiatrist had to work to change structures that were harmful to the human race, e.g., wars, unemployment, etc. (1934). Many eminent psychologists today share the same view. Nearly a decade ago Carl Rogers (1977) wrote:

> Those individuals (person-centered) can see no reason why rigid schools, glaring maldistribution of wealth, depressed ghetto areas, unfair racial or sexual discrimination, unjust wars should remain unchanged. They expect to change these situations.

It would seem, then, that the work of the supervisor should include not only an awareness of social justice questions, but also a concern for and a commitment to them, for they form a part of the total human reality. As the supervisor assists the counselor in the delicate and intricate task of leading the client toward health, that task is most effectively carried out when there is a deep awareness of the social, economic and political milieu of the client's world. There is no other way by which a client can be guided toward total health except in the context of the total picture of his or her reality. Social myopia on the part of the counselor or the supervisor can only impede the work of therapy.

I. Justice Dimensions in Counseling

Social justice, of course, is not something new in supervision. It has always been taken very seriously on at least three levels. (a) There is the consideration of the just relationship between supervisor and counselor; this concerns the quality of one's presence, professional attention, an understanding of the supervisee's personal dynamics and a grasp of the countertransference issues. (b) There is the concern for the counselor's justice toward himself or herself. Is the counselor taking sufficient care of his or her own needs? Are there signs of overwork, depression, etc.? (c) There is the question of justice toward the client. Is the counselor fulfilling the contract with the people seeking professional help? Here the concerns are ones of preparedness, competency, confidentiality, etc. Because of the proliferation of lawsuits against professionals, this dimension of justice is, understandably, receiving an enormous amount of attention today. These three levels of justice have always been a primary concern for supervisors (and rare exceptions would only bear out the rule). However, there seems to be another dimension of justice that is demanding attention in both counseling and supervision: it is the structural or institutional level of justice. In this century human endeavor has moved from merely discovering the world to actually giving shape to it! Modern technology has enabled us to alter substantially our reality. At the World's Fair in New York in 1939, visitors to the General Motors Exhibit sat spellbound as they watched "The World of The Sixties." They saw miniature automobiles racing down superhighways while industrial parks and clusters of suburban homes dotted the landscape. By the 1960's, of course, that world was a reality. General Motors did not have a crystal ball in 1939, nor were they just making educated guesses. They envisioned, designed and created the world of the 1960's.

The structures of society, therefore, are not accidents, but the result of human decisions and planning. Unfortunately, not all of the shapes and forms of social organization are just; many, in fact, are terribly unjust. Consider, for example, from the distant and not so distant past, child labor, segregation, etc. The problem becomes more serious, however, when we consider that not only are there unjust structures, but their power to harm is not immediately evident to the victim. They weigh heavily but are not recognized as such. They are the "silent killers" of a socio-political-economic system. The power that unjust structures can exert on one's unconscious was brought home to me many years ago when I worked on construction with two carpenters. They were great buddies and used to play tricks on each other. One day one of them put two five pound lead weights in the other's tool box and let him carry it around for a month before finally letting him in on the joke. Although he took it in good fun, the victim of the hoax remarked that he had, indeed, felt the extra weight but thought that it was probably due to his age or simply not feeling well. In other words, he blamed himself when, in point of fact, he was the victim of an "unjust" situation. That is precisely how societal injustices function: they create heavy burdens but the victim very often does not recognize or realize the structural nature of the problem, and so tends to blame himself.

This structural dimension of social injustice can easily become an issue in supervision. For instance, Joan is supervising John as he counsels a fifty-five year old male client who is suffering from feelings of worthlessness and depression. The client had suffered a heart attack two years previously but was taking care of himself and had a clean bill of health from his physician. However, his company retired him quite suddenly a month ago and that precipitated the present clinical situation. He feels that he is a "failure" and "just no good anymore."

Joan is aware of actuarial studies and of the fact that large companies will prematurely retire someone whose death "on the job" would be more costly to them than his death "off the job." She feels very strongly that there is a justice issue involved here. How should she proceed with the supervision? (The problem becomes more complicated, of course, if John does not share Joan's views on the justice dimension.) Should she suggest supportive therapy, behavioral techniques, life-planning workshops? Should they address the symptom or the cause? Do they help the client "adjust" to reality or do they broaden his vision so that he sees reality in a different light? What would be more *just* to the client? In other words, what are the limits of the counseling and the supervisory contracts? When does the attempt to lead toward a broader horizon actually become the imposition of one's own opinion? Does the counselor have the same commitment as the social caseworker who, as Carel Germain (1979) comments, "groped for ways to implement the dual commitment to helping people and changing environments"?

There seems to be emerging, then, an important justice dimension to supervision and it concerns that mysterious area of inter-relation between the individual and society. We are the products of our world and our culture, but we also have influenced and produced our world and our culture. The presence of nuclear arms has a devastating effect on the human psyche, yet the build-up of the nuclear arsenal is itself the result of collective feelings of inadequacy, if not paranoia. We are, at once, the victims and the cause; we suffer from the results of what we have created. Yet, it is ultimately our responsibility; we cannot blame it on the serpent, as Eve did in the Genesis story. What counselors and supervisors seem to be facing today is a twofold challenge: first, they must be conscious of the power that social forces have on the people coming for therapy; second, they must bring their professional talents to bear on those very forces in order to humanize them. Those in the mental health profession are in that very privileged position of being present to so many people in their pain and being able to alleviate that pain. However, since the cause of pain can be identified in structures as well as in the individual's unconscious, counselors are being challenged to address the collective as well as the individual source of human misery. Judith H. Katz (1985, p. 621), quoting an impressive array of experts in the field, writes:

> More recently, research in community psychology indicates that interventions made in the environment may be more effective in promoting mental health than interventions made on the individual level.

What appears to be happening is that the communications media have made everyone, professionals and clients, aware of social problems. Also, both the therapist and the client find themselves walking by more "street people," "bag ladies" and soup kitchens than most post-Depression people can remember. Even in the seclusion of the home one is faced with such issues as Marxism in Latin America, the foreign debt and international terrorism, and because therapy is a humanizing process, many clients are not only forming opinions about how society functions, but, in some cases, they are taking action on these issues. This coming to consciousness becomes the subject of the therapy session. In fact, the awareness of broader issues and the concern for the structures of society are signs that the client is making significant progress on the road to health and maturity. They signal a movement away from self-absorption and narcissism. Nearly ten years ago Carl Rogers, reflecting on the process of counseling, wrote:

> Our purpose is facilitating personal and political consciousness-raising, by educating about the political dimension of personal vision, and about the human dimension of political lives and social issues (1977, pp. 276–277).

Culture: A Parallel. The social justice dimension of supervision is very similar to culture and the way it affects the counseling or supervisory process. The effective therapist informs himself or herself as to the cultural background of the client, and any failure in this area would tend to cause difficulties that would most likely surface in supervision. For instance, a black, male client may not open up very easily or quickly to a white counselor, thereby inducing the counselor to consider the client as "resistant."

However, there are important historical and cultural dimensions to be taken into consideration. The black male had to learn to repress his true feelings when dealing with whites in order to survive in the white man's world. Segregation is now illegal, but its impact on black culture is still very severe, and the cultural phenomenon of the black's reticence to expose his feelings to a white person is likely to remain for some time. Justice issues, therefore, function in very much the same fashion as cultural ones in that they weigh heavily on the life of the client, yet, for the most part, go unrecognized. If the counselor fails to recognize their presence and their impact, then the supervisor must point them out.

II. Supervisory Tasks

The principal supervisory tasks and how they relate to the issue of social justice will be our next order of business. We will consider: (a) Counter-Transference, (b) Ethical Sensitivity, (c) Values, (d) The Religious Perspective and (e) Integration.

1. *Countertransference.* It is incumbent on the supervisor to assist the therapist-in-training to be aware of countertransference feelings. Failure in this area will only inhibit the counseling process. Few issues have the power to enkindle a negative reaction as does the issue of social justice. For instance, a financially well-off counselor, whose income is derived in whole or in part from stock dividends, may experience very negative feelings when dealing with an unemployed, poor client. In fact, he may find it much less threatening to himself to diagnose the client as an "inadequate personality" or a "malingerer" than to consider the sociological situation in which the client lives. Although many lazy people are unemployed, the converse is not necessarily true. There may be other reasons, deriving from the very way that society is structured, that cause unemployment. The supervisor will, therefore, help the counselor in dealing with countertransference issues but will also have to assist the counselor in an appreciation of the intricate ways that society and individuals are interrelated.

> Personal pain and joy are intricately tied to institutional policies and power. Pastoral counselors participate in the decisions that monitor institutional change, particularly in institutions that are working with health care issues. Change in personality is intricately interwoven with change in institutions. One process cannot be addressed apart from the other (Ewing, 1983, p. 288).

2. *Ethical Sensitivity* is well covered in this book by R. Davenport in

Chapter 17, but a review of the threefold distinction that he makes is important for our consideration here. Davenport credits H. Richard Niebuhr for distinguishing (a) the "deontological" or "what *must* I do or abstain from doing?" approach to ethics, (b) the "teleological" or the "what is the *goal* or what are the ends?" approach, and (c) the "situational" or "What is the fitting or appropriate *response* to what is happening?" approach. The third of these, which is the one usually called "situational" or "contextual" ethics, is the one most generally accepted as the ideal in counseling or supervision. At the same time, this approach is curiously allied with the second or teleological one which has us consider the *goals or the reasons* in ethics. Social justice calls us to consider our "ability to respond" (situational approach) in the light of the goals (teleological approach.) In other words, the goal of therapy is not the individual apart from society but the individual *as a member of society*. The most effective therapy is done when societal as well as individual well-being is taken into consideration. The most ethical *response* is the one that *responds* to the *situation* in its entirety. A curious shift in ethical approaches sometimes occurs in those counselors and supervisors who have experienced profound structural injustice. In matters that pertain to personal human limitations they usually tend to use a "situational" approach, i.e., they will assist clients in coming to terms with the realities of the human condition. In addressing justice issues, however, these same individuals sometimes shift to the "deontological" approach, challenging the structures which they perceive to contribute to the dehumanized situations they have experienced. Such counselors may be deeply sensitive and accepting of individuals and, at the same time, categorically rejecting of unjust structures. While on the surface such a stance might suggest a certain rigidity of personality, in reality it may be indicative of a healthy and integrated sense of social justice.

3. *Values.* The supervisor must walk the delicate line between having a personal value system yet not imposing that system on the supervisee. Although most everyone in the profession would adhere theoretically to this principle, its application in practice is a very different matter. As Samler (1972) points out: ". . . to say that the counselor manifests no values is to require that he have no feelings and whatever great drama this may be it is not counseling."

The question is, then, how to work from a value system while not imposing it on another. Specifically, how does a supervisor with a highly developed sense of social justice deal with a supervisee who is generally unaware of that dimension? Consider the case of an elderly male client who has recently been confined to a nursing home by his family. He is angry because he feels that he can still look after his own needs and attend to his own affairs. The counselor feels that his responsibility is to assist the client in dealing with his anger, his depression, and the problems of the aging process and also to help him adjust to the new reality of his life. The supervisor, however, feels that there are other values involved in the case. She feels that the man's family acted unjustly in that they denied the client his right to lead his own life. If the counselor does not see the justice dimension, the supervisor has a serious dilemma. She feels that helping the client to "adjust" would be very unjust to him. How does she proceed? To what extent can she make "suggestions" without imposing her value system on the supervisee? The problem becomes even more complicated for her if she is in a position to evaluate or give a grade to the therapist-in-training.

4. *The Religious Perspective.* An awareness of the nuances of the variety of religious beliefs and traditions can assist the supervisor in being sensitive to the justice issues which, frequently, are part and parcel of the supervisory session. For instance, the God of the Jewish Scriptures is the one who intervenes on behalf of his people enslaved in the political, economic and cultural slavery of Egypt. "I have *seen* the miserable state of my people in Egypt. I have *heard* their appeal to be free. . . . I am *aware* of their sufferings. I mean to deliver them" (Ex 3:7–8). The same Scriptures are replete with references to God's concern for the "widow, the foreigner and the orphan," i.e., the defenseless ones of society (cf. Dt 14:29, 16:11 and passim). Jose Miranda, in his book *Marx and the Bible* (1974), points out the interpenetration of faith and justice, i.e., of the "knowledge of God" and social concerns put into effective action. "He defended the cause of the poor and the needy; this is good. Is not this what it means to *know* me?" (Jer 22:16). To *know God* in the scriptural sense is to *do justice*. Christian faith is equally explicit on the integration of faith and justice. Jesus proclaimed it by his very self definition in Luke 4:18: "He sent me to bring good news to the poor, to proclaim liberty to captives, and to the blind, new sight, to set the downtrodden free." Each portion of this statement speaks of concrete action on behalf of those who are unjustly treated. The practical application of this principle has been well laid out by Francis X. Meehan, a Roman Catholic theologian, who writes: "Most clearly it means that not only does our love of God overflow to our brothers and sisters but it also impels us to regard the social structures that affect those brothers and sisters" (1982, p. 8).

There is an interesting "turn-about" occurring in the religious field in both North and South America. It involves many socially-conscious people who had abandoned their religious practices (Protestant, Catholic and Jewish) because their churches or synagogues seemed disinterested in political and economic questions. Now, since many churches have taken a more active role in these matters, more and more social activists are finding that they can express their concerns within the context of their faith groups. This means that some pastoral counselors are finding themselves facing some rather "militant" clients in their counseling sessions. Because activists often carry a certain degree of anger, it could be a temptation for the therapist to dismiss social commitment as unresolved anger. Such an analysis may be correct (in part, at least) but that does not alter the validity of the issue. Uncovering the psychoanalytic roots of the anger will not, or should not, dissuade the client from commitment to the cause. It may well be true that resentment at an overly-strict father or a cold, unfeeling mother impelled him toward involvement in the struggle against racism, but that does not mean that the struggle is invalid. Mature supervisors or therapists know that unadulterated motivation or pure altruism simply does not exist and they would, therefore, always be cautious not to presume that the analytical roots of the client's involvement would negate the validity of his commitment.

5. *Integration,* both personal and professional, is the last but not the least in this somewhat sketchy list of supervisory issues. Integration is both the journey and the goal and would seem to be concerned with such components as the self as person, the self as counselor, one's value system, academic knowledge and counseling techniques. Here we are not so concerned with these dimensions individually as we are attempting to see them in a holistic fashion. The supervisor could be attentive to each of these components as such, even seeing them in relation to each other, and still miss the "big picture." By the "big picture" is meant the total social context in which we live.

The reality of today's world and the nature of the therapeutic and supervisory processes call us to look not only at individuals and their interrelationships but also at the structures that so seriously affect the human reality of our world. This has been the thesis presented in this chapter but the element of integration brings us to a new level of consideration, namely, the ability to move from awareness of an issue to a *feeling* for it. Anthony deMello (1984, p. 2), in his book *The Song of the Bird,* uses an example from the Sufi wisdom to illustrate the feeling level of awareness:

Uwais the Sufi was once asked,
    'What has grace brought you?'

He replied,
    'When I wake in the morning I feel
    like a man who is not sure he will
    live till evening.'

Said the questioner,
    'But, doesn't everyone know this?'
Said Uwais,
    'They certainly do.
    But not all of them
    feel it.'

Until this point what has been principally addressed is the importance of *awareness* of social structures in order to do effective counseling and supervision. But our very humanness calls for the supervisor to promote not only awareness of, but also a *feeling* for, the social reality. In this way the counselor's social concerns would emanate as naturally as do the empathic or interpretative responses. Integration, in its deepest dimension, implies a connectedness of all of one's humanity with all humanity.

There is a fascinating parallel to this feeling dimension of awareness in the life of Leon Tolstoy, the famous Russian novelist. Tolstoy was a teacher, soldier, writer and aristocrat. But, what is more important, he had a deeply sensitive nature that brought him into contact with the hungry and the poor. He was able to integrate his feelings, his social awareness and his artistic ability so well that many of his works were extremely disturbing to his fellow aristocrats. They were sometimes unpopular with his wife too, as she would have preferred that he write books that brought in an income rather than criticizing the social realities of his day. The point, however, for our purposes here is that Tolstoy presents a model for therapists in that he integrated his feelings, social awareness and artistic talent and, because of that integration, took effective action to change the reality that surrounded him. It is the hope of every supervisor that the therapist-in-training progress from technician to artist. The supervisor can help the counselor in that journey by encouraging him or her to make the journey from awareness to feeling and, finally, to commitment in relation to the social reality of our world.

III. The Past, Present and Future of Social Justice in Supervision and Counseling

Social psychology has, from its beginnings, been concerned with the relationship between the individual and society, but mostly in an attempt to discover how the environment affected the individual. The "Social Casework" approach, however, has attempted to apply clinical procedures to the environment as well as to the client. This approach deals with "systemic evaluation" and "systemic prevention." As Carol Swenson (1979) describes it: "The objectives of treatment include providing an environment where the person's progressive forces are encouraged and the nutritive qualities of the environment itself are enhanced." In some areas, then, there is a decided movement toward involvement in systemic change as an integral part of therapy.

Significant work has also been done in the "systems" approach to family therapy as developed by Satir, Munuchin, Haley, Bowen, et al. Instead of dealing with the family as individuals or employing the techniques of group counseling, these therapists have developed the strategy of addressing the *structural* level of the family problem. Rather than investigate the psychodynamics of each individual, they examine how the family system is malfunctioning. Therapy consists in addressing the structural rather than the individual level and so helps the family members to relate to one another in new and healthier ways. Thus, they have learned and in an impressive way demonstrated how attention to structure or institution is essential to the counseling task.

Professional mental health associations are making more and more explicit statements concerning the social responsibility of their members. The American Association for Counseling and Development (AACD) considers its members as ". . . dedicated to the enhancement of the worth, dignity, potential, and uniqueness of each individual and *thus to the service of society*" (1981; italics mine). It also states that the primary obligations of the counselor are "to respect the integrity and promote the welfare of the client(s)." As with any good statement, these provoke more questions than they answer. How does one determine what is for the "welfare" of the client? And what happens when the client's welfare is at odds with the welfare of the rest of society, or when the counselor's or supervisor's ethics collide with those of the client? A wealthy client in marriage therapy mentions in an offhand manner how he had to pay off some union officials in order to settle a strike. He not only does not evidence any guilt but actually feels good about his handling of that situation and says that it was the "responsible" thing to do for his stockholders. What does the counselor do or the supervisor suggest especially if they both have a deep sense of justice? If it is not an issue for the industrialist, should one *make* it an issue? How widely can that area be stretched between our responsibility for the individual and our responsibility for society? The American Psychological Association (APA) adopted the "Ethical Principles of Psychologists" (1981). These principles speak not only about concern for the "public interest" but go on to state: "Psychologists are guided by the primary obligation to aid the public in developing informed judgments, opinions and choices." This would seem to be a significant step in the very delicate matter of a professional association enunciating the responsibility for its members to concern themselves with social justice issues. Just how much more clearly the Association can enunciate such principles without drawing excessive criticism for being political is yet to be seen. Another significant step taken by the APA in this matter was the publication of the October 1985 issue of *The Counseling Psychologist*. It contains some of the most thought-provoking and challenging articles to be published in some time and deals with such topics as the predominance of the white culture in counseling and the sociopolitical nature of counseling.

There is also a growing awareness among pastoral counselors of the need to integrate counseling and social justice. Notable in this regard is the recently established "Pastoral Care Network For Social Responsibility, Inc." The founders of the group, in a recent brochure, describe its purpose as attempting

> to promote increasing awareness among pastoral care specialists of the impact of this enormous crisis of our planet, on the lives of the persons and the institutions with whom we work. To provide pastoral care and counseling to those facing anxiety and stress, and to develop constructive responses to the crisis using the insights, skills and resources derived from our training in pastoral care.

Eminent leaders in the field of psychology (A. Ellis, C. Rogers, A. Maslow, S. L. Halleck) have long been interested and active in social concerns and, most recently, in the major concern of our times: nuclear arms. Drawing on these and on the wisdom of other experts in the counseling profession, Jo Anne Gearhart makes some very explicit statements concerning the responsibilities of counselors in the nuclear age:

> Counselors should become aware of nuclear issues, counsel clients who express fear and uncertainty about the future, and act in ways consistent with personal beliefs to bring about changes in public policy (1984, p. 69).

In conclusion, it would seem, then, that we are definitely in a new era in the fields of counseling and supervision, an era in which we see our task not only in terms of the individual but also in terms of the institutions that affect the individual. The integrated counselor and supervisor are persons who have an understanding not only of the client's personal unconscious but also an awareness of the power that institutions have on the human psyche. The task is taking on enormous proportions but there is really no other option. As members of the human race we will be either part of the problem or part of the solution. S. L. Halleck has pointed out: "There is no way in which the psychiatrist can deal with behavior that is partly generated by a social system without either strengthening or altering that system" (1971, p. 27).

The demands on both counselor and supervisor are taking on new proportions, but that is the nature of the work and also a characteristic of our age. Carolyn Saari remarks: "New knowledge is growing so rapidly that all professional groups must integrate discoveries from other fields in order to remain relevant" (1986, p. 2). The supervisor, then, must have some knowledge of how social institutions function and how they affect people, i.e., some knowledge of sociology as well as psychology in order to carry out the task of supervision effectively.

References

A. Adler, *Mass Psychology*, from *The Individual Psychology of Alfred Adler*, by Heinz Ansbacher, Ph.D. and Rowena Ansbacher, Ph.D., Basic Books, N.Y. (1956).

American Association for Counseling and Development, *Ethical Standards* (1981), Alexandria, Va. (originally published by the American Personnel and Guidance Association).

American Psychological Association, *Ethical Principles of Psychologists;* printed in *American Psychologist*, June 1981, Vol. 36, No. 6, 633–638.

The Counseling Psychologist, Vol. 13, No. 4, October 1985. Sage Publications, Inc., Beverly Hills, Calif.

A. deMello, *The Song of the Bird*, Image Books, N.Y. (1984).

James Ewing, Ph.D., "Pastoral Counseling Issues: Current and Future," Chap. 16 in *Pastoral Counseling*, ed. B. Estadt, Prentice-Hall, N.J. (1983).

Jo Anne Gearhart, "The Counselor in a Nuclear World: A Rationale for Awareness and Action." *Journal of Counseling and Development.* October 1984, Vol. 63.

Carel Germain, *Social Work Practice: People and Environments*, Columbia Press, N.Y. (1979).

S. L. Halleck, *The Politics of Therapy*, Harper & Row, N.Y. (1971).

Judith H. Katz, "The Sociopolitical Nature of Counseling" in *The Counseling Psychologist*, Vol. 13, No. 4, October 1985.

F. X. Meehan, *A Contemporary Social Spirituality*, Orbis, N.Y. 1982.

J. Miranda, *Marx and the Bible*, Orbis, N.Y. (1974).

C. Rogers, *Carl Rogers on Personal Power*, Delacorte, N.Y. (1977).

C. Saari, *Clinical Social Work Treatment*, Gardner, N.Y. (1986).

J. Samler, "Changes in Values: A Goal in Counseling," chap. 3 (II), page 132. From *Counseling: Readings In Theory And Practice*, ed. John F. McGowan and Lyle D. Schmidt. Holt, Rinehart and Winston, Inc., N.Y. (1962).

C. Swenson, quoted in *Social Work Practice: People and Environments*, ed. C. Germain. Columbia Press, N.Y. 1979.

19

Theological and Pastoral Integration

Alicia had been struggling with an important dilemma for her and her community. As a Franciscan she felt drawn to use her newly acquired counseling skills in service to the poor. This was one of the ways she understood the charism of her order for today. However, as with many communities of religious women, there is a critical need for income to meet the financial demands of the order's growing elderly population. With fewer active women earning salaries, the community depends heavily on the working sisters in order to meet their obligations to the retired religious. Alicia knew that if she decided to do counseling with the poor, she would bring in only a minimal income.

How could she balance the realistic need of her community with her sense of vocation and fidelity to the charism of her order? How could she live out her faith commitment and her sense of solidarity with her sisters at the same time? How would she live out her identity as a pastoral counselor? This was the situation which Alicia brought to the pastoral reflection seminar.

This is just one of the many concerns and issues which we have been processing regularly since we added the pastoral reflection seminars as an integral part of the program of the Loyola Pastoral Counseling Department. Later in this chapter, by means of an extended sample session, we will see how Mark, as a man of faith, dealt personally with the reality of suicide in his own family as well as its implications for his work as a pastoral counselor. Both of these people faced questions of integration and attempted to blend a sense of professionalism with a faith perspective. It was just for this type of need, not met in such a explicit way in any other place in the program, that these seminars were first inaugurated as an experiment in 1985.

As the program developed, we knew from regular feedback sessions with our students that they felt good about our ability to initiate them into sound counseling practice. Being people committed to ministry, they were already grounded in various credal worldviews. They were appreciative of the rich electives offered in the program which assisted them in updating their theology. However, they sensed a need for some place to bring the professional and faith dimensions of their lives together, not just to have them nurtured separately. We were encouraged in this direction by the accrediting team from the American Association of Pastoral Counselors who noted the absence of disciplined theological reflection in our program.

Thus in the spring of 1985, we began the first of the pastoral reflection seminars. We decided to use the method of theological reflection proposed by James and Evelyn Whitehead in their book *Method in Ministry* (1983) and adapt it for our own needs. The Loyola Program was first introduced to this approach through a fine workshop given by Michael McGinnis, F.S.C. and Mary Irving, S.S.N.D. as part of an alumni enrichment day on October 6, 1984. Some of the material they presented then has inspired parts of this chapter. I am grateful to them. This experiment with theological reflection has worked well and now these seminars are a required part of our full-time curriculum. They seem to be meeting the need expressed by our students. As several participants expressed in recent evaluations, "It puts the *pastoral* in pastoral counseling."

This last comment may help to understand why a chapter on pastoral reflection seminars appears in this book on supervision. Clearly not everyone in the helping professions will relate in the same way to this need for the integration of faith and profession. However, in the process of becoming a pastoral counselor, this connection is essential. Individual supervision can help somewhat in this development if the supervisor is appreciative of and comfortable with the theological perspective. However, even in that situation, the greatest amount of time and energy is devoted to the clinical development of the candidate. This is as it should be.

Small group and interdisciplinary work can also at times address the pastoral issues as such, but again most of the time is needed to assure the growing therapeutic competence of the student. Furthermore practice has shown that it is quite difficult to shift gears from a clinical to a theological perspective in the same session. As you will see in the course of this chapter, the search for pastoral integration is demanding enough to require a moment of its own in the program.

Thus the pastoral reflection seminars have proven to be important to the ongoing development of our candidates. They have become a necessary element in the overall process by which committed lay people, religious and clergy become competent as professional pastoral counselors, a profession which of its very nature requires an integration of faith, theology and clinical skill.

These seminars assist our students, in the five following specific areas:

1. They help them to develop a personalized understanding of what it means to be a *pastoral* counselor.

2. They help them to focus on the ministerial role of the pastoral counselor.

3. They assist them in dealing with personal integrative questions which arise from doing pastoral counseling or from other dimensions of the program, e.g., exposure to new theological perspectives.

4. They offer them a community of shared faith and trust where they can raise questions which they often have never been able to process before in such a setting.

5. They help them to appropriate a contemporary and relevant theological method.

It is in this type of collaborative role then that these seminars are a part of the Loyola program's overall supervisory process which seeks by disciplined personal interaction to promote the applied professional competence of our pastoral counseling candidates. It is from this perspective that this chapter is included in the present book.

I. Our Approach to Pastoral Reflection Seminars

When Alicia brought her question about the future shape of her counseling work to the pastoral reflection seminar, she had already been thinking and praying about it. She had been doing her own personal theological reflection as a woman of faith committed to ministry in the Church. The seminar offered her a structure and a community in which to deepen and enrich this process of discernment. The community was that of her peers along with a theological resource person. As I mentioned earlier, the structure was adapted from the Whiteheads.

We can describe this approach as the process of attending to the sources of theological reflection which are within us and around us in such a way that we are enabled to have better pastoral insight and to make decisions which will lead to building up the Christian community in the service of God's reign.

In contemporary theology these sources of reflection are three: our lived experience, the tradition and the culture. Such has not always been the case. In the recent past theology focused mainly on the tradition and attempted to represent it to successive generations. People's experience and the cultural matrix provided the language, as it were, into which the tradition was translated when possible. Often the tradition was merely restated. Church members and other interested people were required to learn the traditional language and find meaning there by cultural reappropriation. Therefore theological reflection required that everyone, not just specialists, learn another language and set of symbols in order to think about God's involvement in their present moment.

Today, many contemporary theologians regard the tradition, which includes both Scripture and the subsequent historical reflection on it, as one source for theology among others. Drawing on these trends, the Whiteheads present three sources.

1. *Lived experience:* This is our own story. It is multi-layered and needs to be unfolded to discover its treasures. This is the present human document taken seriously as a source of God's revelation. This valuing represents a strong American sensitivity. In particular, the base communities (*communidades de base*) now common in several Latin American countries are models and sources for understanding the richness of this approach.

2. *Tradition:* This is the process of handing on the experience, values and insight from the past. It represents the larger story of God's interacting with humanity over time and space. This tradition is pluriform in three ways. (See also Whiteheads, 1983, pp. 15–16.)

a. *Over time:* Doctrine and practice have evolved during the centuries both within the scriptural account itself and in the subsequent centuries. For example, our understanding of immortality has developed significantly since the early biblical writings. Also on a practical level, current liturgical practice represents a major evolution beyond the forms of worship found in early Jewish and Christian practice.

Furthermore within the Jewish and Christian traditions there have been strong denominational differences or sub-traditions which have developed in this history of evolving doctrine and practice.

b. *Over space:* In the context of this evolution there have always been geographic and cultural adaptations which have asserted themselves. Many of them have been incorporated into the mainstream and have become universalized.

c. *Through sin and grace:* All our traditions have been ambiguous in their fidelity to the purity of their original inspirations. Thus listening to tradition as a source of theological reflection entails the discernment to sort out the wheat from the chaff.

3. *Culture:* This is the "intricate web of learned responses to the world" (McDermott, 1984, p. 5). Culture is made up of the symbols and

languages through which we understand and interact with reality. Generally cultural influences are implicit. They are taken for granted as the only or at least the best way of viewing ourselves and the world in which we live. This theological reflection method seeks to make them explicit so that we may interact with them and learn from them. For example, today we are very conscious of how much sex role stereotypes have conditioned the way in which we have allowed ourselves to experience being either a woman or a man.

These three sources for reflecting on God and God's involvement with us is what the Whiteheads call their *model*. This model is inserted within a *method* which has three related moments: attending, asserting and decision making.

Attending: In this phase of the method we try to listen and understand as faithfully as possible what each of the three sources of theological reflection have to say to us. This is no simple task since none of the three reveal easily their core. For example, think of how much labor and expertise has been poured into the effort to understand the Scriptures. This exegetical enterprise is phenomenal. On a more personal level, who can claim to grasp the depth of his or her own experience, especially where it is often complex and partially obscured? As far as cultural influences are concerned, we are just beginning to develop methodologies to probe their significance.

It is obvious that in a given pastoral seminar session it is impossible to attend fully to these sources. However, the goal is to further this undertaking by applying appropriate methodologies in a setting where the education, experience and insight of the group can enrich significantly the reflection of the individual.

Asserting: This expression refers to the dialogue between the three sources which follow upon the effort to hear what they have to offer us at this point in time. Once this *asserting* is underway, the seminar enters into a process where the outcome is unknown. New insights as well as deeper and often challenging perspectives open up for the participants. Thus the culture can call the tradition to task for its myopia and vice versa. Lived experience can question the most hallowed of doctrines, just as traditional value systems can challenge contemporary enthusiasms. This is an exciting and demanding phase of the reflection process. It requires the necessary discipline to keep the three poles in tension. We are not used to doing this and tend to become fatigued, falling back to one or other of the three sources as our preferred lens for discernment and decision making. It is the role of the group to help keep the dialogue alive as long as it is profitable.

Decision making: As helpful as the asserting phase is, the goal of the reflection seminar is informed pastoral activity, since we are preparing women and men for applied counseling ministry in the contemporary Church. In practice the seminar moment generally brings the person and/or the group closer to an informed pastoral decision. It enriches the process and supports the person's need to delve deeper into the sources of theological reflection in preparing to make the pastoral decisions which will flow from this process. In Alicia's case, the session allowed her to attend more deeply to the various aspects of the question. In particular it helped her to refocus the immediate question away from her future ministry to her own further needs for training and integration. The relation of service to the poor and responsibility to her community's financial needs took on a different shape. The question became: Could she ask her community for another year of advanced study to complete her preparation as a minister and counselor, given the financial crunch her order is facing?

This is the approach which has been in use in the Pastoral Counseling Department since 1985. Experience continues to refine the process but it remains substantially the same. Before giving an example of a session, I will simply outline the procedure which we follow in implementing this model and method.

We use a basic small group format. It opens with a *prayer* which is led either by the presenter or by another member of the seminar. From experience, there seem to be advantages and disadvantages to both. Then we *read the presenter's write-up*. This is a key element which facilitates the session and determines to some extent its quality. The student presenting an issue is asked to begin the disciplined theological reflection process prior to the actual session. Therefore, he or she will attend to the three sources and do what reading and reflection is necessary to listen well to these approaches. This preparation generally entails theological and biblical research, as well as some investigation into the relevant cultural sources. Some people have more training and facility in doing this. For others it is a new enterprise and they need help in finding the resources and in making good use of them. The facilitator can play an important role here before, during and after the actual session.

The write-up serves two important purposes. First, it helps the presenter to enter the issue with more discipline and therefore with more depth. Second, it helps orient the group to the presenter's progress within the reflection process. It will generally include an introduction to the question, a laying out of each of the three sources (experience, tradition

and culture) and whatever fruits are emerging from the asserting phase.
Typically in our seminars, most of the asserting phase of the method is
done in the actual session. Generally at the end of the write-up, the presenter will formulate one or several questions which seem most important
at this stage of the process.

After some *brief clarification,* when necessary, the group joins the
presenter in the process of theological reflection. The ensuing discussion
and sharing forms the heart of the session.

Toward the end of the session, the presenter is invited to share how
this session has been helpful in the search for informed pastoral activity.
The theological resource person may wish to add a few brief reflections
and/or indicate tools or means for continuing the process. The sessions are
one hour and fifty minutes long and it has been clear that this time frame
only permits the consideration of one issue per session.

Despite the limitations of time many important things happen in
these sessions, which make them quite worthwhile to the group as a
whole. Because of the nature of most of the issues presented, it is generally
possible for all of the seminar members to relate meaningfully to the subject at hand. Here is a sampling of some of the questions we have discussed:

identity as a pastoral counselor
role of women in ministry
evangelization and culture
pastoral approaches to gays and lesbians
ministering to undocumented aliens
inner healing
abortion
addiction and conversion
transference and countertransference in formation work
divorce
suicide
sin and grace in the counseling process
masturbation
sexuality and celibacy
poverty and professionalism
forgiveness and guilt
dying with dignity and medical codes
experience of Church and base communities
caring vs. curing
loneliness and isolation of the pastoral counselor
surrender vs. control in ministry

As you can easily guess, the assertion of the three sources of theological reflection around these topics has been challenging and quite helpful in the effort to do informed pastoral counseling in today's ministry.

Two final notes before looking at a sample session: the role of the facilitator and the style of group interaction. For the first, I will speak from my own experience. I have found my role to be fourfold:

1. Giving an opening didactic presentation of the method. Then in a follow-up session, I have demonstrated the process by making the first presentation of the semester. I have generally taken some issue which was important to me at the time. In the evaluations the seminar groups have consistently said that my original setting of a personal tone allowed and invited them to do the same. They have also said that they are not sure if they would have been as personal as they were if I had not led the way.

2. Guiding one group and also individuals in the use of the method. After a few sessions, most people seem to understand how to proceed, but at times there is need for some refinement during the semester.

3. During the session and together with the rest of the group, helping the presenter respect the integrity of each of the three sources of theological reflection. In particular as a pastoral theologian, I have helped attend to the tradition. Often before or after the session, I have been able to assist the presenter in focusing the question and locating resources for attending and asserting.

4. Helping the group to stay with the process and not attempt to solve a complex issue too quickly. This generally means leaving a question still in process for further reflection by the participant and/or the group after the session.

Secondly, I would like to say a few things about the quality of group interaction. It is important that the atmosphere be one of openness and trust. More concretely this means that the group needs to be:

Supportive: Accept the presenter where he or she is with a given issue, valuing his or her experience and insight. This also includes emotional support for the person who is often feeling very vulnerable sharing his or her question with the group.

Non-defensive: Given the nature of some of the issues, other members of the group may have strong feelings and beliefs which may seem challenged by the way in which the presenter is approaching the question. As in counseling, it is important here not to let one's own issues interfere with the ability to attend to the presenter. It is not helpful in this reflection process to get into arguments or debates, because if there is not a supportive atmosphere everyone loses and no one wins.

Challenging: The ability to challenge while respecting the integrity of the presenter's own process grows as the trust level in the group increases. This is often a way in which the facilitator can help the group by modeling a style of challenge appropriate to the pastoral reflection seminar.

Confidential: This should be explicitly agreed upon at the beginning of the group. Nothing of the session is to be discussed with anyone outside the group. All the write-ups should be destroyed at the end of the semester unless some other arrangement is made with the presenter.

It has been relatively easy to experience this type of group interaction in our program because of the quality of our people and also due to the overall atmosphere of the Pastoral Counseling program which promotes these qualities in a variety of settings.

II. Sample Fictionalized Issue

Mark is a thirty-seven year old married Roman Catholic layman studying to be a pastoral counselor in a suburban parish. This is his second year in the Loyola Program. He finds his work in a county mental health agency to be very enriching and rewarding. He is particularly grateful for the excellent clinical supervision he is receiving at his placement.

He has been counseling Margaret, a middle-aged woman who has been suicidal for several weeks. She had attempted to take her own life by an overdose a year and a half ago which brought her into counseling. Her depression had been lifting, but a recent diagnosis of breast cancer has brought her to a sense of the futility and emptiness of her life. She has no desire to undergo treatment and would like to die. Four years ago her husband and three young children were killed in an auto accident involving a drunk driver. She feels there is little reason for her to live. The question she constantly asks is: "Do I not have the right to decide to end my own life?"

Margaret has a strong religious background and has been active in her church which is of a more liberal Protestant tradition. Recently she has read of people who have decided to take their lives rather than undergo months or years of pain and suffering. In the last session she even brought in her Bible and showed Mark a few passages where some key scriptural figures apparently committed suicide (1 Sam 31:4–5; Jgs 9:54).

Mark is able to process the clinical dimensions of the case at the agency as well as the professional ethical questions involved. However, the religious aspects of this situation cannot be dealt with adequately there. Mark is a man of deep faith and he believes that God is the author of life and therefore that only God can give or take life. For Mark human life is the most holy reality on this earth. On the other hand he is able to understand something of Margaret's assessment that her life has no longer any value for her. How does he integrate his own strong religious faith with his role as Margaret's counselor?

Furthermore Mark finds this situation painful for a personal reason. A little over two years ago, his younger sister committed suicide by consuming a bottle of sleeping pills. As he said in his write-up for the pastoral reflection seminar: "The whole world tips upside down when you have to absorb the reality of suicide. . . . It took me months before I could work through a whole day without the recurring thought: 'Why did she do it?' " With the help of counseling and the support of his family, wife and friends, Mark has been able to come to some peace with his sister's death and not allow her decision to diminish his appreciation of the beauty of his own life. Obviously this situation with Margaret, who is about the same age as his sister, brings back many of the feelings which he has struggled with during the last two years.

The pastoral reflection seminar offered Mark a place where he could bring this issue with all its dimensions. He found doing the write-up both difficult and helpful. He set out the three sources of theological reflection and began the process of attending to them and asserting them in dialogue. It was helpful to look more carefully at the Scriptures including the material which Margaret brought to her sessions. He read some theology on the topic and also learned more about the historical evolution in his Church's pastoral approach to death by suicide. His sister had been buried in consecrated ground with a meaningful funeral liturgy, neither of which would have happened a few decades ago.

He understood how much the cultural input of the behavioral sciences had helped the Church to make this change by documenting the influence of great emotional stress on free will and human decision making. This concrete example of the dialogue of tradition with culture helped Mark to appreciate the value of the theological method we were using for the seminar. Furthermore he looked more closely at the various contemporary trends around this issue, especially those movements which are campaigning for the right to "die with dignity" and, in particular, to choose deliberately to end one's life. He allowed himself to face the questions: "Is the decision to commit suicide a basic human right or not? How do I as a man of faith respond to these positions?"

As you may suspect, the actual session was powerful and quite helpful for Mark and for the group as a whole. It would be impossible to attempt a summary of the hour and fifty minutes. Rather, I will simply indicate how the session helped Mark in the following three ways:

Personal healing: It had been the first time that he was able to present this experience to a group such as this. He felt deeply cared for in his own pain and struggle. The session helped him to own more fully the reality of his sister's death and to further the healing process.

Theological reflection: The pastoral reflection experience helped reinforce in Mark his own deeply held belief that life is a God-given gift. This freed him to be able to move further beyond his own issues and enter more genuinely into Margaret's struggle without placing judgment on her questions and feelings. He was enabled to trust that his own valuing of her life may challenge the meaninglessness that she is experiencing now.

As a pastoral counselor: It seems clear to Mark that counselors will be called upon to respond to this question of the right to take one's own life more and more as many people live longer and face lingering, painful deaths. He feels that it is one of those questions which we will hear about much more in the future. It was therefore very helpful to explore the various dimensions of the issue, to understand the various points of view and to come to a clearer sense of his own beliefs and feelings. He felt that he was more integrated as a man of faith and a professional therapist, in other words, a better pastoral counselor.

This fictionalized account is typical of the pastoral reflection process as we have been practicing it in the Loyola Program. The results have varied from session to session. Some have renewed their theological understanding of important ministerial issues. Others have furthered their own integration where it was needed. Some have made decisions related to their personal life and ministry. Others have been encouraged in their work for systemic change to serve better the interests of clients suffering various forms of oppression. Some have experienced more than one of these outcomes. In ai .iost every case, the sessions have made an important contribution to the ongoing development of all of the pastoral counselors involved: presenters, other seminar members and the facilitators.

A few weeks after her session, Alicia finally took the initiative and asked her order if they would underwrite another year of further training and development for her as a minister and pastoral counselor. To her great relief and joy, they graciously agreed. She felt a deep sense of respect for the courage and trust which the decision represented for her order in these difficult financial times. She knew (and the community trusted) that she would be a better pastoral counselor because of what the added year would offer her.

Of course in another few months she would need to face her original question as to where and with whom she will counsel. In any case she would be better prepared for the ministry. Furthermore she knows that having been able to value and affirm herself in such a responsible way was a deep act of trust in her call to this ministry. In the very ability to make this act of faith she believed she had heard clearly the echo of a call from God.

Conclusion

In this chapter I have shared something of our brief and very rewarding experience with theological reflection seminars in the Loyola Pastoral Counseling Department. It is clear that they have met an important need for our students. I believe that as we continue to live this experience, these seminars can make a contribution to the study of the interplay between the emotional and the spiritual. Theological reflection has been one of the privileged moments in the program where we focus carefully on the relationship between these two powerful forces in human experience.

References

James D. Whitehead and Evelyn Eaton Whitehead, *Method In Ministry: Theological Reflection and Christian Ministry.* New York: Seabury Press, 1983.

Brian O. McDermott, *What Are They Saying About the Grace of Christ?* New York: Paulist Press, 1984.

Lucy Malarkey, M.S., C.A.S.
Rea McDonnell, Ph.D.

Epilogue

Approaching Mystery

In approaching mystery we move beyond ourselves into a world of intuition, overwhelming wholeness, surprises of joy, unitive experiences, depth and openness, love, light and life. A sense of mystery occurs at moments when we least expect it. A nine-year-old boy riding his bicycle along the beach on his way to play softball suddenly, without previous expectation, experiences a moment bursting with joy. This joy is far greater than the environmental setting or the tasks he is about. The joy brings a sense of well-being, of happiness far beyond himself.

A mother rocks her crying child. At last the child falls asleep and is placed gently in the crib. The mother looks at her sleeping child and is overwhelmed in an instant by a sense of peace, of wonder, of a rightness about life that is so marvelous that for a moment she has no concerns or worries.

A helper (anyone in a helping profession) is listening to the helped. There is sudden awe at what is being shared, a deep reverence at being so trusted. One feels a great respect and union with this person who is pouring out his or her story. At the same time there is an intuition of something greater here, something far bigger than these two people in conversation. Each of these situations touches into mystery. None of us made such moments occur but they happen to all of us throughout our lives. Often we are not sensitive to them or do not reflect upon them or are embarrassed to share them with one another.

In our society today this sense has been dulled. At the Association for Humanistic Psychology meeting in San Francisco in 1985, Rollo May referred to the current dramatic increase in drug use and suicides among the young: "We have taken away from them something to love. We have deprived them of art, music, poetry. Philosophy is practically dead, theology is dead, except in a few seminaries, generally Catholic. As a character in one of Nietzsche's stories once proclaimed, 'We have no directions, no

287

north and south, no up and down. Things are getting colder.' "[1] Many have lost creativity, beauty, wonder, curiosity in their lives. Many have lost touch with the appreciation of mystery that invades, inspires, breaks open and fills with the human transcendence and hope and meaning and joy.

At the same meeting Carl Rogers was interviewed.[2] He spoke of religious institutions on a continuum. At one pole, institutions desire to have power over others. At the other pole they aim to heighten the individual's spiritual life in order to help him or her grow in self-esteem or self-confidence. The latter seems to encourage, to enable attention to mystery. Rogers finds that his own most significant spiritual experiences are in relationships with others. At times he discovers that something comes together in a relationship in such a way that more is there than can be accounted for by the two participants. This seems to him to deserve the name spiritual. Rogers, however, hesitates to use religious terminology because he finds it so easily misunderstood.

Without, then, using religious terminology, we invite you now to look at your own experience of mystery in your life. Please reflect on your lived experience and try to remember those moments when mystery broke in upon or flowed through your relationships, specifically supervisory relationships.

Remember when you were being supervised in a helping relationship. Remember moments, experiences, sessions, that were:

   healing
   threatening
   full of insight
   full of power
   confusing.

What was it in these situations, with these persons, which led you eventually to freedom, to peace? What was there that blocked this movement?

   Reflect on your experience as supervisor, on experiences
   of silence in the session
   when your supervisee burst into tears
   when you felt choked up
   when you wanted to hug your supervisee
   when you felt angry
   when you felt helpless
   when you felt awe.

As you reflect on these experiences, what have you learned about mystery? How do you articulate the wholeness and freedom that can happen

---

1. *National Catholic Reporter*, March 22, 1985, p. 6.
2. *National Catholic Reporter*, March 22, 1985, p. 24.

in the supervisory relationship? What is it like to help another encounter the mystery and find meaning in his or her life? How does a person plumb the depths to reach the core of the inner self where authenticity and integrity are found?

Images of Mystery

To encounter mystery is a depth experience. To discover mystery is like diving. A diver explores the depths of the ocean. He or she does not remain in the surface turmoil of swells, kelp, wind driven waves but descends slowly into the bowels of the sea. As he or she goes deeper, distractions decrease, light becomes dimmer, one's attention is more focused, and one contemplates a single object or facet of life. There is silence, stillness of water, in the depths. The mystery of the deep lures one ever further down. At times a kind of rapture pervades the senses. One is permeated within and without by the environment. One has to confront oneself.

Diving is an experience of being alone face to face with self, with mystery, with essence. One can feel suspended, yet fully in touch with what is central to existence. One has entered a new world and things do not seem at all as they are on the surface. One desires to remain at mid-depth for the joy of what is revealed and yet at the same time suffers the pressures of the depth. It is difficult to pull away and resurface. This must be done slowly. To surface too quickly causes a loss of equilibrium. In much the same way, if one has truly encountered mystery one can never again be quite the same. One meets mystery within at the core of one's being, as the diver meets it below the sea.

Bob was a strong extrovert, concerned for others, who made conversation easily. A pleasant person, he engaged others immediately in a seemingly effortless way. The main problem in his work, ministering in a hospital to the sick and dying, was that it went nowhere. As his supervisor, I told him he could converse with the Rock of Gibraltar for hours, be chatty and entertaining but never get below the surface. Bob was blocked because he had never plumbed the depths of his own feelings. He had a strong need to be perfect, to strive continually to eradicate storms and waves from his life. An experience of rejection in early adulthood convinced him that living life in a defended way on the surface would protect him from further hurt. Much of this was unconscious.

For a year our meetings were congenial and superficial. Bob dealt with me as he dealt with everyone in his life. He kept relationships neat, antiseptic, measured. He was always in control. His work with others was far less productive than it could have been. Bob had fears and was lonely but denied this by rationalization and intellectualization. He covered his loneliness by his ability to be charming.

Gradually he began to change. He started to encounter mystery as others risked pouring out their hearts to him whether or not he responded with depth. His own sensitivity was touched by these stories. Over time in our sessions, as he learned to trust my unconditional acceptance of him, he began to look at his own feelings and to share his deeper concerns with me and with others. As he was able to probe his own depths with greater honesty, many of his defenses began to crumble. He experienced that he was accepted and loved in weakness in a way that he never had been in strength. He learned to accept himself as loving and lovable and his need for perfection decreased. He learned to plunge into the depths with others and the quality of his work vastly improved.

The image of the diver portrays the mystery deep at the heart of the human. An image of a midwife facilitating birth elucidates mystery's unexpected, uncontrollable leading from darkness to light, from constriction to freedom. Like a midwife, in approaching mystery our senses, minds and hearts must be open to receive the light and freedom which may or may not be born in any relationship. This receptivity could be called a contemplative approach to the human, a paying attention to the hints and signs of mystery revealing itself in relationship.

For example, when society is mired in such hopelessness, a therapist awed me with her openness, her passion for hope, which for her brought her into communion with mystery. She was reflecting on her experience of silence with her clients. "I am longing, hoping for something to be born from deep within them." She was able to see, claim and rejoice in her gift of midwiving very difficult, very disturbed people into peace. What was the healing factor? Her hope, trust in the mystery within the human, that energy which overcomes darkness and fear.

I had a very different experience with a rigid, highly defended man whom I supervised in a training program for spiritual directors. Session after session, I felt clubbed by him. I realized how clubbing he must have been with those who trusted him with their spiritual vulnerabilities. Thinking that unconditional love would soften him, I tried to receive him—for a while. He was a married man who "never got angry" with his wife, let alone his directees, yet his subtle violence in sessions with me, his continual denial of all anger in his life, finally caused my anger to erupt. He erupted in return, immediately suppressed his rage, and could not talk about our shared experience.

His unresolved anger, expanding our previous metaphors, became like a toxic lagoon for the diver, like a stillborn child for the midwife. He could not be open and receptive to his own life, nor to whatever might be coming to birth in his directees. I could not recommend him, without this receptivity to mystery, for this particular helping relationship.

Other experiences of mystery have been imaged as Love-Light-Life. Tom was a religious brother in his mid-sixties. He was brilliant, a scientist who had traveled the world delivering papers and improving agricultural methods in third world countries. Tom came to make a thirty-day retreat, an intense kind of prayer in solitude with a brief conference each day with a director. I was Tom's director.

From the beginning it was obvious that he had many fears. Tom's whole sense of self-worth was tied up in what he did rather than who he was. He had spent his life producing results in the academic world. Now he was to take time for solitude, to look at his own life and relationship with mystery. He was terrified.

He met with me each day, bringing me detailed written accounts of his dreams with which he had dialogued. He read these to me and then would look up as if to say, "Is this okay?" The dreams dealt with themes of evil, death, violence, pain. I saw the dialogues as his safe way to cope with issues too frightening to talk about directly. Unsure how to best help this man in four weeks, I felt all I could do was to be loving, patient, accepting. Gradually his dream dialogues became less important and Tom began to speak more really of what was happening in his solitude.

After about three weeks Tom was walking in a nearby park. Several people were seated at a picnic table listening to a tape recorder. The tape was of a sermon. As Tom walked within earshot he heard the words, "God will send your sins into infinite forgetfulness." He burst into tears and sobbed for over an hour. Tom had met the mystery of his own being. At long last light penetrated the darkness of his fear and self-doubt. He knew with an assurance never before experienced that he was loved and accepted for who he was and because he was.

The next day he shared this event with tears streaming down his cheeks. Much of his fear had dissolved because he felt loved by me and because he had allowed the light of mystery to fill him with a new sense of self-acceptance and worth. Tom was able to begin to live life on a different level because he experienced love. The following day old habitual defenses and intellectualization returned but Tom remained changed by his experience. New life emerged in laughter. Tom began to take himself less seriously. Joy gradually replaced his hesitancy as he moved tentatively forward with new life.

Naming the Mystery

Let us begin to name the mystery, to identify mystery, surely as an undefinable, unnamable holy who is beyond all names. Yet most of the Western world, the people of the Book, Jews, Moslems, and Christians, believe that Mystery has initiated personal relationship with all that is human and has revealed the personal name (analogous though that name will always be) of the Holy. Since ninety percent of the United States population (and undoubtedly the rest of English speaking nations) operates from spiritual beliefs,[3] we hope that our reflection together on Mystery will speak to and enrich those supervisors who are among the ninety percent.

To enter into life—the goal of all helping relationships—is to enter into mystery. Theologian Brian McDermott concludes that to enter into life is really to enter into God.[4] As you have reflected on the mystery of life earlier in this chapter, perhaps you have already named this transcendent presence: God. We agree with Paul Pruyser, who has written on the interaction of psychology and religion, that focusing on the God of Judeo-Christian-Moslem revelation can only enhance the strong among our readers.

Because religious language can so easily be misunderstood, as Carl Rogers and countless others in the field have pointed out, let us begin with our own experience of the Mystery whom we now name God, and our experience of God's work within the supervisory relationship. We will begin to formulate a theology of supervision. Theology may be defined as a process of systematically reflecting on God's activity in the experience of human beings.[5] Thus we write from our own experience of supervision and invite you to join us, continuing to reflect on being supervised and supervising, as together we move toward a theology of supervision.

It is our own experience that in the helping relationship between supervisor and supervisee, God can communicate God's self and can work with and for the supervisee. The supervisor and the relationship then can be sacraments, signs of God's activity on behalf of the supervisee.

We begin our naming of Mystery, discovered in the supervisor's activity and in the supervisor/supervisee relationship, with the usual categories of Western thought, categories of being. Mystery is sometimes

3. Robert M. Theodora, "Utilization of Spiritual Values in Counseling: An Ignored Dimension," *Counseling and Values* (July 1984), p. 163.

4. Brian McDermott, S.J., *What Are They Saying About the Grace of Christ?* New York: Paulist Press, 1984, p. 44.

5. Monika Hellwig, New York: *Whose Experience Counts in Theological Reflection?* Milwaukee: Marquette University Press, 1982, p. 20.

named Ground of all being, our ultimate concern. God, however, also is known in our lived experience as active, a worker, creator, savior, healer, and so many other names which indicate God's functioning, God's serving people. Thus we will primarily focus on God's activity, on God as worker. God graces, loves unconditionally, stands faithfully with, gifts, energizes, heals, educates, frees. If our readers are among the ninety percent who operate out of spiritual beliefs, naming God's work in the supervisory process may uncover even deeper riches in the supervisory relationship.

Mystery, the Holy, the ultimate concern is often named Grace. Grace, *hesed* in Hebrew, is at the core of God's self-communication. God is grace, that free, extravagant, and unconditional love which/who transforms us. Out of God's fullness "we have all received grace upon grace upon grace upon grace," writes John, the Christian evangelist. God's own self, unconditionally offered, creates space for the human to change and grow. God's own self welcomes the human heart home. This welcome, *hesed*, unconditional love, is undoubtedly the most healing factor in any simply human or professionally helping relationship. In offering this kind of open, receptive care, the supervisor can act as instrument of God who graces the supervisee, and through the supervisee's unconditional acceptance in turn, God who graces the client/patient.

Jesus told a parable which illustrates this parallel process, although in a negative way. A servant owed his master an immense amount of money. When the master was about to arrest the servant, the servant begged for mercy and the master remitted the entire debt. That servant then called due some debts owed to him and had a man who owed an insignificant amount tortured "till he paid all he owed."

The servant is like a supervisee who is learning, for example, how to be a therapist. In his or her relationship with the master, the supervisor, the servant is taught responsible stewardship, and, more importantly, unconditional love and forgiveness by receiving unconditional acceptance. The master, the supervisor, offers and models strength and compassion, a kind of justice which goes beyond exacting just what is owed.

When the servant relates with his or her own "client," however, it is obvious that he or she has not yet learned, internalized, appropriated the freeing "justice" of the master's acceptance. The master is just; the servant does justice. The supervisee does therapy, whereas the supervisor is therapeutic.

God graces the supervisory process with unconditional love. God also stands with the supervisor and supervisee, is committed, is faithful. Just as *hesed* characterizes God, so does *'emet*, that truth, fidelity so often linked with *hesed* in the Jewish scriptures. We have experienced Mystery as truth, light, insight which breaks through barriers in the helping relationship. If we name the Mystery God, then we know that God's truth and fidelity are active on our behalf. Even if the supervisor cannot mark achievement in the supervisory process God remains committed to it, to both supervisor and supervisee. The supervisor's own fidelity to the supervisee, despite misunderstanding, incoherence, seeming lack of movement, even failure, can mirror God's fidelity.

The supervisor affirms the supervisee's gifts. In a relationship in which Mystery can be named, gifts for therapy, nursing, ministering can be supported as greater than the sum of the supervisee's achievements. Because the source of these gifts is outside the self, because they are God's gifts, the self may be more able to look less defensively at the concomitant weaknesses, working them through with the supervisor. The supervisor affirms gifts for the supervisee's work. If, however, the affirmation leads to a focus chiefly on self-understanding and/or on issues of personal growth, the supervisor needs to suggest counseling for the supervisee. God's gifts, as the Christian tradition affirms, are always for the sake of others.

A supervisor, who, with God, graces with unconditional acceptance, stands faithfully with, affirms gifts for the sake of others, can mediate for the supervisee new power and energy in very complex, stressful work. Power, energy in Greek is *dynamis*, another name for the Spirit of God. It is our experience that the energy that often is released or which more gently flows in the supervisory session could be named Spirit.

Another way in which the supervisor can share in God's work is providing the atmosphere for healing. Healing, as R. Callahan points out in her chapter, is an intransitive verb. All any therapist or minister or supervisor can ever do is create a climate in which healing happens from the inside out. As we have emphasized, acceptance allows for major healing, but so does challenge, as when, for example, the supervisor refuses to rescue the supervisee from pain or to sidestep issues in which both supervisee and supervisor may be vulnerable. A supervisor may be tempted to play god, savior, healer. The supervisor who reverences Mystery, however, is vulnerable to having his or her self-idolizing smashed by an overwhelming sense of helplessness in the supervisory relationship. In our experience this is a renewed invitation to relax and trust the healing energy of God. "Make me an instrument of your peace . . ."

Perhaps within the supervisory process, the peace, the wholeness, the sign of salvation, the *shalom* which can happen in the presence of and by the power of Mystery, might best be summed up as the experience of freedom. Fears and angers and superficial attachments, blocks in the supervisee's helping relationships, can be released in the supervisory session. The supervisee is invited to freedom from self-preoccupation.

Breaking any cycle of self-defeating thought or behavior because of the supervisor's unconditional love can be named and gratefully claimed as breaking the stranglehold of evil. The supervisor shares as God's instrument in God's chief work—liberation. Whether our religious tradition sees God's freeing work in the exodus of Israel from slavery, the resurrection of Jesus from death, the homecoming at Mecca from alien lands, God frees.

The supervisor is active witness, instrument to the movement of Mystery within the supervisory relationship. What response can the supervisor make? We have presumed that the supervisor's first and major response is to be open and receptive to the freeing, healing power of Mystery. That is a contemplative attitude which leads the supervisor further from religious certitudes and deeper into a humble waiting for God to work. We have presumed, too, that the supervisor has responded with a commitment to the supervisee and with a commitment to truth. These two fundamental stances of receptivity and commitment are prerequisite responses to Mystery. But in practical action, in moment to moment decisions within supervisory sessions, how can the supervisor respond?

The supervisor wants to enable growth in peace and freedom. To do this the supervisor needs a gift for discernment, the ability to discriminate. The supervisor must decide when to focus on the client because of legal liability and ethical responsibility and when to focus on the supervisee. The supervisor must decide whether to probe or to listen unconditionally, to critique or to support. The supervisor must decide what to pursue, what to let go, in all that the supervisee presents. In other words, the supervisor must interpret his or her own experience as well as that of the supervisee and the client.

Sensitivity to Mystery can enable those immediate decisions. An experience of "rightness" even greater than intuition can operate for the supervisor who is alert, and acts within the ambience called life-force or Spirit. Discernment is made in deepest tune with the movement of Mystery.

Supervision is an art. Skills can be learned and refined. Supervision of supervision can be obtained, but ultimately the art of supervision is a gift that is given, not one that can be achieved. As supervisors, we are challenged and invited to love tenderly, to act justly and to walk humbly with God and with one another. We enable others to move from darkness to light, death to life, slavery to freedom, self-hatred to self-love first of all by loving them. The supervisor sometimes loves tenderly and sometimes with tough love but which is love nevertheless. The supervisor acts justly by being responsible in his or her stewardship, by becoming a discerning person. The supervisor walks humbly by seeking the good, the best interests of the other in truth. Humility is truth, the painful with the pleasant, the bad news shared along with the good.

To be alert to, responsive to Mystery, God, in the supervisory relationship is to enable our supervisees to love tenderly, act justly, walk humbly and helpfully. As a spokesperson for God, Jesus capsulized the helping professions and their mysterious connection with the divine:

> "For I was hungry and you gave me food,
> I was thirsty and you gave me drink,
> I was a stranger and you welcomed me,
> I was naked and you clothed me,
> I was sick and you visited me,
> I was in prison and you came to me" (Mt 25:35–36).

As believers and participants in the Mystery, something greater than ourselves, one who is beyond us, God, we are invited to bring this healing and helping to our brothers and sisters.

Notes on the Contributors
(follow the order of the articles)

ROBERT WICKS is Director of the Graduate Program in Pastoral Counseling at Neumann College, Aston, PA, and maintains a private practice in Philadelphia. He is also visiting Assistant Professor at Hahnemann University. Dr. Wicks is the author/editor of seventeen books, the latest of which is *Clinical Handbook of Pastoral Counseling* (Paulist Press, 1985).

BARRY K. ESTADT, O.F.M. Cap. is Director and Chairman of Pastoral Counseling Programs at Loyola College of Maryland. He holds a Diplomate in Counseling Psychology from the American Board of Professional Psychology and a Diplomate from the American Association of Pastoral Counselors, and is a Certified Supervisor with the National Association of Catholic Chaplains. Fr. Estadt is a licensed psychologist in Maryland, the District of Columbia, and Pennsylvania. He is the editor of *Pastoral Counseling* (Prentice-Hall, 1983).

JOHN R. COMPTON, an ordained minister of the American Lutheran Church, is a member of the graduate school faculty at Loyola College of Maryland. He holds an M.Div. from Trinity Lutheran Seminary, an S.T.M. from New York Theological Seminary, and a D.Min. degree from Lancaster Theological Seminary.

MELVIN C. BLANCHETTE, S.S. is an Associate Professor in the Department of Pastoral Counseling at Loyola College of Maryland. In addition to teaching, he is a licensed-certified psychologist in private practice. He received his Ph.D. in Professional Psychology from the United States International University.

SHARON E. CHESTON is Associate Chairperson of the Pastoral Counseling Department at Loyola College of Maryland. She holds a doctorate in Education from Northern Illinois University. Dr. Cheston has spent eleven years as a pastoral counselor and has held several administrative positions including Deputy Executive Director at the Baltimore Regional Chapter of the American Red Cross.

JAMES W. EWING is Visiting Professor of Pastoral Counseling at Loyola

College of Maryland. In addition to his teaching and supervisory roles, Dr. Ewing is currently the Executive Director of the American Association of Pastoral Counselors. He received his S.T.M. from the Eden Theological Seminary and his Ph.D. from St. Louis University. Dr. Ewing is a Diplomate with the American Association of Pastoral Counselors.

DAVID LUECKE serves on the core faculty of the Loyola College of Maryland Pastoral Counseling Master's Program. He is the founder of the Relationship Institute which provides marriage counseling and enrichment materials and training. Dr. Luecke is a Lutheran pastor in Columbia, Maryland. He is the author of *Relationship Manual* and the *Guide* for using this resource for counseling couples, and a contributor to *Pastoral Counseling* (Prentice-Hall).

RACHEL CALLAHAN, C.S.C. is a member of the Core Faculty of the Graduate Program in Pastoral Counseling at Loyola College of Maryland. Dr. Callahan is Clinical Coordinator of the Consultation Center of the Archdiocese of Washington and maintains a private practice as a clinical psychologist.

ROBERT F. DAVENPORT is Director of the Annapolis Center of the Pastoral Counseling and Consultation Centers of Greater Washington, D.C. and is Adjunct Associate Professor of Pastoral Counseling at Loyola College of Maryland. Rev. Davenport holds a D.Min. degree from Vanderbilt Divinity School.

RICHARD W. VOSS is a Supervisor of Social Services at Catholic Social Services in Chester County, PA. He holds a Master of Theological Studies (MTS) from the Washington Theological Union and an M.S.W. from Fordham University. Mr. Voss is an Adjunct Assistant Professor at Loyola College of Maryland. An eclectic practitioner, he provides marriage and family therapy, and supervision to counseling and casework staff and students.

JOSEPH CIARROCCHI is Director of Addictions Services at Taylor Manor Hospital, Ellicott City, Maryland, and Assistant Professor in Pastoral Counseling Department, Loyola College of Maryland. He holds a Ph.D. in Clinical Psychology from Catholic University of America and is a licensed psychologist. He is a contributing author to pastoral counseling textbooks and journals.

LOWELL M. GLENDON, S.S. is on the faculty of the Counseling Department of Loyola College of Maryland. He holds an S.T.L. from the University of Montreal and a Ph.D. from Fordham University, both in Spirituality. Father Glendon has taught in seminaries in Canada and the United States, and has had extensive experience directing retreats and offering workshops in various aspects of theology and spirituality.

JOSEPH A. HEIM, M.M. has served as a missionary with the Maryknoll Society in Venezuela for some twenty years in a variety of local and diocesan-wide ministries. He completed the Master's and Certificate of Advanced Study at Loyola College of Maryland from 1984 to 1986. Father Heim has returned to Venezuela to serve in a leadership capacity with the Maryknoll lay and religious missionaries.

REA McDONNELL, S.S.N.D. teaches Scripture at Emmanuel College in Boston and Loyola College of Baltimore in graduate programs for pastoral counselors. She offers retreats and workshops on biblical spirituality, and has authored *Prayer Pilgrimage Through Scripture* and *Prayer Pilgrimage With Paul* (both Paulist Press), *The Sacramental Spirituality of John's Gospel* (Sheed and Ward), and *The Catholic Epistles and Hebrews* (Michael Glazier).

LUCY MALARKEY is Assistant Professor of Pastoral Counseling at Loyola College of Maryland. Sr. Lucy is a member of the formation faculty at Theological College, a part of The Catholic University of America, and serves as a formation advisor for many seminarians. During the summer she is a retreat director for a 36 Day Program of the Spiritual Exercises of St. Ignatius Loyola. Sr. Lucy holds several academic degrees, including an M.A.S. from the University of San Francisco, and an M.S. and C.A.S. from Loyola College. She is licensed as a Marriage, Family, and Child Counselor in California and is a National Certified Counselor.

Index

tation outline for, 60–61; rationale for, 59–60

Interpretation: confrontative, 72; and counseling, 69–74; and counselor, 69–72; definition of, 70; description of, 17–18; facilitative, 71; implications of, psychotherapeutic, 73–74; importance of, 69; issues of, technical, 73; reflective, 70–71; summary of, 81–82; tentative, 71; and therapy, 69–70; time-related, 71–72; and timing, 72–73

Intervention, in addiction counseling, 221–222, *see also* crisis intervention

Intimacy, 147–148

In vivo learning, 24

In vivo observation, 159

Irving, Mary, 276

Issues, supervisory, *see* specific topics of; supervision

Ivker, Barry, 174

Jargon, 156

John of the Cross, 225

Johnson, 27

Johnson, Harriet C., 196

Justice issues, *see* social justice issues

Kadushin, Alfred, 162, 170, 182

Kahn, Robert, 169

Katz, Judith H., 265

Kniskern, David P., 196

Laws, certification and licensing, 30

Learning: process of, 5; and teaching, 67; in vivo, 24

Licensure laws, 30

Lindemann, 165, 168

Living Flame of Love (John of the Cross), 225

Long term psychotherapy: and core process, supervisory, 131–134; countertransference in, 130; description of, 122; initial phase of, 124–125; resistance in, 125; settling in phase of, 125–128; and short term counseling, 113–116; summary of, 134; and supervision, 122–124, 131–134; termination of, 101, 130–131; working through phase of, 128–130

Lovinger, Robert, 244

Loyola Pastoral Counseling Department, *see* LPCD

LPCD (Loyola Pastoral Counseling Department): background of, 228–230; counselors in, 44; example of, fictionalized, 233–236; formats of, supervisory, 53–54, 65; and integration of theology and pastoral counseling, 275–277; and pastoral reflection seminars, 277–283; and sample issue of pastoral reflection seminars, fictionalized, 283–286; and skill acquisition, 26; structure of, 230–233; summary of, 287; and supervision of spiritual direction, 226; theory of, 228–230

Luke 4:18, 268

Luke 12:49-53, 209–210

"Making Family Therapy Easier for the Therapist: Burnout Prevention" (Friedman), 200

Male dominance, 257